Business Plans For Canadians For Dummies®

What makes a business plan work?

- **Leadership:** The ability to influence and encourage others around you
- **Plans:** Your company's mission, vision, goals, and objectives, which all work together
- **Organization:** A structure for your company that makes sense
- **Procedures:** Efficient and effective ways of doing things
- **Skills:** The talents and expertise that your people need to succeed
- **Culture:** Values and attitudes that lead to doing the right thing

Customers, competitors, and you

Three customer questions

- Who's buying?
- What do they buy?
- Why do they buy?

Three competitor questions

- How big are they?
- Which customers are they after?
- What's their strategy?

Three ways to win

- Keep your customers happy.
- Offer something unique.
- Cut costs to the bone.

Basic financial statements

- **Income statement:** Your bottom line — subtracting costs from revenue to come up with net profit
- **Balance sheet:** A financial snapshot that shows what you own, what you owe, and what your company is worth
- **Cash flow statement:** A cash monitor that follows the flow of cash into and out of your company
- **Budget:** Your financial forecast that indicates where you plan to make and spend money

Major pieces of a business plan

- Executive summary
- Company overview
- Business environment
- Company description
- Company strategy
- Financial review
- Action plan

Business Plans For Canadians For Dummies®

Checklist of planning essentials

- Get everyone involved in setting goals and objectives.
- Find out all you can about your customers.
- Understand who your competitors are.
- Identify your strengths and weaknesses relative to opportunities and threats.
- Determine which capabilities you absolutely need to succeed.
- List all the things you do that add customer value.
- Make sure that you do your financial homework.
- Imagine several different versions of your company's future.

What small businesses need to succeed

- A long-term company vision and strategy
- Clear goals and objectives
- Knowledge of the customer
- An eye on the competition
- Plenty of financial resources
- Good leadership
- Satisfied employees with talent and skills
- An implemented business plan

Hot spots and shortcuts

- **Statistics Canada** (www.statscan.ca): Quick access to economic and market research
- **Canada Business** (www.canadabusiness.ca): Services for entrepreneurs
- **Legal Line** (www.legalline.ca): Free legal advice
- **Industry Canada** (www.ic.gc.ca): In-depth industry information
- **Canadian Federation of Independent Business** (www.cfib.ca): An independent business lobby

For Dummies: Bestselling Book Series for Beginners

Business Plans
For Canadians

FOR

DUMMIES®

Business Plans For Canadians

For Canadians

FOR

DUMMIES®

by Paul Tiffany, PhD
Steven D. Peterson, PhD
Nada Wagner, MBA

John Wiley & Sons Canada, Ltd.

Business Plans For Canadians For Dummies®

Published by
John Wiley & Sons Canada, Ltd.
6045 Freemont Boulevard.
Mississauga, ON L5R 4J3
`www.wiley.ca`

Library and Archives Canada Cataloguing in Publication Data

Tiffany, Paul

   Business plans for Canadians for dummies / Paul Tiffany, Steven D. Peterson, Nada Wagner.

Includes index.

ISBN 978-0-470-15420-5

   1. Business planning—Canada. I. Peterson, Steven (Steven D.) II. Wagner, Nada III. Title.

HD30.28.T576 2008   658.4'012   C2008-902117-7

Printed in Canada

1 2 3 4 5 TRI 12 11 10 09 08

Distributed in Canada by John Wiley & Sons Canada, Ltd.

For general information on John Wiley & Sons Canada, Ltd., including all books published by Wiley Publishing, Inc., please call our warehouse, Tel 1-800-567-4797. For reseller information, including discounts and premium sales, please call our sales department, Tel 416-646-7992. For press review copies, author interviews, or other publicity information, please contact our publicity department, Tel 416-646-4582, Fax 416-236-4448.

For authorization to photocopy items for corporate, personal, or educational use, please contact in writing The Canadian Copyright Licensing Agency (Access Copyright). For an Access Copyright license, visit `www.accesscopyright.ca` or call toll-free, 1-800-893-5777.

WILEY

About the Authors

Paul Tiffany, PhD: Paul Tiffany is a Senior Lecturer at the Haas School of Business at the University of California, Berkeley, and an Adjunct Professor of Management at The Wharton School of the University of California. He teaches courses in strategic management, global strategy, and business and its environment to students in the graduate program as well as to participants in executive education programs. Dr. Tiffany is also a Visiting Professor at Sasin, the graduate school of business administration at Chulalongkorn University in Bangkok (Thailand), and CEIBS, the graduate school of business in Beijing (China). He received an MBA from Harvard University and a PhD from the University of California, Berkeley. In addition, he has provided management training programs to firms throughout the United States and the world. He can be reached at `tiffany@haas.berkeley.edu`.

Steven D. Peterson, PhD: Steven Peterson is founder and CEO of Strategic Play, a management training company specializing in hands-on software tools designed to enhance business strategy, business planning, and general management skills. He is the creator and developer of the Protean Strategist, a business simulation that reproduces a dynamic business environment where participant teams run companies and compete against each other in a fast-changing marketplace. Each team is responsible for developing a business plan along with the strategies and programs to put it to work. For more information, check out the Web site at `www.StrategicPlay.com`.

Steven has worked with both large and small companies around the world on strategy and business planning, strategic marketing, new product development, and product management. He uses the Protean Strategist simulation to help managers improve their skills in teamwork and collaboration across functional areas and even across cultures. Prior to founding Strategic Play, Steven served for many years as a consultant to companies in the United States and abroad. He holds advanced degrees in mathematics and physics and received his doctorate from Cornell University.

Nada Wagner, MBA: Nada Wagner is a business consultant, Principal of Next Wave Marketing Inc., and an instructor at The Business School, Humber Polytech in Toronto, Ontario. She consults on business planning, performance management, and teaches courses in entrepreneurship, marketing, and sales. Nada assisted numerous start-up ventures with business planning and implementation, and was the former Director, Centre of Entrepreneurship at Centennial College, Toronto, Ontario. Nada earned an MBA from Ivey School of Business, University of Western Ontario. She can be reached at `nada.wagner@nextwavemarketing.ca`.

Authors' Acknowledgements

Paul Tiffany: I would like to thank the executives and students who have used this book and offered wise counsel in how it could be improved. I would like to acknowledge the many insights and suggestions provided by Dr. Tamara St. Claire, one of the first people to read the U.S. edition of this book and utilize it to create a winning business plan for a successful start-up firm.

Steven D. Peterson: Many people helped us in the writing of this book. I especially want to thank our U.S. editors at Wiley, Sherri Pfouts and Josh Dials, for all of the time, effort, and hard work they put in.

Nada Wagner: Many thanks go to the clients and students who have taught me as much as I have them, and to talented colleagues who have generously shared their insights and wisdom. There are a number of people at Wiley I would like to acknowledge. I especially want to thank our Canadian editor Robert Hickey for his guidance, direction, and encouragement; the project team of Elizabeth McCurdy, Pam Vokey, Lindsay Humphreys, and Laura Miller for their hard work and diligent effort keeping the project on target; and to Erika Zupko and Denise Koch for their enthusiasm and professionalism to bring this book to the market place. It has been a delight to work with such a dynamic and dedicated group.

Publisher's Acknowledgements

We're proud of this book; please send us your comments at canadapt@wiley.com.

Some of the people who helped bring this book to market include the following:

Acquisitions, Editorial, and Media Development

Project Editor: Sherri Cullison-Pfouts, US edition

Editor: Robert Hickey

Copy Editor: Laura Miller

Cover Photos: © iStockphoto.com/Alex Nikada

Cartoons: Rich Tennant (www.the5thwave.com)

Composition Services

Vice President Publishing Services: Karen Bryan

Project Manager: Elizabeth McCurdy

Project Coordinators: Lynsey Stanford, Pamela Vokey

Layout and Graphics: Nikki Gately, Melissa K. Jester, Julie Trippetti

Proofreaders: Laura Albert, Laura L. Bowman

Indexer: Cheryl Duksta

John Wiley & Sons Canada, Ltd.

Bill Zerter, Chief Operating Officer

Jennifer Smith, Vice-President and Publisher, Professional and Trade Division

Publishing and Editorial for Consumer Dummies

Diane Graves Steele, Vice President and Publisher, Consumer Dummies

Joyce Pepple, Acquisitions Director, Consumer Dummies

Kristin A. Cocks, Product Development Director, Consumer Dummies

Michael Spring, Vice President and Publisher, Travel

Kelly Regan, Editorial Director, Travel

Publishing for Technology Dummies

Andy Cummings, Vice President and Publisher, Dummies Technology/General User

Composition Services

Gerry Fahey, Vice President of Production Services

Debbie Stailey, Director of Composition Services

Contents at a Glance

Table of Contents

Introduction

So, you picked up this book and decided to give us a try. Smart move. You've taken a good first step. You may not know how to build a business plan just yet, but you're clever enough to know that a plan is really important. We know from working with organizations large and small, from start-up to ongoing concerns, that a business plan is vital for success — and following it is the only way that you can get where you want to go.

Some people think business planning is just an exercise to please a banker or another financial investor. On the contrary — you don't create a business plan just to raise money. It's much more than that! View it as your personal, powerful business tool — one that can make your company a more successful venture and a better place to work.

Is a business plan magic? Nope. But it does dispel a lot of the unknowns facing your business. A business plan works because it makes you take stock and think about what you're doing and where you're going. It presses you to picture what you want your venture to be in the future and how you intend to make it happen. You become the architect of your destiny; your plan acts as the blueprint — or, at the very least, a road map — that guides you to reach your goals. For example, a business plan

- Requires you to look carefully at your industry, your customers, and the competition to determine what your real opportunities are and what threats you face

- Allows you to take a good hard look at your company so that you can honestly and objectively recognize your capabilities and resources, your strengths and weaknesses, and your true advantages

- Coaxes a financial report, a forecast, and a budget out of you so that you know where you stand today and what the future holds

- Prepares you for an uncertain future by encouraging you to come up with business strategies and alternatives to increase your chances of success down the road

About This Book

Business Plans For Canadians For Dummies lays out a series of stepping stones that can help you create your business plan. You find out information about your business that can help you position it competitively and play to your strengths.

This book can help your business succeed, no matter who you are or what your job description says, whether you have an existing enterprise or are just starting up, whether you're part of a large conglomerate or are a one-person show. Depending on your circumstances, you may find yourself exploring the book in different ways:

- ✔ If business plans are new to you, you may want to start at the beginning and let us be your guides. We take you from determining your company's mission all the way through to making your business plan work, and we keep on route the whole way.

- ✔ If you have a little more experience, you may want to head straight for one of the more interesting pit stops: how to recognize the critical success factors in your business, for example, or where to look for your company's strengths and weaknesses. After dropping in anywhere along the way, you may discover yet another section where you want to spend some time.

No matter where you are in your business development, it's never too late to start a business plan, and it's never too late to make the plan that you have even better. In each case, you can find what you're looking for between these bright-yellow covers.

Throughout this book, we provide many examples of successful — and not so successful — Canadian businesses. We also relate stories of some well-known multinational companies. Hopefully, those stories can inspire you to look into foreign business opportunities. After all, with the right plan, just about anything is possible.

Conventions Used in This Book

To help you navigate your way through *Business Plans For Canadians For Dummies,* we use the following conventions:

✔ *Italics* are used for emphasis and to highlight new words or terms that are defined.

✔ **Boldfaced** text indicates keywords in bulleted lists or the action part of numbered steps.

✔ Monofont is used for Web addresses.

What You're Not to Read

You don't have to read the sidebars scattered throughout the book. Just because we find these little facts and tidbits fascinating doesn't mean you will. And you won't hurt our feelings if you don't read *Business Plans For Canadians For Dummies* from cover to cover. Feel free to skip around; pick and choose what you're really interested in.

Foolish Assumptions

Believe it or not, we don't need to be psychic to know a bit about your background. In fact, we can assume that you're probably in one of the following situations:

✔ You have a great idea for a brand-new gizmo and can't wait to get your own company up and running.

✔ Your boss just turned over a new leaf and wants a business plan from you in three weeks.

✔ You've always run the business without a business plan, and you're the one who turned over the new leaf.

✔ You thought you had a business plan for the company, but it doesn't seem to be doing the job that it should.

Are we close? Whatever your situation, you don't need a sixth sense to make a business plan; just read this book and follow our guidance. We can't tell you the future of your business. But the business plan that we can help you put together prepares you for the future. And we're here with you every step of the way.

How This Book Is Organized

We divide *Business Plans For Canadians For Dummies* into six parts, based on the major elements of your business plan. You don't have to read all the parts, however, and you certainly don't have to read them in order. We devote each chapter to a particular business-planning topic, and you may need some chapters more than others.

Part 1: Knowing Where You Want to Go

Before you can put together a business plan, you have to decide where you want to end up in the future. This part of the book starts by convincing you that planning is important when it comes to reaching your destination. We help you identify who your plan is for and how it can help you bring your great business ideas into clearer focus. We identify planning resources for you, discuss the planning process, and summarize the major pieces of a business plan. We also help you examine your company's values and your vision for the future. Finally, we help you get on track quickly by establishing a mission for your company, along with well-defined business goals and objectives.

Part II: Describing Your Marketplace

To plan a meaningful route for your business, you have to know something about the market you want to go after. In this part, we help you analyze your customers so that you can understand who they are, what they need, and how you can group them together to better serve them. We also help you examine your industry and figure out the keys to success by identifying where your opportunities and threats come from. Finally, we help you scope out your competition to determine exactly what you need to succeed.

Part III: Weighing Your Company's Prospects

In this part, we turn our full attention to your company. We help you look as objectively as you can at your capabilities and resources, identifying the strengths that you can count on and the weaknesses that you need to deal with. We also help you zero in on what you do best, enabling you to figure out the real value that you provide your customers and the true advantage that you have over your competitors. Finally, we help you put together a business model, and we guide you through your finances as you put together a financial forecast and a budget.

Part IV: Looking to the Future

The main reason you put together a business plan in the first place is to get ready for the uncertainties that lie ahead for your business. Part IV encourages you to look into your future and helps prepare you for change. We introduce several standard tools that can help you think strategically about the future, and we show you how you can use them to come up with alternative scenarios and strategies of your own. We also consider the different directions that you can take while your company continues to grow.

Part V: Putting Your Business Plan into Action

Too many mighty business plans sit on shelves, gathering dust, because someone neglected to act on them. In this part, we help you shape your company to be as efficient and effective as it can be. We also help you prepare the people in your company so that they have the skills they need to accomplish the goals that you set in your plan. Finally, we point you to the Appendix and a sample of a real business plan, so that you know — start to finish — what you should aim for.

Part VI: The Part of Tens

The Part of Tens is a collection of reminders, hints, observations, and warnings about what to do — and what not to do — while you work through your business plan. These chapters focus on the big picture, so look at them when you need a little perspective on where you stand and where you're headed.

Icons Used in This Book

To guide you through your business plan preparation, we include icons in the left margins of the book. Here's what they mean:

This icon indicates tips to put you way ahead of the competition.

This icon calls your attention to illuminating examples from the business world.

This icon flags situations that apply mostly to large companies, but that may help small companies, as well.

Ouch; you may get burned unless you heed these warnings.

Don't forget these timely tips.

Where to Go from Here

Take a minute to thumb through the book and get comfortable with what's inside. Pick one or two chapters that tickle your fancy. Better yet, turn to a chapter that covers something you already know about. Or, if you're really daring, turn the page and start at the beginning.

Remember to use the Table of Contents for a chapter-by-chapter breakdown. You can also turn to the Index to find a specific topic right away.

Part I
Knowing Where You Want to Go

The 5th Wave

By Rich Tennant

"It's quite a business plan, Ms. Strunt. It's the first
one I've read whose mission statement says,
'...keeps me out of trouble.'"

In this part . . .

No matter what task you plan to complete, from assembling book shelves to hooking up a home theatre, you may be tempted to pass over all the groundwork and sink your teeth right into the meat of the project. Fess up, the preliminaries seem bland and ho-hum. But for the really important things in life — and in business — preparation is everything. So, *preparing* to create your business plan ranks right up there in importance with each of the other major steps of actually *creating* a plan.

In this part, we take a big-picture view of a business plan. First, we lay out the blueprint for the plan. Then, we convince you of the importance of the plan, just in case you're still undecided. We outline a planning process for you and review the major sections of a business plan. We also point out why values and ethics are so important to your company and show you how you can make practical use of them in your planning. We look at how a vision for your company gives you something to aim for and a direction to take. Finally, we look at how to establish a mission for your company and develop effective business goals and objectives to fulfill that mission.

Chapter 1

Preparing to Do a Business Plan

● ●

In This Chapter

▶ Getting your planning resources together

▶ Figuring out who needs to work on the plan

▶ Checking out what the written plan looks like

● ●

*P*lanning is serious business. For many companies, a solid business plan is the difference between success and failure. Many people going into business for the first time want to rush right in, print business cards, hang up the sign, and start making money — a natural response for anyone excited about a new business idea. But taking a little extra time up front to prepare can pay off in many ways down the line; especially when it comes to writing a business plan. Face it, after your company is up and running, you won't have all the time you need to devote to writing the major pieces of your plan.

Identifying Your Planning Resources

Having the right resources at the right time can make business planning easier and more successful. Fortunately, you can now find more useful and usable business-planning resources than ever before, from books and software to Internet Web sites and real, live experts. Of course, you may also find plenty of stuff that isn't worth looking at — much less paying for. And you can't always judge a book (or software program) by its cover.

As you begin to put together your business plan, you may discover that you need some additional tools — a book devoted to marketing, for example, or business-planning software that can help you create and maintain your written document.

Hitting the corner bookstore

Obviously, you already selected one of the best hands-on, business-planning books around. But okay, you can also find other useful business-planning books out there — particularly books that concentrate on specific areas, such as marketing or financial planning, and books that focus on particular kinds of businesses, such as nonprofits or sole proprietorships.

You can find out a lot about a book by reading through its table of contents. You should also try dipping into the first chapter. If you're browsing on the Web, booksellers such as Chapters.Indigo.ca often include an About the Book section, customer ratings and reviews, and experts' recommendations directly on their Web sites. Readers' reviews and ratings that you find online can also help steer you toward other particularly useful books. And don't forget to ask your colleagues, business advisers, or investors to list their favourite business books and resources.

The basic principles of business planning may be timeless, but certain subjects — Internet marketing, for example — change rapidly. A book that was published three years ago may already be ancient history. If you want to find timely information, such as details about tax considerations for a small business, be sure to check the book's publication date.

For the timeliest info, turn to magazines, newspapers, and journals. They offer a terrific way to keep up on what's happening in the world of business, in general — and your industry, in particular. The business press also provides an efficient way to routinely scan the business environment for trends or new developments that may affect your business plan. If you're not sure what periodicals focus on your particular industry or your region, do a quick search on the Internet (see the following section for more details).

Surfing the Internet

Today, hundreds of Web sites offer information on business planning. You can access the information on some of these sites for free; other sites tease you with a sample of what they have to offer and then charge you for more details. In our experience, some of the freebies can be just as helpful as the subscription sites, so we suggest that you check first to see what's free for the asking before you plunk down your hard-earned cash. In particular, the federal government offers heaps of solid information on planning, starting, and operating your own business through its Canada Business site (www.canadabusiness.ca) and its network of provincial and regional sites. Even the Canada Revenue Agency (CRA) has helpful planning tips, which you can find on the Web at www.cra-arc.gc.ca.

Internet hotspots for business-planning info

You can find a treasure trove of business-planning information and resources online. To help you sort through all the riches, we put together a list of popular sites that provide useful and reliable tips, tools, and examples — including dozens of real-life business plans:

✔ www.canadabusiness.ca: The Canada Business site is far and away the best source of information about planning, funding, starting, and running a small business. You can find useful FAQs, as well as counselling help and shareware software programs.

✔ www.ic.gc.ca: Industry Canada's Web site has a wealth of information. Check out the Programs and services menu by subject and look for the business tools and resources, especially under the Planning and management menu. The site offers a number of diagnostic and benchmarking tools, as well as useful financial figures comparing the performance of other SMEs.

✔ www.statcan.ca: Statistics Canada is our nation's statistical agency. It has the most current information, including statistics and data on population, economy, industry, import/export activity, and special subject areas. You can also find links to other useful sites here.

✔ www.cra-arc.gc.ca: A useful site if you run a small business or are self-employed. The CRA provides all kinds of bookkeeping, accounting, and tax information. The site also includes links to other helpful non-CRA business resources on the Web.

✔ www.cfib.ca: The Canadian Federation of Independent Business (CFIB) calls itself the big voice for small business, representing small and independent businesses in Canada. Its Web site features tools, tips, and research reports that small business owners may find useful.

✔ www.bdc.ca: The Business Development Bank of Canada Web site has a number of business tools, from planning templates to e-business diagnostics. The Ask a Professional section enables you to post your own questions and review previous Q&As.

✔ www.legalline.ca: You can't find a better place than Legal Line to turn for basic information on the legal aspects — federal and provincial — of key business issues. The Web site also offers free information in 35 areas of law, including info on insuring your home business, independent contractor arrangements, trademarks and copyrights, debts, bankruptcies, and employment law.

Lists of the hottest business-related Web sites have a way of going out of date fast. And a resource that appears hot to one entrepreneur may not be suited for another. Your best bet is to prowl around the Internet yourself, looking for useful resources. On search engine sites, using the keywords *business* and *plan* leads you to plenty of generic business-planning information. For a more efficient hunt, tailor your search by using keywords specific to your business area (*technology*, *retail*, *travel*, *financial services*, and so on) along with the words *business plan* and see what you come up with. Bookmark any promising Web sites so you can return to explore them later in more detail. Check out the sidebar "Internet hotspots for business-planning info," in this chapter, for helpful Web site addresses.

Beyond sharing some basic business-planning tools, the Internet is also a great place to turn for the latest information about competitors, markets, business trends, and new technologies — all the things you need to know to put together a complete picture of your business environment. We're constantly amazed at how much information you can find in corporate press releases, company home pages, executive bios, online business magazine articles, the Canadian Securities Administrators' (CSA) System for Electronic Document Analysis and Retrieval (SEDAR) at www.sedar.com for public company document filings and news releases, and thousands of other online documents.

The Internet may be a gold mine of business information, but you may also find plenty of fool's gold. Unlike magazine articles, which are typically checked for accuracy, much of the info on the Web hasn't been validated. Often, the Web site providing the info is also trying to sell you something.

Follow three simple rules when you use the Web for business research:

- ✔ **Make sure the material is current.** Many Web documents aren't dated, so you may not know whether what you read is the latest scoop or ancient history. Look for a date. If you can't find one, dig a little further to make sure that the information is still relevant; you can often confirm the facts on another Web site.

- ✔ **Know your sources.** In the wide world of the World Wide Web, you may be hard-pressed to know exactly where the stuff you read comes from. If you read a rave review of a new business-software program, and the review comes from a respected business magazine, you can put your faith in it. If the review appears without a source on the software company's Web site, however, be suspicious.

- ✔ **Double-check key facts and statistics.** If you use specific pieces of information — about business trends, markets, competitors, technology, and so on — as the central building blocks of your business plan, make darn sure they're correct. If you build your financial projections on a forecast that the market for digital widgets will grow at 40 percent a year, for example, you better make sure that information is true and not some widget inventor's private dream.

Installing business-planning software

Business-planning software allows you to automatically assemble all the components of a business plan, turning them into a printer-ready, spiffy-looking document. The best programs also make easy work of the financial parts of business planning — creating income statements and cash-flow statements, for example, or making financial projections. Some software programs add graphics, such as tables and charts, which provide an easy way for your audience to see what you describe in the written document.

Business-planning software programs can sometimes make the job of business planning *too* easy. With all their bells and whistles, they may trick you into skipping the serious (that is, difficult) work of creating and writing an effective plan. Remember, the best software-planning tools guide you through the important aspects of business planning and then keep track of your words, sentences, and paragraphs. But they don't think for you. You should still do the serious mental work yourself.

Investors and bankers who make a living reviewing and funding business plans are all too familiar with the look and feel of the most popular software-generated, business-planning documents. If you use one of these programs, make sure you customize your plan to make it unique. The last thing you want is for your business plan to look exactly like a hundred others that cross a venture capitalist's desk every month.

Seeking professional help

No one knows the ins and outs of planning and running a business better than people who have done it. And most business people are happy to share their experience and expertise, as long as you don't plan on becoming a competitor! Many will even mentor first-time entrepreneurs. Don't be afraid to turn to a grizzled veteran for advice if you run into questions that you can't answer or run out of ideas to get your business off the ground.

Finding expert advice is surprisingly easy. The first place to look is in your own address book. You may have an easier time getting help from someone you already know on a personal level. Ask your friends and colleagues for suggestions. Other good places to look for help are the Chamber of Commerce, provincial government business centres, a local college or university, or the business section of your newspaper. Of course, you may end up paying for expert advice. But when you really need help, the advice is well worth the cost. Later on, your advisers may pay you back by becoming your advocates, cheering for your business while you search for funding or your first customers.

Choose experts with experience in a business similar to the one you're planning. After you identify a person, decide exactly what kind of assistance you need. You can't ask someone to plan your whole business for you, after all. But you can ask them to fine-tune your marketing strategy, for example, or review and critique your financial projections.

Finding friendly advice

Many local communities sport organizations of business people who convene to share ideas, exchange contacts, help each other out, and just plain socialize. Some organizations focus on helping specific groups, such as women, Aboriginals, immigrants, youths, homosexuals, or freelancers; other organizations, made up of local people across the business spectrum, are open to the public. Thanks to the Internet, you can find business groups that regularly schedule online support meetings.

Business networking organizations are an invaluable resource for help in planning and running your business. For information about what's available in your community, check with your local Chamber of Commerce. Ask whether they have a mentoring program. Because Web sites change so fast, look for a networking organization online by using a search engine.

Assembling Your Planning Team

The first step in creating a business plan is realizing that creating a plan is vital (see Chapter 2 if you're still wavering). The first question you may think of after your realization is this: Who's supposed to put the darn thing together? In some sense, the answer depends on how big your company is:

- **Small businesses:** If your business is really just you — or maybe you and a couple of other people — making a plan for the company is your responsibility. But don't fret: Who better to create a view of the future and set business goals and objectives than the person responsible for reaching those goals and making the future happen?

- **Medium-size companies:** If your company is a bit bigger, the process of creating your written plan requires more organization — and more people. Putting together a plan is a big job, and involving all your key people has a certain advantage: Everyone involved in the plan has a stake in making sure that your company succeeds.

- **Large corporations:** If you're part of a big company, you may need to hire people who work on business planning full-time. Make certain, however, that you don't create an independent planning staff: You don't want your plan to take on a life of its own and get completely divorced from what's happening with your business.

Make sure that your planners don't create the plan all by themselves. Your planning staff should always work alongside the managers and owners who actually have to carry out the business plan.

Setting the ground rules

Putting together a business plan resembles any project that involves team-work, from building a house to running a relay race. The clearer the ground rules, the smoother the process — and the happier your team. Make sure that your ground rules do three things:

- ✔ **Identify key steps.** Typically, the process of writing a business plan includes five distinct steps: research, first draft, review, revised draft, and final review. You can specify as many or as few of these steps as you think you need. Just make sure that you spell them out up front.

- ✔ **Clearly assign duties.** Everyone involved needs to know exactly what you expect from them. You can use the key steps you identify to create separate sets of tasks, and then you assign each task to members of your team (see the following section, which begins with recruiting a few people keen on being involved and ends with assigning one person to lead and another to wordsmith).

- ✔ **Establish a schedule.** Although writing a business plan is a big job, the process doesn't need to be a long and drawn-out affair. A business plan has to be timely, responding to the current business environment — not the way it looked six months ago. After you complete the preliminary research, the rest of the steps are fairly straightforward. To keep your project on track, set due dates for each component of the plan and each step in the process. Give the members of your team as much time as they reasonably need, but no more.

Delegating responsibility

If your company is large enough to boast a management team, you should divvy up the work involved in putting together your written business plan. We're not suggesting that you delegate responsibility simply to make your job easier (although it certainly does). Different people bring different perspectives to your plan. With a team in place, you have a group of people ready to read and review drafts, offer suggestions, and fine-tune the document to make it as good as you possibly can.

We can't give you a simple formula for putting together your team. Every business is different. We can't even tell you the ideal number of people to choose — that depends on the size of your company and the complexity of your plan. But here are a few tips that can help you create an efficient and effective team:

✔ **Keep your team lean and mean.** Too many planners are like too many chefs in the kitchen — they get in each other's way. A bloated team can mean endless meetings and too many points of view. Involve only the number of people you think you really need to get the job done.

✔ **Appoint people who want the job.** Sure, you may have trouble finding volunteers who jump up and down at the chance to work on a business plan. But you need to make sure that whomever you choose is at least willing and able to complete the task. To spark your planners' enthusiasm, take time to explain why creating a written business plan is so important. Refer to Chapter 2 if you need help convincing your team of the importance of a plan.

✔ **Organize your team around the plan.** By accomplishing this, you make sure that your people know the purpose of their tasks and how their work fits into the larger picture. Some of the assignments are straightforward. Your financial person takes charge of the financial review. Your marketing head puts together the business environment section. However, if certain pieces of the plan are more complex than others, think about assigning a small group to work on the more complicated pieces.

✔ **Put one person in charge.** Keeping track of the whole process can be a job in itself, especially if you have a large team or a complicated plan. Name one person as the project director to manage the team and ensure that employees complete tasks on schedule. Make sure every person on the team understands that the person you choose has the ultimate authority.

✔ **Appoint a wordsmith.** A business plan is a written document. If you're lucky, you have someone on your team who enjoys writing — or at least has the talent to put words down on paper. Pick a lucky person to be in charge of writing key sections of your plan, such as the executive summary. He or she can also serve as senior plan editor, checking grammar and spelling, and making sure that the writing style is clear and consistent throughout the plan.

Putting Your Plan on Paper

When you first set out to create a business plan, the task may seem overwhelming. Right off the bat, you need to answer fundamental and sometimes difficult questions about your company and what you see for the future. You have to decide what targets to aim for when you look ahead and set business goals and objectives. To succeed, you have to take the time to know your

- ✔ Industry
- ✔ Customers
- ✔ Competitors
- ✔ Company resources
- ✔ Company's unique qualities
- ✔ Company's advantages
- ✔ Basic financial condition
- ✔ Financial forecast and budget

You also need to prepare for changes that you make to this list down the road. That means thinking through other options and alternatives, and being on the lookout for new ways to make your company prosper.

You don't want to scare people — yourself included — with a giant written plan. The longer your plan is, in fact, the less likely people are to read it. Ideally, your written plan should be 15 or 20 pages, maximum. You can always support the main text with all the exhibits, appendixes, and references that you think it needs. If you want to glance at a sample business plan, check out this book's Appendix.

To remind yourself and others that your written plan is forever a work in progress, you may want to keep it in a three-ring binder. You can also keep an up-to-date version of your plan on your company's internal Web site or intranet. That way, you can add or delete pages and swap entire sections in or out when your business plan changes — and it *will* change. Fortunately, however, the format you use — all the major sections of a business plan — stays the same.

To avoid becoming overwhelmed, and to keep the business-planning process in perspective, break the plan up into the basic sections that every good business plan needs to include. The following sections outline the sections of a business plan.

Executive summary

Your executive summary touches on every important part of your business plan. It's more than just a simple introduction; it's the whole plan, only shorter. In many cases, the people who read your plan don't need to read any further than the executive summary; if they do, however, the summary points them to the right place.

You don't need to make the executive summary much longer than a page or two, and you can wait until you complete the rest of the business plan before you write it; that way, you only have to review the plan to identify the key ideas that you want to cover.

If you want to make sure that people remember what you tell them, summarize what you're going to say, say it, and then reiterate what you've just said. The executive summary is the place where you summarize what your business plan says.

Company overview

The company overview provides a place to make general observations about the nature of your business. In the overview, you highlight the most important aspects of your industry, your customers, and the products and services that you offer or plan to develop. Although you should touch on your company's business history and major activities in the overview, you can leave many of the details for later sections.

To put together a general company overview, you need to draw on several key planning documents, including the following:

- ✔ **Values statement:** The set of beliefs and principles that guide your company's actions and activities
- ✔ **Vision statement:** A phrase that announces where your company wants to go or paints a broad picture of what you want your company to become
- ✔ **Mission statement:** A statement of your company's purpose; establishes what it is and what it does
- ✔ **Goals and objectives:** A list of all the major goals that you set for your company, along with the objectives that you need to meet to achieve those goals

To begin constructing these statements, turn to Chapters 3 and 4.

Business environment

Your business environment section covers all the major aspects of your company's situation that are beyond your immediate control — the *macroenvironment.* The macroenvironment includes the nature of your industry, the direction of the marketplace, and the intensity of your competition. Look at each of these areas in detail to come up with lists of both the opportunities that your business environment offers and the threats that your company faces. Based on your observations, you can describe what it takes to be a successful company.

Pay special attention to how your industry operates. Describe the primary business forces that you see, as well as the key industry relationships that determine how business gets done. Talk about your marketplace and your customers in more detail, perhaps even dividing the market into sections that represent the kinds of customers you plan to serve. Finally, spend some time describing your competition: Their characteristics, how they work, and what you think you may see from them in the future.

For more information on how to explore your business circumstances and the overall environment that your company competes in, check out Chapters 5, 6, 7, and 8.

Company description

In this section, go into much more detail about what your company has to offer. Include information about your management, the organization, new technology, your products and services, company operations, and your marketing potential — in short, anything special that you bring to your industry.

In particular, look carefully and objectively at the long list of your company's capabilities and resources. Separate the capabilities that represent strengths from the ones that show weaknesses. In the process, try to point out where you have real advantages over your competitors.

Examining your company through your customers' eyes helps. With a consumer viewpoint, you can sometimes discover something of value to the customer that you didn't know you provide, and as a result, you can come up with additional long-term ways to compete in the market.

To start to put together all the things that your company brings to the table, flip to Chapters 9 and 10.

Company strategy

Company strategy brings together everything that you know about your business environment and your company to come up with future projections.

Map out your basic strategies for dealing with the major parts of your business, including the industry, your markets, and competition. Talk about why your strategy is the right one, given your business situation. Describe how you expect the strategy to play out in the future. Finally, point out specifically what your company needs to do to ensure that the strategy succeeds.

Everybody knows that the future is uncertain, so you need to talk about the ways your business world may change. List alternative possibilities for action, and in each case, describe what your company is doing to anticipate the changes and take advantage of new opportunities.

To prepare for change in your business world and to get info on how to think strategically about your company's future, turn to Chapters 13, 14, and 15.

Financial review

Your financial review covers both where you stand today and where you expect to be in the future.

Describe your current financial situation by using several standard financial statements. True, these statements don't make for the liveliest reading, but the people who are interested in the financial part of your business plan expect to see them. For everyone else, make certain that your financial statements are referenced in the text and that they support the assumptions and arguments that you make in the other sections of the business plan. The basic financial statements include the following:

- ✔ **Income statement:** A list of numbers that adds up all the revenue that your company brings in over a month, a quarter, or a year and then subtracts the total costs involved in running your business. The total is your *bottom line* — the profit that you make during the period.

- ✔ **Balance sheet:** A snapshot of your financial condition at a particular moment, showing exactly what assets your company owns, what money it owes, and its resulting net worth (assets owned minus money owed equals net worth, also known as equity).

- ✔ **Cash-flow statement:** A record that traces the flow of cash in and out of your company over a given period, tracking where the money comes from and where it ends up. The cash-flow statement tracks money when you actually receive it or spend it.

Your projections about your future financial situation use exactly the same kind of financial statements. But for projections, you estimate all the numbers in the statements, based on your understanding of what may happen.

Make sure to include all the assumptions that you made in other sections of your business plan to come up with your estimates in the first place.

To get a head start on your financial planning, flip to Chapters 11 and 12.

Action plan

Your action plan lays out how you intend to carry out your business plan. It points out proposed changes in management or in the organization, for example, as well as new policies or procedures that you expect to put in place. Also, include any new skills that you, your managers, and your employees may need to make the plan work. Finally, talk about how you plan to generate excitement for your business plan inside your company, creating a culture that supports what you want to accomplish. Only then can you have real confidence that your business plan is going to succeed.

For more direction on how to make your business plan work, head to Chapters 16 and 17.

Chapter 2

Understanding the Importance of a Business Plan

In This Chapter

▶ Focusing on your business ideas

▶ Planning for the past, present, and future

▶ Identifying your audience

*M*ost of us go through life thinking ahead. We always seem to have a plan or two in the works, whether we want to paint the house next summer or begin setting aside a little something extra in our RRSPs. Why do we plan so much? We certainly can't predict what's going to happen, so why bother? We may not know the future, but each of us knows that tomorrow will be different from today, and that today isn't the same as yesterday. Planning for those differences allows us to move forward and face the unfamiliar and uncertain. Planning is a strategy for survival.

Different companies make business plans for many of the same reasons. Planning is one way to improve the odds of success in a business world that constantly changes. Business plans don't guarantee prosperity, of course. Business planning isn't a science that offers right and wrong answers about the future; it simply gets you ready for what's to come. And making a plan increases the likelihood that your company will be sitting in the right place at the right time down the road.

In this chapter, we look at why having a plan is so important and how you can use your business plan in different ways. We talk about your business plan as a guide to your company's future, and as a record of where you've been and how you've done. We help you take the first steps in describing what you actually plan to do and how you plan to do it. Finally, we look a little closer at two important groups: investors who may want to own a piece of your business and bankers who may loan you money to help you grow.

Bringing Your Ideas into Focus

The concept of a plan originated with the early builders of, well, buildings, not businesses. If you've had a house built or have remodelled one recently, you know that this kind of plan is still around (and is expensive). Over the centuries, however, the meaning of the word *plan* has expanded to include time, as well as space. A *plan,* in the modern sense, also refers to a view of the future, as seen from the present. You make plans for a birthday party next week or a business trip next month.

A *business plan* is a particular view of your company both today and in the future, planning for the following things:

- ✔ What markets you want to compete in
- ✔ What value you can provide customers
- ✔ What products and services you want to offer
- ✔ What your industry will look like
- ✔ What competition you'll be up against
- ✔ What long-term advantages you think you'll have
- ✔ How big and profitable your company can become

To create this detailed view of the future, you have to make a whole bunch of predictions about what's going to happen down the road. If your company manufactures crystal balls, of course, you're in luck. If not, you have to find other ways to make some basic business assumptions about the future.

In the end, your business plan is only as good as all the assumptions you put into it. To make sure that your assumptions make sense, much of your planning should involve trying to understand your surroundings today — what goes on right now in your industry and marketplace. By making these assumptions, you can better predict the future of your business. Will your predictions actually come true? Only time can tell. Fortunately, the planning process better prepares you for what lies ahead.

Looking forward

A business plan provides a view of the future. Whether your company is large or small, whether you're just starting a business or you're a part of a seasoned company, you still need some sort of planning process to point you in the right direction and guide you along the way:

✔ A brand-new company makes a business plan to get its bearings and often uses the plan to get funding.

✔ An up-and-running company uses a plan to prepare for the inevitable changes in the marketplace.

✔ A large company needs a plan so everybody sees the same view ahead.

✔ A small company constructs a plan to make sure it has the necessary resources to survive year in, year out.

In fact, a small company needs a business plan most of all; unfortunately, small businesses are often the *last* to prepare a formal business plan. If you own or manage a small business, you already know that you're the Jack-or-Jill-of-all-trades. You hardly have enough time to get your daily business chores done, much less plan for next week, next month, or next year. But because you run a small business, you simply can't afford *not* to plan. Failing to plan is planning to fail!

When a giant corporation stumbles, it usually has the financial reserves to break the fall and get back on its feet. If your resources are limited, however, a single mistake — such as exaggerating the demand for your product or underestimating how long you have to wait to get paid — can spell the end of everything you've invested in and worked so hard to achieve. A business plan points out many dangers, alerting you to the hazards and obstacles that lie ahead, so that you can plan to avoid such pitfalls.

Three quarters of all new businesses fail within two or three years. And untold numbers never even make it off the ground. Smart business planning up front can reduce these scary casualty rates.

Create a schedule for reviewing your plan — quarterly is good, monthly is better, and annually is a must. This regular review helps keep you on track, and it reminds you where you were heading when you started out and what adjustments you need to make. You can easily lose track of your direction when you're busy dealing with day-to-day activities that can put you on a different route. So, review, assess, and adjust.

Looking back

A business plan paints a picture of where your company has been and how it has changed over the years. By reviewing your past performance or the track records of your competitors, you can use your plan to figure out what worked and what didn't. In effect, your business plan offers you an opportunity to keep score, allowing you to set goals for your company and then keep track of your achievements. For example:

✔ **Your plan creates a view of the future.** In years to come, you can use old copies of your plan to look back and determine just how well you predicted the future.

✔ **Your plan maps out a direction in which to go and the route to take.** You can use it to gauge how skilfully you accomplish what you set out to do.

✔ **Your plan forecasts where you want to be.** You can use it to check out how close you come to your targets for the industry, your market, and your finances.

Your history, as described in your business plan, teaches you important lessons about the business you're in — so you aren't doomed to make the same mistakes over and over. If you can't remember exactly where your company has been, you probably can't see where you're headed. Past performance is an indicator of future performance, unless you map and monitor a new route.

Looking around

You can use your business plan to tell the world (or at least anyone out there who displays an interest) meaningful information about your company. No matter whom you deal with or why, your plan has a ready-made description to back up the claims you make. Your plan comes in handy when you deal with the following people:

✔ Customers with whom you want to establish long-term relationships

✔ Distributors that are interested in carrying your product or service

✔ Suppliers that you want to work with on a regular basis

✔ The board of directors or other advisers who want to offer their support

✔ Outside consultants that you hire to help out with specific issues

✔ Bankers who decide to lend you money or shut you out

✔ Investors who show interest in taking a stake in your company

All these people have their own special reasons for wanting more information about you. Each group is probably interested in a different part of your plan. A well-written business plan satisfies all these groups and makes your company stronger in the process.

Taking the first step

With so many people to keep in mind and so many issues to think about, you may be feeling a little overwhelmed. Well, we're not going to sugar-coat this: Business planning does take time and effort. But if you're excited about the business you're putting together, the process can be a lot of fun. In fact, maintaining your sense of excitement and enthusiasm and making sure you reflect it in your business plan are important.

Now's the time for you to capture the spirit of that gung-ho, can-do, let-me-at-'em enthusiasm and take the first step: Get your big ideas captured on paper. Imagine that you're at a cocktail party. Someone introduces you to a high-powered investor who instantly takes a liking to you and what you plan to do. "I may be able to help," she says. "Can you jot down a quick description of your business idea so that I can talk it over with some of my colleagues?"

Sure you can, you say. So give it a try. Grab the back of an envelope or a scrap of paper and write down the essentials of your plan. Don't worry about writing beautiful prose. Get right to the point. Devoting no more than a sentence to each of these items, explain

- Who your customers will be
- What you want to offer to them
- Why customers should come to you instead of going to the competition
- How you plan to achieve that competitive advantage
- The number-one reason you're convinced that this business will succeed

After you finish, staple the paper to the front of your business-planning folder or place it prominently on your bulletin board. During the planning process, if you ever feel as if you're losing sight of some of your original ideas or enthusiasm, look back at your first description. You can probably recapture some of the initial excitement that got you started in the first place. (For more information on describing your business in 50 words or less, check out Chapter 4.)

The Planning behind the Plan

Some companies think that planning is a total waste of time. They'd never think of using the term in the context of their own organizations. These companies still move forward; they just don't talk much about it ahead of time. So why does planning have such a bad reputation in certain quarters? More than likely, the companies that don't plan don't understand what it really means to plan. Planning has become such a buzzword in today's business world that it has lost its real meaning.

Is planning an art or a science?

Planning is both an art and a science. Putting together a serious business plan requires you to gather data, analyze the information, and then turn it into knowledge about your situation. A serious business plan requires that you think strategically. What do we mean by that? The word *strategy* comes to us from the ancient Greeks and translates literally as *the art of generalship*. So you shouldn't be surprised that when you start thinking strategically about your business, you feel like you're suiting up for battle and jousting with your competitors for the hearts and minds of customers.

Modern definitions of the word *strategy* have become a bit fuzzy. You don't really need to know what strategic thinking *is,* but rather what it *does.* When you think strategically about business plans, you

- ✔ Take into account the personal and social values that surround your company (see Chapter 3).
- ✔ Clearly describe how to reach the goals and objectives that you set for your company (see Chapter 4).
- ✔ Create an advantage in the marketplace that you can sustain, despite intense and determined competition (see Chapters 10 and 14).
- ✔ Think about how to allocate and deploy your human and financial resources (see Chapters 12 and 16).

Make sure you don't forget the strategy behind your business planning. Without strategic thinking, business plans often turn into those neatly bound documents that begin and end with numbers — revenue projections, cash flows, expense allocations, and the like — that alone don't help you figure out what to do. These business plans (in name only) end up gathering dust sitting on a shelf. They don't represent planning; they represent a waste of time.

What can you do to make sure your business plan includes a strategy? When it comes to strategic thinking, a healthy dose of plain old common sense and logic works wonders while you pull all the pieces of your plan together. Experience in your industry and some smarts are advantages, too. Unfortunately, we can't give you any of these gifts. But we can offer you some solid advice to keep you on track.

Always keep the following questions in mind as you begin to formulate your business plans strategically:

✔ What markets and customers do you intend to serve? What are their needs, wants, and demands?

✔ Which products and services do you plan to develop and support?

✔ Where's your company's competitive advantage in these markets?

✔ How can your company sustain that competitive advantage over time?

Your answers go a long way toward keeping your plan focused and on target, so you want to return to these questions from time to time at each phase of the planning process.

Planning versus tactics

With all the fuzziness surrounding the definitions of business terms, business people sometimes confuse *planning* with the various *tactics* that they intend to use to accomplish their goals. The two terms are closely related, and you need both to succeed, but they don't carry the same meaning.

Here's a useful analogy: Think of planning and tactics in terms of a symphony orchestra delivering a musical performance. In this case, the musical composition represents the overall plan for what the performance sounds like. The conductor's guidance and the individual musicians' efforts represent the tactics for achieving the plan. The tactics are only as good as the design of the instruments and the quality of the musicianship, introducing a human element into the process.

You can reach some important conclusions about the relationship between planning and tactics in this case:

✔ No matter how good the musical composition is at the planning level, without the individual musicians (the tactics), the end result is a resounding silence — no musical performance at all.

✔ Without the pieces of the plan (the notes on paper) working together, the result is an unpleasant noise.

✔ And without a conductor (the manager in charge of implementing the plan through the use of tactics), the end result is chaos.

So, when you put your business plan together, remember to concentrate first on thinking strategically. After you put your strategy in place, you're in a position to develop the tactics that bring your plan to life. For insights into practical ways to tie your own strategic thinking to successful tactics, see Chapter 4, which includes guidelines for setting company goals and objectives.

Why planning matters

Planning doesn't guarantee success, but it does go a long way toward bettering your chances. We've seen it with our own eyes. And a recent survey of close to 1,000 small businesses backs up the claim. The survey found that companies with business plans enjoy 50 percent more revenue and profit growth than companies without plans. It's that simple.

Planning works best when your company integrates strategic thinking into every aspect of your business, every day of the week, and every week of the year. An ongoing process means that you

- ✔ Observe customers and markets, tracking their wants and needs.
- ✔ Always question what makes your company successful.
- ✔ Relentlessly examine the competition and what progress it makes.
- ✔ Steadily work at maintaining your competitive edge.
- ✔ Continue to search for ways to take better advantage of what you do best.

Some managers may follow all these tips automatically and intuitively. But if you want to make sure that strategic thinking extends into all parts of your company, you need to create a framework. When you make planning a basic responsibility, you get the added benefit of including all levels of employees in the process. Employees often have different and equally valuable viewpoints about shaping strategy, and having a planning framework ensures that you hear their voices.

To start the ball rolling in your company, pull together employees who represent different functions and various levels of your organization. Meet on a regular basis to talk about strategy and planning. Concentrate on how to set up a framework to promote strategic thinking and focus on problems associated with the planning process itself. The group members can then take what they find out back to their own areas and begin to integrate strategic thinking and planning into the way that they do business.

Satisfying Your Audience

Whether you write your business plan on your own or do it by committee, always keep in mind who reads the written document. A business plan is meant to communicate your vision and strategy — what you plan to do and how you intend to do it. You can best convey your message by considering your audience. You don't speak German to someone who speaks only Italian, right? For the same reason, you don't want to fill your business plan with all kinds of techno-jargon if your audience is made up of people who don't know the first thing about the new-fangled technology you work with.

What if your whole business idea is based on something brand new? Don't you need to describe it in detail? Sure, you do. But you can address different audiences within the same document. For example, your plan may include an overview of the new technology, written so that anyone can understand it; and, if necessary, you can put the technical nitty-gritty into an appendix. Before you can really think about how to speak to different audiences, however, you have to know your readers.

You come in contact with all kinds of people in the course of doing business. Your employees and customers are on the list, of course. And you probably have contact with suppliers, outside consultants, lenders, investors, regulators, and competitors, just to name a few.

For the sake of simplicity, we lump them all together and call them your *stakeholders* — meaning everyone who has a possible stake in what your company does or how it operates. Some of these people may have direct stakes: You owe them money, for example, or they own a piece of your business. Others may have less tangible interests: suppliers who want to continue selling to you or civic organizations that want to make sure you remain a good corporate citizen.

Whatever the interest group, your business plan is one of the most important tools you have to communicate with them. But there's a catch: Each of these groups probably looks at your plan in a different light. So, the following sections take a closer look at two very important types of stakeholders: investors and lenders.

Venture capital and angels

If you need money to fund your business and you want to minimize your financial risk, you may decide to turn to the venture capital (VC) marketplace. Venture capital firms are in the business of raising money and then putting it in the hands of businesses that make their money grow. They usually invest capital in new ventures; hence their name. So, when it comes to the business plan, new companies face a very important (and discerning) audience in venture capitalists. You can bet that venture capitalists read your plan very carefully before handing over any cash.

Fancy financing lingo

As you may expect, the world of venture capitalists and angels has a language all its own. Most of it has to do with the various types of financing available — which is closely tied to the different stages of a company's development. Here's what you need to know:

✔ **Seed financing:** The money you need to prove that your basic business concept is a rock-solid one that can generate gobs of additional money. Seed financing may go into building a prototype of your very cool new technology or conducting market research to show that customers really want what you have to offer.

✔ **Start-up financing:** The initial level of investment required to get your business off the ground. You can use the funds for everything from assembling your business team to developing your product or service, testing it, and bringing it to market.

✔ **First-stage financing:** Additional money that comes in after your initial start-up funds run out. You often use the funds to support further growth by ramping up new product development, production, marketing, or your sales efforts.

✔ **Second-stage financing:** Money raised further down the road, after your business has initially proven itself. You typically use the funds to allow the company to expand even more by supporting growth in all areas of the company's operations.

✔ **Mezzanine financing:** We're not talking about buying theatre tickets here. *Mezzanine* means in between. In a theatre, the mezzanine level is between the orchestra and the first balcony. In the business arena, mezzanine financing falls between an equity investment and a standard bank loan. The money allows your company to expand in a particular direction without necessarily having to give up additional ownership in the business.

✔ **Bridge financing:** Like a bridge over troubled waters, this kind of financing can help your company over temporary rough spots. For example, you sometimes use bridge loans before an Initial Public Offering (IPO) to smooth out any cash shortfalls that may occur before the IPO is completed.

Sounds simple, right? Well, lining up venture capital funding isn't easy. Would-be entrepreneurs have been led to think that a great idea and plenty of enthusiasm are enough to shake the money tree. You need both, of course, but now you're only at the beginning. According to a recent survey, venture capitalists fund less than 1 out of every 500 business pitches.

What do you need to succeed in the venture capital sweepstakes? First, it helps to know about the nature of VCs. Venture capitalists come in all sizes, from small, independent operators to large VC firms that evaluate thousands of new business proposals every year. Some VCs specialize in certain industries — biotechnology or Internet services, for example. Others tend to stay close to home, funding companies in their own geographic area so that they can keep tabs on their investments. Some VC firms prefer to invest in companies working in the early stages of development. Others look for companies that need a final push into the big leagues.

Venture capitalists, by the way, aren't the only funding game in town. You can find another source of start-up cash in so-called *angel financing*. This money typically comes from high net-worth individuals (also known as rich people) who have an interest in getting richer by investing in promising new businesses. You call them angels because they place fewer demands on a company than venture capitalists do (see the section "Bankers and other backers," later in this chapter, to get a whiff of some demands). And angels also show a little more patience when it comes to cashing out and receiving their monetary reward.

Now comes the $64,000 question — or if you're lucky, make that $64 million: What's the best way to get your business idea and plan in front of real, live investors? We wish we could give you a sure-fire, one-size-fits-all answer. There isn't one. Still, entrepreneurs who've been successful before can provide you with valuable knowledge. A few Web sites organize Canadian VCs, angel investors, and entrepreneurs, and those sites offer case studies and guidelines to help you. Two good sites to get you started are www.angel investor.ca and www.cvca.ca. Use a good Internet search engine to find others. The following sections give you a few tips that can help you distinguish yourself.

Make connections

As almost all successful entrepreneurs can tell you, it's not just what you have, it's who you know. The more contacts you make — those people who say nice things about you, your business idea, and your plan — the better your odds of actually getting onto some venture capitalist's or angel's radar screen. Include accountants and lawyers in that list as they are channels to those screens.

Put together a top-notch team

Face it: So many eager entrepreneurs have gone after start-up gold that you may find it almost impossible to come up with an idea that someone hasn't thought of before — several times. So how do you set yourself apart? What's just as important as a great idea, according to many venture capitalists, is convincing backers that you have a team of experienced managers in place who can turn your idea into a real business success story. In fact, some VCs say that the very best thing you can do with your first infusion of cash is to put together a knock-'em-dead management team. (If you want to know more about how to create a high-performing team, check out Chapter 17.)

Do your homework

Venture capitalists and angel investors have been around the block more than once. And although they love to see excitement and enthusiasm in the entrepreneurs they talk to, they absolutely need to know that you've also done all your homework — everything from scoping out the competition and sizing up the market to crunching the numbers and identifying the strengths, weaknesses, and uncertainties inherent in your business model (see the section "Bringing Your Ideas into Focus," earlier in this chapter, for tips on finding this info). In short, they want an ironclad business plan.

Perfect your pitch

What do successful entrepreneurs have in common with hotshot Hollywood script writers? They know how to give a good pitch. And knowing how to pitch your idea is absolutely critical in both of these fast-moving worlds. Like movie producers, venture capitalists have crowded schedules and short attention spans. You have to wow them fast and keep them listening. If this sounds a bit scary, start simple. Imagine that you're in an elevator and someone asks you about your new business idea. Think about how you can describe it to them before you reach the 25th floor. For more help, turn to Chapter 4.

Bankers and other backers

Before you jump on the venture-capital bandwagon, here's something to remember: VCs are definitely not philanthropists. They take a big chunk of your company in return for the cool cash they provide. And they often demand a role in directing or even running your business. You get their talent, along with their cash. You need to decide whether their presence can help or hinder your business.

If you decide to fund your start-up the old-fashioned way — with a business loan — you get to keep all your equity in the company. And you get to run your business any way you please. So, unless you have very large start-up costs, you may be able to take the route that many businesses still take, paying your way with a business loan.

By securing a loan to fund your company, you get to use other people's money to build up your business, keeping all the growth and profits for yourself — at least, in theory. But borrowing money isn't without risk. Somebody has to pay back the loan, after all, and that somebody is you. To minimize your risk, make sure that your business idea is sound and that you have a solid business plan in place. Rest assured, your banker also does the same.

Help from your government

The federal government helps small and medium enterprises (SME) by offering a number of financial programs. So, if you're a small company, you may use Industry Canada as an important source of funding. The Canadian government does its good deeds through four specific programs:

- ✔ **The Canadian Small Business Financing (CSBF) Program:** This loan program facilitates access to loans for SMEs. Industry Canada provides administration of the loan program, and banks, credit unions, or caisse populaires make the credit decisions and loans. You can use this program to establish, expand, modernize, and improve your small or medium enterprise.

- ✔ **Community Futures:** Through this program, the feds, along with regional partners, established more than 250 community economic and business development corporations that assist small businesses and rural communities with access to financing and business services. Visit www.community futures.ca for your local office and programs.

- ✔ **Business Development Bank of Canada (BDC):** BDC boasts leadership in flexible financing and affordable consulting services, as well as venture capital for technology-based businesses. If you're starting a business, buying a business or assets, or growing your enterprise (domestically or internationally), find the details at www. bdc.ca.

- ✔ **Industrial Research Assistance Program (IRAP):** The National Research Council (NRC) supports innovative research and development and commercialization of new products and services through IRAP. This program provides financial support to growth-oriented SMEs.

To foster innovation and competitiveness, both federal and provincial governments provide other services or tax incentives for specific industries. To find out more, check out Industry Canada's Web site (www.ic.gc.ca) and your provincial government's Web site.

Local branches of most banks are more than willing to lend money to local businesses, provided that those businesses can present convincing business plans. The simplest arrangement is a standard commercial loan. In this kind of loan, the bank lends you the money, and you pay it back, usually in monthly instalments and with interest. But you can find all sorts of variations on this theme, from real estate loans on commercial property to loans secured by your inventory or accounts receivable (see Chapter 11 for more info). If business assets secure the loans, you usually pay a lower interest rate.

If you don't intend to use all the money all at one time, consider applying for a commercial line of credit. A credit line allows you to draw on the funds when you happen to need the cash. Banks don't usually require collateral to secure small lines of credit. Larger lines (some banks loan up to $10 million or more) are typically secured against accounts receivable, inventory, machinery and equipment, or real estate.

Chapter 3

Setting Off in the Right Direction

● ●

In This Chapter

▶ Discovering the importance of values

▶ Identifying your company's current beliefs and principles

▶ Declaring your company's vision

● ●

*Y*ou may ask yourself why on earth you're reading a chapter on values and vision in a book on business planning. We can hear what you're thinking: Hey, I'm in the 21st century. Today's business principles revolve around survival in the marketplace. Cater to your customers, beat the competition (heck, demolish them!), make a ton of money, and run.

Yet even in a business world dominated by market economies, global competition, and the laws of the jungle, ethics still matter. Shareholders can launch (and have launched) class action suits against large corporations for misreporting results. Even not-so-noble lords can be brought down by financial scandal and fraud, and they end up trading their black business suits for pretty orange prison jumpsuits.

Now, don't get us wrong here — we have no quarrel with profits. We absolutely love them, and we expect to earn a lot for ourselves over time. But short-term profits aren't the measure of business success. And accumulating any kind of fake profits (or expenses) can land you in jail.

We're convinced that a successful business plan must start with a statement of company values, as well as a vision for the future. *V*alues and a *v*ision give your business a moral compass that guides you if you encounter trouble along the way. The two Vs also keep everybody in your company — even if that means only two of you — on course and heading in the same direction. What if you're a company of one? Taking time to establish your values and vision still guides you as your business grows.

In this chapter, we point out why values are so important in the first place. We help you identify your company's values by evaluating the beliefs and business principles that you already hold. We show you how to put together a values statement, along with a set of rules to work by. Finally, we encourage you to create a vision statement for your company.

Understanding Why Values Matter

Your company faces all sorts of options, alternatives, and decisions every day. If you take the time to define your company's values, your principles and beliefs can guide your managers, employees, or just you (if you're in business for yourself) as your company wades through complicated issues that sometimes don't have easy answers. When the unexpected happens, you can react quickly and decisively, based on a clear sense of what's important. Even when your company is in smooth waters and sailing along just fine, a strong sense of value helps motivate you and your employees.

Facing tough choices

Consider one scenario. Frank Klein is an independent consultant working for a large Canada-based petrochemical firm that we'll call Canuck Oil. Frank conducts market analysis for one of the company's largest divisions and is involved in an important project concerning the development of new overseas business.

Frank sketches out several options for the production, distribution, and pricing of petrochemicals in three countries.

In one of his most promising scenarios, the numbers for a country that we'll call Friedonia yield substantially higher short-term profits than the other two — primarily because the nation doesn't yet have expensive pollution-control procedures in place. The other two nations have environmental laws similar to those in Canada.

Here's Frank's dilemma: By introducing the Canuck Oil product line into Friedonia, Frank's client could make huge profits. Sure, the resulting pollution may cause ecological damage that environmentalists could possibly trace back to Canuck Oil. But the company would do nothing illegal, according to Friedonia's current laws, and Frank stands to get a lot more business from Canuck Oil if the project goes ahead.

He agonizes over the situation and his report. What should Frank recommend to senior management? His options include

- Going for the short-term bucks
- Voluntarily enacting procedures to control pollution, even though the company isn't legally required to do so
- Forgetting Friedonia until the country has stronger environmental laws

Maybe you can relate to Frank's quandary, having faced similar kinds of ethical questions and tradeoffs in your own business.

If Frank has taken the time to set out his core values in advance, those values can help him out of his quandary. Values provide a framework to guide people who confront difficult choices, especially as a business grows and more people have to face tough decisions. Also, research suggests that principled companies with strong values tend to attract and retain better employees, and those companies are often more successful as a result.

Having no fundamental guidelines to follow — or, worse yet, being told to play it safe or "don't rock the boat" — business people in Frank's position are forced to choose the easy path paved by profit opportunity. But the easiest path isn't always the best. When profits are the only guide, you may find it easier to cut corners or even bend the law — and that has spelled serious legal trouble for many companies in recent years, bringing some very high flyers crashing down.

Applying ethics and the law

A *values statement* is a set of beliefs and principles that guide the activities and operations of your company, no matter what its size. To make the statement mean anything, the people at the top of your company must exemplify your stated values, and your company's incentive and reward systems should lead all employees to act in ways that support your company's values.

Having a values statement can keep you and your colleagues on the right side of the law. After a spate of stunning financial scandals in the United States, Canada moved to protect and build confidence with investors. The Canadian Security Administrators developed new rules that include stringent standards of disclosure. The rules require senior managers of publicly traded companies to certify the accuracy of their financial statements and take responsibility for internal financial controls. Failing to do so can land you in jail. No longer can top-level executives say they don't really know what's going on in the companies that they run. Now, the executives are responsible for every number on a financial statement.

If your company isn't big enough to be publicly traded, you're still certain to come up against the law every time you file a tax return, whether you run a corporation, a partnership, or a sole proprietorship. Having a clear set of values can keep you from getting too well acquainted with the Canada Revenue Agency (CRA).

Getting caught lost and unprepared

You probably remember some headline-grabbing stories of companies suddenly faced with crises. Establishments that have come under fire include

- **ExxonMobil (oil manufacturer and exporter):** One of the world's most profitable companies is still the company environmentalists love to hate. Exxon operated the infamous oil tanker *Valdez* that spewed millions of gallons of crude oil into a pristine Alaskan bay, causing incalculable economic and environmental damage to the area.

- **Ford Motor Company (automobile manufacturer):** After a series of roll-over accidents involving Ford sport utility vehicles, investigations revealed problems with the Firestone tires. The result was a massive recall, class action lawsuits, a congressional investigation, and a mountain of bad publicity.

- **Liberal Party of Canada (federal government):** Results of the Gomery Inquiry into the Sponsorship Program from 1994 to 2003 revealed that the granting department circumvented contracting procedures for federal tax dollars intended to promote federalism in Quebec and funnelled that money through private advertising companies to secret contracts, as well as to political and bureaucratic officials.

These companies all stumbled over so-called externalities (to use economics doublespeak). *Externalities* refer to those circumstances that extend beyond a firm's immediate control to issues that go deeper than simply making a buck. Over time, the failure to see the power of these outside forces — and to account for social and ethical values when you make decisions — can result in serious or even disastrous consequences for your company. As the examples in the preceding list illustrate, we're not talking about one unhappy customer; we're talking about big-time trouble.

You can find examples of externalities in episodes involving companies of every size in all industries, from daycare centres to giant investment firms. Faced with unexpected events, unprepared companies often react as though they're in total disarray. When a company lacks stated values to which everybody subscribes, the interpretation of important issues is left up to anyone and everyone in the company. The company finds itself speaking with many voices and going in several directions, resulting in confused employees, unhappy customers, an angry public, and disappointed investors.

To see how a company with strong core values responds to a potentially disastrous situation, check out the Johnson & Johnson example in the following section. In this case, J & J pulled through a major crisis and, in the process, became a corporate role model. When you begin to think about your own business values, remember

> ✔ A *values statement* is a summary of the beliefs and principles that guide your company's activities.
>
> ✔ Clearly stated values can help your company react quickly and decisively when the unexpected strikes.
>
> ✔ Everybody in your company must understand and embrace your company's values.

Understanding the value of having values

A clear values statement can be most important when the unexpected happens.

In the late 1980s, the United States experienced what many consider a terrorist attack. Someone in the Chicago area tampered with bottles of Tylenol, the best-selling pain reliever from McNeil Laboratories, a subsidiary of the health care giant Johnson & Johnson. An unknown number of Tylenol capsules were laced with cyanide, and eight people died. The tragedy created a business crisis for Johnson & Johnson.

Johnson & Johnson reacted quickly and decisively to the threat against its customers. The company pulled every bottle of Tylenol from retail shelves throughout America — a massive undertaking that ultimately cost the company more than $100 million — and it did so immediately upon discovering the problem.

When the crisis was over, Johnson & Johnson became a corporate role model. It's lightning-fast response to the Tylenol incident earned it a reputation as one of the most responsible companies in the world, one that takes its civic duties seriously and is willing to put the public good ahead of its profits. Johnson & Johnson's many businesses benefited accordingly.

Why did Johnson & Johnson behave so well when so many other companies act paralyzed in sticky situations? The reasons are summed up in the company's statement of values, an extraordinary document called the Johnson & Johnson Credo (see the "The Johnson & Johnson Credo" sidebar, in this chapter).

For more than half a century, the Credo has successfully guided behaviour and actions across the sprawling Johnson & Johnson empire, currently a $53 billion worldwide corporation with more than 122,200 employees.

The Johnson & Johnson Credo

We believe our first responsibility is to the doctors, nurses, and patients, to mothers and all others who use our products and services. In meeting their needs, everything we do must be of high quality. We must constantly strive to reduce our costs in order to maintain reasonable prices. Customers' orders must be serviced promptly and accurately. Our suppliers and distributors must have an opportunity to make a fair profit.

We are responsible to our employees, the men and women who work with us throughout the world. Everyone must be considered as an individual. We must respect their dignity and recognize their merit. They must have a sense of security in their jobs. Compensation must be fair and adequate, and working conditions clean, orderly, and safe. Employees must feel free to make suggestions and complaints. There must be equal opportunity for employment, development, and advancement for those qualified. We must provide competent management, and their actions must be just and ethical.

We are responsible to the communities in which we live and work and to the world community as well. We must be good citizens — support good works and charities and bear our fair share of taxes. We must encourage civic improvements and better health and education. We must maintain in good order the property we are privileged to use, protecting the environment and natural resources.

Our final responsibility is to our stockholders. Business must make a sound profit. We must experiment with new ideas. Research must be carried on, innovative programs developed, and mistakes paid for. New equipment must be purchased, new facilities provided, and new products launched. Reserves must be created to provide for adverse times. When we operate according to these principles, the stockholders should realize a fair return.

The Johnson & Johnson Credo works so well because each employee takes it seriously. With the active encouragement and involvement of top management, from the chairperson on down, the Credo is invoked, praised, and communicated throughout the company. Old-timers and new hires alike are reminded of the importance of the message. Promotions depend, in part, on how well managers live up to and disseminate the values of the Credo within their areas of responsibility. The Credo is a significant factor in Johnson & Johnson's continued performance near the top of its industry — and an indication of why the company is so well regarded by so many people.

Clarifying Your Company Values

Values statements often address several audiences. The Johnson & Johnson Credo (refer to the sidebar "The Johnson & Johnson Credo," in this chapter), for example, speaks to doctors, patients, customers, suppliers, distributors, employees, stockholders, and the community and world at large.

You put together a values statement primarily for the benefit of your employees, of course (or just for yourself, if you operate a business alone). But your company's values have an obvious impact on all your stakeholders, including the owners, investors, bankers, customers, suppliers, regulators — and heck, even your mother if she loaned you $10,000 to start your business. (See Chapter 2 for more info on stakeholders.) When you start to identify your company's most important values, you have to consider different viewpoints, including the following:

- The demands of your investors (if you have any)
- The interests and expectations of all your stakeholders
- The beliefs and principles that you and your company already hold

After you come up with a preliminary list of company values that you feel are most important, you're in a good position to create your values statement.

Strong coffee and high principles

Second Cup has grown from a single java kiosk selling whole bean coffee in a Toronto shopping mall, opened in 1975, to an international company with more than 360 cafés across Canada and 15 in the Middle East. Second Cup is Canada's largest specialty café franchisor and second largest retailer of coffee. Its tag line proudly boasts, "Independently owned; uniquely Canadian." The company owes its success to many savvy decisions. But it also credits its guiding principles, which allow the company to measure the appropriateness of everything it does. Here are Second Cup's guiding principles:

- Work in harmony with both the environment and people.

- Treat our coffee growing environment with the utmost respect and dignity.

- Ensure that no coffee purchased from Second Cup is harvested from child or forced labour.

- Provide a safe and healthy work environment.

- Provide fair and equitable compensation.

- Offer financial payment for quality coffee beans to directly benefit the farmers, workers, and mills.

Focusing on existing beliefs and principles

Drawing up a list of beliefs and principles is one thing; putting those beliefs to the test is another. Tough choices are bound to come along, and they force you to examine your beliefs closely. If you run a one-person company, you already know something about what you stand for. In a bigger company, certain beliefs and values are inherent in the ways that the company does business. The best way to get to the heart of your company's beliefs and principles is to imagine how you'd respond to tough dilemmas.

Think about the situations described in the Beliefs and Principles Questionnaire (see Figure 3-1). Ask other people in your company, or trusted colleagues from outside your business, how they'd react to these situations. Include a box on the questionnaire labelled Other or Don't Know. And remember, the whole point of situations that put your values to the test is that they're not always easy.

Figure 3-1:
Answers to the questionnaire point to the beliefs and principles that your company's managers and employees already hold.

Beliefs and Principles Questionnaire

Situation	*Possible Response*
A disgruntled customer demands a full sales refund on a product. The product isn't defective but can't be resold. The customer insists that it just doesn't work right. Would you be more inclined to	❏ Send the customer away, keeping the sale on the books ❏ Refund the customer's money, absorbing the loss but betting on repeat business and loyal customers
You're faced with filling a key position in your company. Would you be more inclined to	❏ Hire a person from the outside who has the necessary job skills but little experience in your industry ❏ Promote an experienced and loyal employee, providing job-skills training
You're forced to let one of your employees go. Would you tend to dismiss	❏ The young, recently hired college grad, inexperienced but energetic ❏ The 55-year-old manager with 20 years at the company, solid and hard-working but somewhat set in his or her ways
You find out that a long-term supplier has been routinely under billing you for services, increasing your own profit margins. Would you be inclined to	❏ Let the matter pass, assuming that it's ultimately the supplier's mistake and responsibility ❏ Take the initiative to correct the billing error in the future ❏ Offer to not only correct the mistake, but also pay back the accumulated difference

Situation	Possible Response
You have a brilliant and creative employee. Unfortunately, this employee continually flouts the rules and disrupts the entire company. Would you tend to	❏ Tolerate the behaviour ❏ Work on ways to correct the situation ❏ Terminate the employee
An employee is faced with a personal dilemma. To meet a deadline on an important project, the employee must work overtime and miss a child's birthday celebration. Which do you tend to think of as the better employee	❏ The one who willingly agrees to work overtime ❏ The one who declines to come in and instead attends the birthday party
To meet your profit target for the coming quarter, you're faced with reducing costs. Would you lean toward	❏ Cutting back on customer-service expenses ❏ Reducing current investment in new product development ❏ Missing the quarterly target, concluding that the long-term investments are both necessary and justified
When developing the compensation packages for managers in your company, would you support	❏ Incentives based primarily on rewarding individual effort ❏ Compensation systems that promote attainment of group or team-based goals
You discover that one of your products doesn't quite meet its published specifications. Would your likely response be to	❏ Immediately alert your customers to the discrepancy ❏ Invest some time and effort into understanding the problem before informing customers ❏ Quietly correct the error, assuming that if customers were having problems, they would have already come to you
Rank the following in terms of their importance to you in your business	❏ Maximize profits ❏ Satisfy customers ❏ Create jobs ❏ Promote new technologies ❏ Win product-quality awards ❏ Beat the competition ❏ Maintain long-term growth ❏ Dominate markets

Keep in mind that there are no right or wrong answers; you don't have to send a note home or give anyone a bad grade. You're simply trying to identify the basic values with which your company already feels comfortable. Completed questionnaires give insights into the general beliefs and principles that your company considers important.

Putting together your values statement

Your company's values statement represents more than a quick to-do list. The description of your values reaches beyond quarterly goals or even yearly targets. Your values should guide you through tough decisions while you build a sustainable business that lasts and grows over years and decades.

Maybe your company has some sort of values credo in place. If so, you're a step ahead of the game. (You lose points, however, if you have to glance at the dusty plaque on the office wall to remember it.) If you can't dig up a ready-made values statement to start with, begin putting together your own.

You may not have the luxury of spending weeks or months developing a values statement, so we show you a quick way to create one that sets your company on the right track. If your company is small, you can follow the steps yourself or with one or two of your colleagues — no need for long meetings and careful review. If you're part of a larger company, however, you have to go through a bit more debate to get a consensus. (Sorry.)

You can't create a values statement quickly, but you *can* quickly begin a process to help capture and articulate the values intrinsic in the leadership and employees of your business.

Follow these steps to start creating a value statement:

1. **Gather your company's chief decision-makers to talk about the general company values that should (and do) guide employee behaviour.**

   Come prepared with an agenda and your own observations, and take careful notes.

2. **Prepare a first-draft list of all the values discussed in the meeting and circulate copies for review.**

3. **Schedule one or two follow-up meetings with senior managers to clarify and confirm a final set of values.**

4. **Create a values statement that captures the agreed-upon values clearly and concisely, and get it approved by the senior managers and chief decision-makers.**

5. **Meet with managers at all levels to make sure that they understand the importance of, and the reasoning behind, the company values statement.**

6. **See that every employee gets a copy of the statement.**

If you're in business for yourself, place a framed copy of the values statement near your desk at work or in your home office. Don't let it gather dust. For a bigger company, print the values statement on wallet-size cards to hand out, and don't forget to include the statement in the annual report. Post it on the company Web site and make sure it reaches all the stakeholders. Refer to and rely on the company values and let them be a guiding force in the actions and activities of every person who represents your company.

If you're part of a larger firm, the procedure in our list relies heavily on the ideas and suggestions of people at the top of your organization. Sometimes, however, the best insights on company values come from employees themselves — people from different backgrounds and various levels in the company who can draw on a range of business experiences. Don't forget to include two other important groups — customers and shareholders. Both can help you figure out what values are essential to your company.

Following through with your values

A values statement can sometimes turn out to be a bit too simplistic, using words that sound good on paper but that are difficult to put to practical use. We recently looked through a stack of values statements from some of the biggest companies around. Over half of them included the word "integrity" or something close ("ethical conduct," "doing the right thing"). The next most popular value showing up was "respect for others," followed by "teamwork," "excellence," and "customer service."

To make your values statement really useful, you need to take the next step and link your values to basic, sensible rules that employees at all levels in your company can follow. A good place to start is to ask a selection of employees to fill out a questionnaire similar to the Beliefs and Principles Questionnaire shown in Figure 3-1. You may also want to create an anonymous suggestion box in which employees can express their own ideas about values and about how your company is fulfilling its stated values.

The values statement of the infamous Enron Corporation, by the way, boasted four key words: "respect," "integrity," "communication," and "excellence." Nice words. But the company went from one of the highest-flying businesses in the country to bankruptcy and scandal in months. The lesson of its fall is a simple one: Values must matter. And you must integrate those values into the way the company operates day-to-day and week-to-week.

When the time comes to conduct those annual employee performance reviews (you know, the ones that everyone loves to hate), use them as an opportunity to promote your company's values. Bring out a copy of the values statement and ask each employee how well his or her individual activities reflect the company's values. At the same time, ask yourself if the incentives and reward systems in your company work toward supporting those values.

Creating Your Company's Vision Statement

Your company's *vision statement* should be a precise, well-crafted document announcing where your company wants to go and painting a picture of what your company wants to become. To people on the inside and outside of your company, your vision statement is a compass, showing the whole world the direction in which your company is heading.

A vision statement not only points the way to the future, it also makes you want to get up and go there. It represents your company's best hopes and brightest dreams. Now, we know that Karl Marx and his vision of socialism seldom come up in conversation at cocktail parties, even in Moscow. But when you hear his message

> *Workers of the world, unite! You have nothing to lose but your chains!*

it's hard not to be roused, even today. Effective vision statements are, in part, inspirational calls to action. What if Marx had come up with this:

> *Hey, guys, let's all get together over here! Maybe we can figure out how to make you more dough!*

You'd say, "Karl who?" And Marx could forget that place in history.

Don't panic if the makings of a dynamic, charismatic leader aren't in your back pocket. An insightful corporate vision is much more likely to develop out of a diverse team of hard-working folks than to spring mysteriously from an inspired moment in the life of a leader.

The best way to create a meaningful vision statement resembles the best way to create a values statement. Just follow these steps:

1. **Select a small group of dedicated employees from various levels across your company.**

If your company is small, get the whole gang together. If you're the chief cook and bottle washer all in one, you can represent yourself. ***Remember:*** The more people you involve, the broader the perspective you receive and the better the chances of creating a vision statement that truly reflects your company's future.

2. **Have the group reread your company's values statement and review the list of stakeholders who have an interest in your company.**

3. **Begin a verbal free-for-all.**

   Allow everybody to volunteer personal opinions and ideas about the company's future, form, and direction. Start taking down a list and forming it into a cohesive statement.

4. **When the vision team feels comfortable with the results, add the finishing touches to the wording and choice of medium to get your vision ready for prime time.**

Keep these tips in mind when you create your vision statement:

✔ Make sure that no one dominates the discussion when the team begins to toss around the ideas and phrases that form your company's vision. Nothing kills creativity faster than having every idea come from one person.

✔ Allow sufficient time for the words to grow on the group, permitting the deeper meanings to sink in. You can't accomplish the vision statement process in one quick take. Good vision statements have a tendency to evolve over time — and over several meetings.

✔ Make sure that your company's vision statement ties in with your company's reality. Nothing is worse than creating a vision that has more to do with fantasy than with the future. Fantasy visions generate nothing but a sense of confusion and alienation among everyone involved.

Although you may end up with only a couple of sentences or even just a phrase, the vision statement is the compass that provides your company's direction into the future. Spend enough time with your statement to make sure that the north on your company compass truly is north — that it does indeed point in the direction in which you want to go.

As a rule of thumb, you should assume that your vision statement could serve the company for the next decade. Does this mean that you can never change the statement? No — but you should change a vision statement only if business conditions truly warrant a new course of action. Keep in mind that no one should cross out or rewrite the ideas that you capture in your company's vision statement on a whim; those ideas represent the lasting themes that guide your company at any time and under any circumstance.

Companies with vision

Check out these vision statements to see how some companies look toward the future:

Ballard Power Systems' vision is power to change the world. Our mission is to make fuel cells a commercial reality.

— Ballard Power Systems, Burnaby, B.C.

A manufacturer of zero-emission fuel cells

To offer the best service and the right product at the right price to North American consumers of housing and home improvement products.

— RONA Inc., Boucherville, P.Q.

A distributor and retailer of hardware, home renovation, and garden products

To make Sobeys the most worthwhile shopping experience in the marketplace by accurately identifying customers' preferences and efficiently meeting their needs.

— Sobeys Inc., Stellarton, N.S.

A grocery retailer and food distributor

A complete commitment to helping clients achieve results.

— CGI Group Inc., Montreal, P.Q.

An international IT and business-process service provider

But only diamonds last forever. If a changing environment throws you an unexpected curve, by all means, alter your vision to reflect the new reality. You should craft your statement in such a way that it's flexible enough to respond to a changing environment. If the words on paper no longer have meaning for your company, they become useless. Again, the company's vision statement is useful only to the extent that it has the power to move your people into the future.

Chapter 4

Charting the Proper Course

. . . .

. . . .

*Y*ou probably have a good idea of what you want your business to become. But how do you make your idea a reality? You start by defining the business activities that your company plans to engage in, the goals that you expect to meet, and the ways in which you're going to measure success.

In this chapter, we help you create a basic overview of your company and its activities, and we guide you as you shape your expectations into a mission statement. We introduce business goals and objectives and show you how to use them to measure the results that you expect to achieve. We also help you prepare to set your company's goals and objectives, and we look at how you can use those goals and objectives to improve the overall efficiency and effectiveness of your future business.

Creating Your Company's Mission Statement

Mission statements have become very popular with business types in the last few years. Many of us remember the days when you'd find a company's mission statement turning yellow on the cafeteria bulletin board, completely ignored by everyone but the people who wrote it. That's no longer the case.

More and more companies, in fact, post their mission statements for everyone to see. Some companies put mission statements in their brochures and even on their letterheads. Many now include them prominently on company Web sites.

In fact, you can search the Web for the name of almost any business, large or small, using terms such as "mission statement" to find what you're looking for. Our favourite local community theatre, Theatre Collingwood, proudly includes their mission statement on fund-raising material: "To produce professional live theatre in the Georgian Triangle by presenting quality productions, events and educational activities which enrich the cultural life of our community." Who wouldn't want to support such a generous mission?

Many companies are finding out that they can use a mission statement as a powerful tool to communicate the purpose of the business to people both inside and outside the organization. It establishes who you are and what you do.

To be effective, your mission statement must

- ✔ Highlight your company's business activities, including the markets that you serve, the geographic areas that you cover, and the products and services that you offer.

- ✔ Emphasize what your company does that sets it apart from every other business out there.

- ✔ Include the major accomplishments that you anticipate achieving over the next few years.

- ✔ Convey what you have to say in a clear, concise, informative, and interesting manner (a little inspiration doesn't hurt, either).

Getting started

A mission statement doesn't need to be long. In fact, the shorter it is, the better. Even so, the task of creating one can seem impossibly daunting — the Mount Everest of business-planning chores. One reason writing a mission statement can be so overwhelming is that it has to sum up some pretty grand ideas in a few sentences. Also, writing a mission statement requires business planners to ask themselves some fundamental questions — and come up with solid answers. And don't forget, your mission statement should closely reflect the values and vision that you set for your company (see Chapter 3 for how to determine your company's values and vision).

A little preparation up front can make the process a bit easier. Ask yourself some background questions when you get ready to work on your company's mission statement. Don't worry if the answers are fairly general at this point because you're only interested in the basics right now. Research your goals and the practices of the competition, and then answer these questions:

- ✔ Which customers or groups of customers do you plan to serve?

- ✔ What needs do you want to satisfy?

- ✔ What products or services do you plan to provide?

- ✔ How will your company's products differ from competitive items?

✔ What extra value or benefits will customers receive when they choose your company over the competition?

✔ How fast do you expect these answers to change?

In other words, a mission statement answers the basic question:

What is your business?

Need some help? You should enlist managers who are familiar with all the aspects of your business. Follow these steps to begin the process:

1. **Get together a small group of people whose responsibilities cover all the major functions and activities of the company.**

   If you run a small company, include trusted friends, former co-workers, and perhaps even your significant other in this group.

2. **Ask the group members to prepare for the meeting by coming up with their own answers to the background questions we list earlier in this section.**

3. **Review the reasons for having a company mission in the first place and go over what the mission statement should include.**

4. **Schedule several informal meetings in which group members can present their own perspectives, brainstorm a bit, and begin to form a consensus.**

5. **Create, revise, and review the company's mission statement over as many formal meetings as it takes for everyone to be satisfied with the final product.**

A well-crafted mission statement is clear, concise, and easily understood. You should also make it distinctive (from the competition) and up-to-date (give the company's current situation).

Capturing your business (In 50 words or less)

Your company's mission statement has to draw a compelling picture of what your business is all about. We often refer to drawing this picture as creating a *tangible image* of the company. Begin with a first stab at a mission statement:

Our gizmos bring unique value to people, wherever they may be.

Not a bad start. This statement says a little something about geography and a bit about being different. But you're far from done. To work toward communicating the company's activities, accomplishments, and capabilities with more clarity and punch, we suggest expanding the statement:

We provide the highest-quality gizmos with unmatched value to the global widget industry, which allows our customers to be leaders in their own fields.

This statement conveys what the company does (provides the highest-quality gizmos), who it serves (the global widget industry), and what sets it apart from its competitors (unmatched value, which allows customers to lead their own fields). The energy makes it a far more compelling mission statement than the earlier version.

How do real companies go about capturing their purpose clearly and concisely, in 50 words or less? The following examples provide useful insights:

- ✔ **Delta Elevator** *(an Ontario manufacturer of elevators):* "Our mission is to develop and manufacture leading-edge elevating devices and provide dependable and honest service, while giving lifelong satisfaction and employment for our people."

- ✔ **Cooper Virtual Office Services** *(a small Saskatchewan administrative support service):* "Our mission is to offer affordable, efficient services to professionals and students locally and around the globe."

- ✔ **ZENN Motor Company** *(an Ontario car manufacturer):* "As a leading developer, manufacturer and supplier of electric vehicles, our goal is to provide drivers with a quality urban transportation solution that positively impacts our environment and greatly reduces operating costs. Working with our internationally respected partners, we bring the world's zero-emission vehicles to you, setting the standard for what electric vehicles can be. The culmination of this passion for quality is the ZENN Neighbourhood Electric Vehicle."

- ✔ **Strategic Leadership Forum** *(a professional association):* "Our mission is to provide our community of members with an independent and intellectually challenging forum that delivers practical insights and interactions on strategic management and leadership."

- ✔ **Canadian Humanitarian** *(an Alberta humanitarian organization):* "Our mission is to provide the basic necessities of life such as nutrition, shelter, health care, and education, to disadvantaged children everywhere."

- ✔ **Magnetic Hill Zoo** *(a New Brunswick zoological park):* "The Magnetic Hill Zoo is committed to safeguarding animal species and raising public awareness of endangered species. The zoo is designed for the well-being of the animals, as well as the safety of the public, in mind."

- ✔ **Cognos Incorporated** *(an Ontario-based software company; prior to the purchase by IBM in 2008):* "As enterprises around the world move to adopt performance management, Cognos will continue to direct our products, support, and services toward helping our customers deliver on its promise."

Mission accomplished

You may think that mission statements represent only businesses. But you can also use them for product categories. And the best statements not only describe the purpose of the products and what they offer, but they also capture something about the images that the products hope to convey. Consider this statement from *Canadian Business Magazine* — a product of Rogers Publishing — which neatly includes both a mission and a message:

Every two weeks, Canadian Business *delivers timely, forward-looking and relevant commentary on the fast-moving stories that characterize business today. As Canada's best-selling business magazine,* Canadian Business *is widely read by corporate leaders, innovators and entrepreneurs, for the insight they need to make informed management decisions.*

By the way, did you know that *Canadian Business* is the longest-published magazine in Canada? It was first published in 1928 by the Canadian Chamber of Commerce before being divested in 1977 because of its profitable success (an apparent no-no for not-for-profits). Could an effective mission statement be the cause of all that longevity and success?

Introducing Goals and Objectives

Your mission statement is a giant step forward; in it, you articulate the purpose of your company by defining the business that you're in. But the definition is just the beginning. When Canada decided to assist the United States with its space shuttle program, it set its sights on building robotic arms (now known as Canadarm 1 and 2). Stating the nature of the mission was the easy part. Actually figuring out, step by step, how to get there was the trick. It involved carefully formulated goals and objectives.

You don't have to be planning a trip to outer space to know that goals and objectives are important. If you've ever planned a vacation trip by car, you know that choosing the destination is essential (and often painful, especially if the kids want to go to Canada's Wonderland and you want to go to the West Edmonton Mall). But the real work starts when you begin to work out an itinerary, carefully setting up mileage goals and sightseeing objectives so that your three-week getaway doesn't turn into a *National Lampoon* vacation. Goals and objectives are vital to successful business planning.

We know you're eager to get going with your business plan. But allow us to take a few moments in the following sections to introduce some important ideas that you can take advantage of when you begin setting your own goals and objectives.

Why bother?

Who needs goals, anyway? You may be the type who plans a trip by filling the hybrid with gas and charging the battery, stopping at the ATM for cash, and flipping a coin as you head out of town. Why waste time trying to decipher a map when you're just out for the ride? Maybe your approach is fine for a quick getaway adventure, but for a company, failing to set business goals can lead to more serious consequences.

Remember the clever exchange between Alice and the Cheshire Cat in Lewis Carroll's *Alice's Adventures in Wonderland?* Alice asks:

"Would you tell me, please, which way I ought to walk from here?"

"That depends a good deal on where you want to get to," said the Cat.

"I don't much care where —" said Alice.

"Then it doesn't matter which way you walk," said the Cat.

If your company doesn't have goals to work toward, you don't know what direction to take or what business efforts to focus on. You become as lost as Alice in Wonderland.

If your business opportunities are so obvious and so overwhelming that you don't need to define a particular course of action to reach your ultimate destination, you've won the business planner's lottery. You're more likely, however, to run into one hazardous crossroad after another, and a lack of careful planning can be dangerous indeed. Just look at the following examples:

- ✔ The manufacturing breakdown of the sports car Bricklin in 1976, which cost taxpayers close to $23 million, resulted from a failure to create sound processes and quality assurance.

- ✔ Monumental planning blunders have been partly blamed for fiascos involving certain infamous product introductions, including the Ford Edsel in the 1950s and New Coke in the 1980s.

Not setting goals and objectives created financial chaos in the situations discussed in the preceding list, and not knowing customers, competitors, and how they play into the company mission resulted in product failure. Setting business goals and objectives provides an important insurance policy for your business: the opportunity to plan a successful course of action and then keep track of your progress.

Goals versus objectives

After you complete a mission statement, your business goals lay out a basic itinerary for achieving your mission. *Goals* are broad business results that your company absolutely commits to attaining.

Goals are typically stated in terms of general business intentions. You may define your company's goals by using phrases such as "becoming the market leader" or "being the low-cost provider of choice." These aims clearly focus the company's activities without being so narrowly defined that they stifle creativity or limit flexibility.

In working toward set goals, your company must be willing to come up with the *resources* — the money and the people — required to attain the intended results. The goals that you set for your company should ultimately dictate your business choices throughout your organization and may take years to achieve. Goals should forge an unbreakable link between your company's actions and its mission.

Simply setting a general goal for your company isn't the end of the story; you also need to spend time thinking about how to get there. So, your company must follow up its goal with a series of *objectives:* operational statements that specify exactly what you must do to reach the goal. You should attach numbers and dates to objectives, which may involve weeks or months of effort. Those numbers help you realize when you reach a given objective.

Objectives never stand alone. They flow directly from your mission and your values and vision (see Chapter 3), and outside the context of their larger goals, they have little meaning. In fact, objectives can be downright confusing.

The goal "Improve employee morale," for example, is much too general without specific objectives to back it up. And you can misinterpret the objective "Reduce employee grievances by 35 percent over the coming year" if you state it by itself. (One way to achieve this objective is to terminate some employees and terrorize the rest of the workforce — effective, but not really the way to run a good business.) When you take the goal and objective together, however, their meanings become clear.

Want an easy way to keep the difference between goals and objectives straight? Remember the acronym GOWN: G for goals, O for objectives, W for words, and N for numbers. For goals, we use words — sketching in the broad picture. For objectives, we use numbers — filling in the specific details.

Ford Motor Company and its China goal

One hundred years ago, the Ford Motor Company had a simple mission statement: "We will democratize the automobile." The company's efforts extended around the world, and in 1913, Ford sold its first Model T in mainland China.

But the turbulent events of the 20th century ended Ford's bid to democratize the automobile in one of the world's most populous countries. To this day, Ford has been slow to re-enter the vast and booming modern Chinese market. With just one car-manufacturing plant in China, Ford lags far behind its rivals, General Motors and Japan's Toyota Motor Corporation.

However, Ford still wants to achieve its original mission in the People's Republic. So, the company announced a new strategic business goal in 2004 to increase its market share and close in on its competitors in China. The company planned to achieve its goal through a set of targeted objectives. One objective was to build a second car plant in Nanjing, close to the bustling eastern provinces, which launched operations in 2007. Another objective was to expand output seven-fold at its existing plant in Chongqing, located in western China.

These key objectives are supported by initiatives that should help Ford make up for lost time. These initiatives include

- Partnering with solid local companies
- Taking advantage of a strong local labour pool
- Developing human resources in the region
- Leveraging its global operations expertise

Whether Ford's new goals and objectives will win it the lion's share of the Chinese market or force the company out of the market for good remains an open question. Although its sales in China increased a whopping 50 percent over the past two years, its hot competition is getting hotter with car prices in China falling as competitors slug it out. Still, Ford should find plenty of room for success. The car market in China is booming, and analysts expect it to soar by at least 40 percent a year for several years to come.

If you already use different definitions for goals and objectives, don't worry; you're not going crazy. What we find crazy is the lack of any standard definition of terms when it comes to business planning. The important task is to settle on the definitions that you want to use and stick with them in a consistent manner. That way, you prevent any unnecessary confusion within your company.

Efficiency versus effectiveness

People have bandied two business terms back and forth for years: efficiency and effectiveness. The terms were first thrown together in an absolutely captivating business classic, *Functions of the Executive,* written by Chester Barnard back in 1939. Old Chester was president of the New York Telephone

Company, and we're afraid that he had a bit too much time on his hands. But he did come up with one useful notion for working with your company's goals and objectives: efficiency versus effectiveness.

We all strive to be both efficient and effective in our individual work, of course. *Effectiveness* is often described as "doing the right thing," whereas *efficiency* is described as "doing things right." Chester came up with the idea that you can apply these concepts to a company and its activities.

In this context, effectiveness — doing the right thing — has a great deal to do with choosing the right goals to pursue. For example, consider our imaginary gizmo company. Global Gizmo's mission statement may emphasize becoming customer-focused and market-driven in all product areas. If Global Gizmos wants to be effective, management must set goals that encourage product designers and engineers to first be in touch with their customers and to be aware of market demands before they start designing and creating new products.

Efficiency — doing things right — is concerned more with how well the company applies resources in pursuit of its goals. To be efficient, Global Gizmo employees must have objectives that ensure that the company can achieve its goals of becoming customer-focused and market-driven. Among other results, these objectives should lead to a proper allocation of the research budget among design, product development, and market testing. Resources are always scarce, and Global Gizmos can't afford to squander them.

Successful organizations aren't just effective or just efficient. The best companies are both efficient and effective on a consistent basis. They achieve both efficiency and effectiveness by taking goal-setting and the development of clear, measurable objectives seriously in the relentless pursuit of the company's mission.

Minding Your Own Business: Setting Goals and Objectives

Your company's goals and objectives reflect your primary business intentions, and they determine both the itinerary and timetable for fulfilling your intentions. In other words, your goals and objectives focus the company on the important work at hand and provide a mechanism for measuring your progress.

Goals and objectives are ultimately meant to make your company more efficient and effective. How can you see to it that setting them is also as efficient and effective as it can be? Here are some guidelines to get you started.

Creating your business goals

Goals are the broad business results that your company commits to achieving. To jump-start the process of setting your company's goals, use this useful list of guidelines:

- ✔ Determine who to involve in setting your company's goals. Because goals are the core of your company's business, the group members should include the people who are responsible for all your major business activities. If you're going it alone in business, try to develop a core group of advisers who can meet with you periodically to set goals.

- ✔ Develop a procedure for monitoring your company's goals on a routine basis, revising or reworking those goals as business circumstances change.

- ✔ Create individual goals that clarify your company's business activities without limiting flexibility and creativity.

- ✔ Confirm that your company's goals, taken together, provide an effective blueprint for achieving your broad business intentions.

- ✔ Make sure that your company's stated goals closely tie in to your company's mission statement (see the section "Creating Your Company's Mission Statement," earlier in this chapter, for more info).

- ✔ Rely on your goals when you communicate your business intentions to people both inside and outside your company.

Laying out your objectives

Objectives are the statements that fill in the details, specifying exactly how you plan to reach each of your company's goals.

As much as possible, you should tie your objectives to cold, hard numbers: the number of new customers you want to serve, products you want to sell, or dollars you want to earn.

This list of guidelines provides a useful template when your company starts to develop business objectives:

- ✔ Determine who should set business objectives in your company.

- ✔ Develop a system for reviewing and managing business objectives throughout your company.

✔ Make sure that objectives are achievable and verifiable by including numbers and dates where appropriate.

✔ Create business objectives that can clearly advance and achieve larger company goals.

✔ Confirm that your company's objectives, taken together, result in an efficient use of *resources* — money and people — in pursuit of broader business intentions.

✔ Consider using a formal method, such as management by objectives (MBO), to involve everyone in your company in the continuous process of setting, reviewing, and meeting business objectives. (For more on the ins and outs of MBO, see the sidebar "Management by objectives," in this chapter.)

Matching goals and objectives with your mission

We say it over and over throughout this book, but this statement is so important that it deserves repeating: Your company's goals and objectives must be closely tied to your mission statement.

Management by objectives

In 1954, management guru Peter Drucker came up with a novel way to generate and communicate a company's intentions (its mission, goals, and objectives): You simply involve all the employees who have to actually carry them out. Not surprisingly, he also coined a term for his method, calling it *management by objectives* (MBO).

MBO turned out to be a wildly successful idea when it was introduced. By the mid-1970s, more than half of the top 500 companies were using the technique. Granted, not everybody was happy with the process. Some companies balked at the time and effort that it took to set MBO goals and related objectives. Other companies failed to carry out the paperwork that the system requires. Still other companies found the entire concept of shared decision-making to be just plain weird and the new culture to be too alien.

For companies that commit to using it correctly, MBO has proven to be a valuable management tool — a process capable of generating new ideas, communicating business intentions, and focusing the company's energy on an agreed-upon set of goals and objectives. Management by objectives works because it involves people fashioning the company's future. Employees commit more to that future because they have a greater stake in the process that gets them there. As you begin to work on your company's goals and objectives, invest some well-spent hours in figuring out ways to bring the spirit of MBO into your collaborative process.

How goals can keep a mission on track

Norco Product Ltd. began producing bikes in Vancouver in 1964. It started with a man, a garage, and a dream of a western Canadian–based bicycle manufacturing company committed to quality products and outstanding customer service. Today it has a staff of 150 in three offices across Canada, domestic manufacturing facilities, and 25 international distributors.

Success hasn't always been easy, though. The industry has taken a number of turns. Bikes have changed dramatically from the simple 3-speed or 10-speed roadsters of the mid-1900s to the complex metal-matrix composite, shock-absorbing, extreme sport versions of today. Cheaper foreign imports lured customers away. Market demand declined.

Norco has managed to ride out these changes by keeping its goals and objectives closely aligned to the company's mission statement. Here's its mission statement:

We are dedicated to building rewarding, long-term relationships with our Employees, our Customers, and our Suppliers. We are driven by our Customers to supply innovative cycle products, outstanding service, *and marketing support that will promote their growth and success.*

Fine words, of course. Making progress can be challenging, however, when competition threatens and markets change. On its Web site, the company shares its strategic business goals for meeting these challenges:

✔ To provide a rewarding and challenging environment where our Employees and the company can grow together on a progressive basis

✔ To be the number one supplier to our Customers, partnering with them in the adventure of cycling

✔ To be an industry leader in developing and delivering innovative performance products

✔ To maintain the financial stability of the company and ensure an adequate return on investment for our Shareholders.

The language of these goals and objectives may not be as stirring as the mission statement, but they represent the wheels and gears that turn the company mission into a reality.

Too many companies become nearsighted and simply forget their broad business intentions when they go about the nitty-gritty work of setting goals and tying them to measurable objectives. Managers start with what's close at hand. They look at employee activities and behaviour, and they come up with incentives and rewards that seem to do the right thing at the time, motivating workers toward specific objectives. But these types of goals and objectives tend to be nearsighted and may be totally out of sync with the larger aims of the company.

Suppose that an Internet-based consumer PC business finds that its profit margins are squeezed. As a result, the company sets objectives and offers incentive bonuses to managers who can reduce expenses by 15 percent during the next six-month reporting period. The manager in charge of customer service, being a rational team player, mandates an immediate reduction in the time service reps spend on the phone with customer inquiries. He delivers this mandate, even though the company has built its reputation on helping customers with confusing hardware and software problems, and even though the company mission states, "The organization is committed to offering the best customer service in the industry."

Hurried conversations inevitably lead to disgruntled customers. Even worse, these objectives send a clear signal to employees that efficiency and cost-cutting efforts are what really count — not customer satisfaction. If the manager had set goals and objectives with the company's mission in mind, perhaps he or she would have come up with a more innovative solution — introducing an Internet-based help system that includes real-time dialogue with an expert online or automated e-mail support, for example. By allowing customers the option of searching online for answers to the most common software questions, the manager could have reduced calls to the service reps and enhanced service at the same time.

Avoiding business-planning pitfalls

Goals and objectives are meant to motivate everyone in your organization. They also help channel every employee's efforts in the same direction, with the same results in mind. When human nature is involved, nothing is certain. But you can improve the odds that your actions will produce the results you expect by avoiding several common pitfalls while your company works toward specific business goals and objectives:

- ✔ **Don't set pie-in-the-sky goals for yourself.** If you don't have a prayer of achieving a particular goal, you shouldn't bother setting it. Goals are meant to motivate; impossible goals tend to discourage. You don't want to mess up a great business opportunity because you need more time, resources, and energy. We find that the best goals are *stretch goals:* goals large enough to propel your company forward without causing you to stumble along the way.

- ✔ **Don't sell your organization short.** Although trying to reach too far with your goals can be dangerous, you don't want to wimp out, either. Goals often become self-fulfilling prophecies. Companies set them, attain them, and then relax — coasting along on automatic pilot — until they get around to setting new goals. If anything, try to err a bit on the high side, creating goals that expand your organization's capabilities. Again, think of setting stretch goals. You may be surprised by the skills and expertise that you discover within your company.

- ✔ **Be careful what you aim for.** Your goals should clearly state what you want to see happen with your venture. If your goals contradict the intentions of the company, you and your employees may actually end up pursuing misguided aims. Goals that appear out of sync with the company's larger mission may lead to behaviour that makes little sense from the broader perspective and purpose of the company (see the preceding section for more info on making your goals and objectives match your mission).

✔ **Beware of too many words or too many numbers.** Remember — a goal is a broad statement of a business intention that flows directly from your company's mission. Objectives are more narrowly defined and always tie in to a specific goal; they fill in the details, specify time frames, and include ways of verifying success. You define goals in words, and you define objectives in numbers. But no rule is hard and fast. In reality, well-designed goals and objectives often mix words and numbers. Words alone are sometimes too vague to carry any real meaning, and you can't reduce all hoped-for outcomes to pure numbers.

✔ **Don't keep your goals and objectives a secret.** If you want goals and objectives to focus and direct your organization's behaviour, every employee has to know about them. We know, we know — this statement seems to be so obvious that it sounds downright silly. But you'd be amazed by the number of managers and owners who carefully set goals and objectives, and then go to great lengths to hide them from everyone else. They protect the goals like corporate jewels. But these jewels have no value unless you communicate them to your employees, who in turn must embrace them. So, prominently display your business goals and objectives in your company newsletter, intranet, or Web site.

Timing is everything

What's the proper time frame for you to reach your goals and objectives? How far out should you place your planning horizon — one year, three years, maybe five? The answer is . . . it depends on the pace of your industry.

Certain industries remain tortoise-like in their pace. Many plastics companies in Canada, for example, operate today much the same as they did 30 years ago, with perhaps the addition of an Internet address. The needs of plastics end-users have changed slowly, and the types of materials used and levels of materials required have stayed pretty much the same. But change is definitely on the horizon, with producers overseas adopting leading-edge innovations, investing in research and development, and delivering quality plastics at significantly lower costs.

Change is perhaps the only constant for other industries. Take health care, for example. The world of doctors and hospitals was at one time a predictable universe in which organization goals and objectives could be developed years in advance. In the last decade, the Canadian health care system has gone through a sea of change. Changes in government regulation, new technology, outdated facilities, labour shortages, and increasing demand from an aging population have all conspired to create a very uncertain world. If you're in hospital management today, you don't worry about five-year horizons; you're now pressured to measure your planning cycles and reviews in months.

You can find plenty of examples of businesses that have lost out because they don't move fast enough to take advantage of changes and to enter new markets. Ford Motor Company was slow to re-enter the booming Chinese market, and when it recently announced plans to build a new plant in China and throw production into high gear, some analysts said the move may be too late. Competitors have already made significant inroads into the Chinese market. Ford pushed forward with aggressive goals and is gaining some market share. Is it enough or still too late? You must identify the forces of change in your own industry. What causes change? How fast do the changes change? Chapter 5 points out how to look for opportunities and threats. And check out Chapter 13 for more guidance on preparing for change.

When dealing with change, business planners have to maintain a balancing act between moving too fast and not fast enough. You need to set business goals and follow them up with verifiable objectives, basing time frames on your comfort level with what you expect to happen down the road. (Chapter 13 helps you manage uncertainty.) Build in some flexibility so that you can revisit your goals and objectives and account for the changes you see.

Part II
Describing Your Marketplace

The 5th Wave   By Rich Tennant

"It's hard to figure. The concept was a big hit in Nunavut."

In this part . . .

To succeed at any venture that you take on, you need to be aware of what you're getting into at the beginning. Think about a road trip you want to take, for example. First, you need to know something about your route and where you want to end up. Next, you need to know what vehicle you'll be driving. Who's going with you? Will you car-camp, use B&Bs, or luxuriate in 5-star hotels? And who said a little road trip was an easy thing to plan?

A business plan isn't much different. In this part, we help you plot out your company's journey for the smoothest trip possible. First, we take a hard look at your industry to see what it takes for you to be successful, and we get you prepared for business opportunities and threats that come your way. We look at how you can divide your customers into groups with similar characteristics and wants so that you can more easily identify and communicate with them. We spend time talking about ways to get better acquainted with your customers — figuring out what motivates them, how they make choices, and what keeps them coming back. Finally, we talk about your competitors — who they are, what they're up to, and how you can plan to compete against them and win.

Chapter 5

Examining the Business Environment

• •

In This Chapter

▶ Defining the business that you're in

▶ Taking a closer look at your industry

▶ Knowing the keys to success

▶ Watching out for business opportunities and threats

• •

*O*ne of the most important questions you can ask yourself as you prepare to create a business plan is "What business am I really in?" The question may sound simple — even trivial — which is precisely the reason why business people too often ignore it. However, if you can answer this basic question correctly, you take the first giant step toward creating an effective business plan.

Remember when crossing Canada on trains, with their elegant dining cars, two-level parlour cars, and smoking lounges, was commonplace? Probably not — but you can visit `www.collectionscanada.gc.ca/trains` and become a bit nostalgic for a long-lost era. Railroad companies in the 1930s, '40s, and '50s thought they knew exactly what business they were in: the railroad business. The question was a no-brainer. As it turned out, however, passengers wanted something a little more general: effective and efficient transportation. Railroad companies soon found competition in the form of provincial highways, General Motors and the Ford Motor Company, Bombardier Aerospace, airlines, and international airports. The forces and players in the railroad business extended well beyond ties and rails. The railroad companies didn't see the big picture — the competition growing everywhere — and they never regained their former glory. Those railroad companies that didn't go up in smoke were engineered into one of the two primary nationals — Canadian National (CN) and Canadian Pacific Railway (CPR).

In this chapter, you can find out how to capture your big picture by defining the business that you're really in. We help you analyze your industry and search for critical success factors, and then we give you some pointers on preparing for the opportunities and threats that may appear on your business horizon.

Understanding Your Business

Okay, so what business are you *really* in? Don't say that you're in the widget business, if widgets are what you produce; go beyond the easy answer that you base simply on what you do or what you make. You have to dig a bit deeper and ask yourself what makes your marketplace tick:

- ✔ What basic customer needs do you fulfill?
- ✔ What underlying forces are at work?
- ✔ What role does your company play?

Eastman Kodak — no longer picture-perfect

Founded way back in 1880 by the entrepreneur George Eastman, Eastman Kodak quickly established itself as the leader in amateur still photography, selling cameras and film, and developing the prints that you stuff into albums, drawers, boxes, and entire closets. Where did the company make its money? Cameras were only marginally profitable, but Kodak wanted people to have cameras so that it could make money on film and even more money on developing that film.

In fact, Kodak has always reaped huge profits from the processing of film. The company manufactures all its own photographic chemicals and coated papers, and it owns the processing labs. Eventually, Kodak came to think of itself as being in the chemical imaging business — they announced this to their stock analysts and anyone else who would listen. While Kodak's executives and managers were busy patting one another on the back, new competitors — and new technologies — snuck in the back door.

As it turned out, customers weren't exactly interested in chemical images for their own

sake. Nobody had a hankering for chemically coated paper or clamoured for the bulk photographic chemicals that Kodak produced so well. People wanted memories, nothing more. They wanted to capture special moments and save them forever. Kodak was really in the *memories* business. And new ways of saving memories were just around the corner.

First, a Japanese firm came along and introduced the video camera to the world. Suddenly, memories were made of electrons, not chemicals. Next came the digital camera revolution. In 2004, Kodak finally recognized the full impact of the train wreck overtaking them. They abandoned their traditional camera markets in North America and Europe to concentrate on digital technology — both digital photography and printing. Kodak's Vancouver and Victoria locations are driving its digital growth globally. Now, the big question is: "Is it too little, too late?" Although snapshots haven't completely gone away, Kodak's exclusive monopoly on memories is certainly over.

You can make sure that your company isn't like the railroads by understanding the underlying forces that shape your business environment. Start by analyzing your industry. (For a closer look at your customers, check out Chapters 6 and 7. The competition gets a once-over in Chapter 8. And we have you take a closer look at your company in Chapters 9 and 10.)

Analyzing Your Industry

No business operates alone. No matter what kind of business you're in, you're affected by forces around you that you must recognize, plan for, and deal with to be successful over the long haul. Ivory-tower types often call this process *industry analysis*. You may have the urge to run the other way when the word *analysis* pops up. We don't want to sugar-coat this step, but we try to make the process as painless as possible.

How much do you already know? Take a moment to complete the Industry Analysis Questionnaire (see Figure 5-1). If you're unsure about an answer, check the ? box.

Your answers to the questionnaire in Figure 5-1 provide a snapshot of what you think you know. The question boxes that you check highlight the areas that need a closer look. In any case, now you can roll up your sleeves and make a serious stab at completing your industry analysis.

The good news is that many smart people have already worked hard at analyzing all sorts of industries. Although no two businesses are exactly the same, basic forces seem to be at work across many industries (see Figure 5-2).

The following sections describe the most important of these forces — those factors in your industry — and provide some hints on how you can think about these forces in terms of your business planning.

Solidifying the structure

Every industry, from fresh-flower shops to antique stores, has a unique shape and structure. Here are a few tips on how to recognize the particular structure of your industry.

Arranging your rivals

The number of competitors, taken by itself, has a major impact on the shape of an industry. An industry can be a *monopoly* (one monster company with no competitors), an *oligopoly* (a small number of strong competitors), or a *multiopoly* (many viable competitors). Actually, we made up the word multi-opoly because we figure that you need a word to represent the vast majority of industries in this competitive world. In addition to the number of competitors, you should check out how many of the companies are big and how many are small, as well as how they carve up the various markets that they compete in.

Industry Analysis Questionnaire

Number of competitors in your industry:	❏ Many	❏ Some	❏ Few	❏ ?
Your industry is dominated by several large firms:	❏ Yes	❏ No		❏ ?
The combined market share of the three largest companies in your industry is:	❏ <40%	❏ In between	❏ >80%	❏ ?
New technologies change the way your industry does business every:	❏ 1 year	❏ 5 years	❏ 10 years	❏ ?
The barriers that stop new competitors from entering your industry are:	❏ High	❏ Medium	❏ Low	❏ ?
The barriers that prevent competitors from getting out of your industry are:	❏ High	❏ Medium	❏ Low	❏ ?
Overall market demand in your industry is:	❏ Growing	❏ Stable	❏ Declining	❏ ?
There's a large, untapped market that your industry can take advantage of:	❏ Yes	❏ Maybe	❏ No	❏ ?
Your industry offers a selection of features and options in its product lines that's:	❏ Extensive	❏ Average	❏ Limited	❏ ?
Customers buy products in your industry based almost entirely on price:	❏ Yes	❏ No		❏ ?
Customers can find other alternatives to take the place of your industry's products:	❏ Easily	❏ With difficulty	❏ No	❏ ?
Suppliers to your industry have a lot of influence when it comes to setting terms:	❏ Yes	❏ No		❏ ?
Customers have a lot of bargaining power when buying your industry's products:	❏ Yes	❏ No		❏ ?
Distributors have a lot of power and play a major role in your industry:	❏ Yes	❏ No		❏ ?
Overall costs in your industry have been:	❏ Declining	❏ Stable	❏ Rising	❏ ?
Profit margins in your industry are:	❏ Strong	❏ Average	❏ Weak	❏ ?

Figure 5-1:
Use the Industry Analysis Questionnaire to test your industry knowledge.

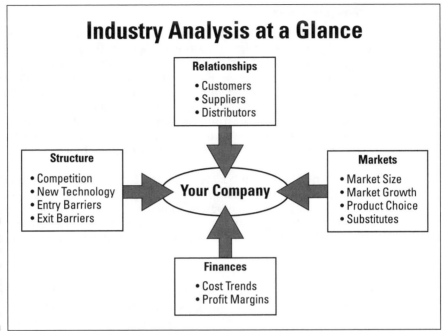

Industry Analysis at a Glance

Relationships
- Customers
- Suppliers
- Distributors

Structure
- Competition
- New Technology
- Entry Barriers
- Exit Barriers

Your Company

Markets
- Market Size
- Market Growth
- Product Choice
- Substitutes

Finances
- Cost Trends
- Profit Margins

Figure 5-2:
The four major components of analyzing an industry.

Make a list of all the major competitors in your industry. Find out their sizes, based on revenue, profits, or some other readily available measure, and estimate their relative market shares for the markets that you want to explore. Take advantage of the extraordinary range of information on the Internet to gather as much data as you can find. Be sure to practice some patience and persistence as you sift through all the raw data to find the gems.

Examining technology

Changing technology drives many industries. Look both at how much and how fast things change in your own business. Although you don't need to become a rocket scientist, you should feel comfortable with the underlying technological issues that fuel the change around you. You should also find out who controls the technologies and how easily you can obtain the technologies.

Identify obsolete technologies, current technology, and future technologies in your industry. How long were old technologies around before they were replaced? Try to predict when new technologies may become important to your business. At the same time, try to keep track of any copyrights, patent protection, or special expertise that could influence the adoption of a new technology. A little digging around in business magazines and journals can really help you.

Overcoming barriers

The "cover charges" that make it more or less difficult for new competitors to join the party are referred to as *entry barriers* (experts call it *barriers to entry*). Some of these barriers are obvious — *high capital costs* (a lot of money needed up front), for example, or complex distribution systems that make it hard to reach customers. Other barriers are easy to miss. *Economies of scale*, in which the bigger you are, the more money you make, often discourage brand-new competitors. Strong customer loyalty, long-term contracts, or high customer costs associated with changing products (called *switch costs*) can also create formidable barriers for new kids on the block.

As you think about your business, list the entry barriers that you think stand in the way of new competitors: capital costs, distribution, organization, raw materials, new technology, economies of scale, regulation, patents, and customer-switching costs, for example. Rank these barriers based on how impenetrable you find them. On which side of each barrier do you stand?

Cashing out

Sometimes, you can find it hard to leave a casino, even when you really want to. How difficult is it for companies in an industry to get out of the market if they want to? The ties and attachments that keep competitors around are called *exit barriers*. Exit barriers can include everything from expensive factories or specialized equipment that companies can't easily sell to long-term labour contracts, extended customer leases, service agreements, and government regulations.

Find out how many companies have left your industry over the past five years. Try to figure out why they got out of the market and what sort of difficulties they ran into as they made their way to the exits. How many of them left voluntarily, and how many were asked to leave, penniless and in tatters? Spend some time prowling through the pages of business magazines and journals — they offer plenty of useful insights.

Measuring the markets

Competition comes down to customers, and customers make up markets. Ideally, the customers you intend to target represent a market that you feel is ripe for new goods or services. The following sections give you tips to help you judge for yourself.

Just how big is big?

The size of a market tells you a lot about what's likely to happen to it over time, especially when it comes to competition. Large markets, for example, are always big news and can't help but attract competitors. Smaller markets don't get the same attention, however, and because competitors can easily overlook them, they often represent business opportunities. You hit the real jackpot if you can turn a small market into a bigger market by discovering a *usage gap* — finding a new use for your product or service that no other company has thought of before.

Try to work out some estimates of the overall size of your market based on current usage patterns. While you're on this subject, try your luck at coming up with novel approaches or applications that have the potential to redefine your market. Make some market projections based on the new uses that you're thinking about.

Growing or shrinking?

If large markets are good news, rapidly growing markets are great news, and competitors are going to come crawling out of the woodwork. A growing market offers the best odds for new players to gain a foothold and unseat the existing competition. As for shrinking markets, you can bet that the old competitors get leaner, meaner, and fiercer. So, as markets change size in either direction, the competition is likely to heat up.

Identify changes in the size of your market over the past five years, in terms of both units sold and revenue generated. If the market is changing rapidly in either direction, look for opportunities and predict the likely effect on both the numbers and the intensity of the competition. Business journals and the Internet are good places to start gathering data. Also, try talking to customers, suppliers, and even other competitors in the market.

What choices do customers have?

A quick survey of the similarities and differences among products or services in a market measures something called *product differentiation*. If each product looks pretty much like every other product (think sugar or drywall), you can bet that price is important to customers in what's known as a *commodities marketplace*. On the other hand, if each product is different and offers customers something unique or special — from laptop computers to hot little roadsters — product features are likely to determine long-term success or failure in the market.

Take a hard look at the products or services that the top three competitors in your market offer. How similar are they? In what ways are they unique? Think about what you can do to differentiate your product — adding special features or offering value-added services — so that you can compete in ways beyond simply raising or lowering your price. Your competitors' Web sites can offer a wealth of inside information.

What about something altogether different?

Every once in a while, a completely new type of product or service suddenly makes a debut in a market, crashing the party, so to speak. The product often comes out of another industry and may even be based on a different technology. The new product becomes an overnight rival for the affections of existing customers — the rise of e-mail to challenge fax machines and snail mail, for example, or the proliferation of digital cameras to overtake film-based cameras. The threat of *product substitution* — new products taking the place of existing ones — is real, especially in fast-changing, highly competitive markets.

Think about what your customers did 5, 10, or even 20 years ago. Did they use your product or a similar one back then, or did a completely different kind of product serve their needs? What about 1, 5, or 10 years from now? What types of products or services may satisfy your customers' needs? Although you can't predict the future, you can envision the possibilities.

Remembering the relationships

Business is all about connections. Connections aren't just a matter of who you know — they involve who supplies your raw materials, distributes your product, and touts your services. Connections are about who your customers are and what kind of relationship you have with them. The tips in the following sections can help you spot the key connections on which your business depends.

Recognizing supply and demand

One obvious way to think about products and services is how a company puts them together. Every company relies on outside suppliers at some stage of the assembly process, whether for basic supplies and raw materials, or for entire finished components of the product itself. When outside suppliers enter the picture, the nature of what they supply — the availability, complexity, and importance of that product or service to the company — often determines how much control they have over the terms of their relationship with a company. That means everything from prices and credit terms to delivery schedules.

Think about your own suppliers. Are any of them in a position to limit your access to critical components or to raise prices on you? Can you form alliances with key suppliers or enter into long-term contracts? Can you turn to alternative sources? Are any of your suppliers capable of doing what you do, transforming themselves into competitors? How can you protect yourself?

Keeping customers happy

You've probably heard the expression "It's a buyers' market." As an industry becomes more competitive, the balance of power naturally tends to shift toward the customer. Because customers have a growing number of products to choose among, they can afford to be finicky. As they shop around, customers make demands that often pressure businesses to lower prices, expand service, and develop new product features. A few large customers have even greater leverage as they negotiate favourable terms.

The last time that you or your competitors adjusted prices, did you raise or lower them? If you lowered prices, competitive pressures no doubt are going to force you to lower them again at some point. So think about other ways in which you can compete. If you raised prices, how much resistance did you encounter? Given higher prices, how easy is it for customers to do what you do for themselves, eliminating the need for your product or service altogether?

Delivering the sale

No matter how excited customers get about a product or service, they can't buy it unless they can find it in a store, through a catalogue, on the Internet, or at their front doors. *Distribution systems* see to it that products get to the customers. A *distribution channel* refers to the particular path that a product takes — including wholesalers and anyone else in the middle — before it arrives in the hands of the final customer. The longer the supply chain, the more power the channel has when it comes to controlling prices and terms, not to mention smart marketers who partner with channel members to create a superior delivery network. The companies at the end of the chain have the greatest control because they have direct access to the customer.

Think about what alternatives you have in distributing your product or service. What distribution channels seem to be most effective? Who has the power in these channels, and how is that power likely to shift? Can you think of ways to get closer to your customers — perhaps through direct-mail campaigns or marketing through the Internet?

Figuring out the finances

Successful business planning depends on you making sense of dollars-and-cents issues. What are the costs of doing business? What's the potential for profit? The following sections give you some tips that can help get you started.

The cost side

With a little effort, you can break down the overall cost of doing business into the various stages of producing a product or service, from raw material and fabrication costs to product-assembly, distribution, marketing, and service expenses. This cost profile often is quite similar for companies competing in the same industry. You can get a handle on how one firm gains a cost advantage by identifying where the bulk of the costs occur in the business and then looking at ways to reduce those costs.

Economies of scale usually come into play when major costs are fixed up front (think of large manufacturing plants or expensive machinery, for example); increasing the number of products sold automatically reduces the individual cost of each unit. (For more information on economies of scale, refer to the section "Overcoming barriers," earlier in this chapter.) *Experience curves* refer to lower costs that result from the use of new technologies, methods, or materials somewhere during the production process. (For more information on experience curves, see Chapter 14.)

Separate your business into various stages and ask yourself where the bulk of the costs occur in your company. Can you take any obvious actions to reduce these costs immediately or over time? How does the doubling of sales affect your unit costs? How are your competitors toying with new cost-saving ideas?

The profit motive

Companies typically have their own rules of thumb when it comes to expected *profit margins* — how much money they expect to end up with after they subtract all the costs, divided by all the money that they expect to take in. In certain industries, these profit margins remain fairly constant year after year. A look at the history of other industries, however, points to cycles of changing profitability. These cycles often reflect changing *capacity levels* — how much of a product or service an industry sells and delivers compared to what it can actually produce.

Knowing where an industry stands along the cycles of profit margin and capacity, as well as the direction in which the industry is heading, tells you a lot about the competitive pressures that may lie ahead. Ideally, you want to find yourself in an industry without much excess capacity — now or in the near future. Try to answer the following questions:

- Is your industry one that has well-known business cycles?

- Traditionally, how long are the business cycles?

- If you've been in business for a while, have your profit margins changed significantly in recent years?

- In what direction do profits appear to be heading?

✔ Do you think that these changes in profitability may affect the number of competitors you face or the intensity of the competition over the next one to five years?

Don't stop with our list here. No doubt we've missed one or two industry forces that may be important and perhaps unique to your business situation. Spend a little extra time and creative effort coming up with other forces while you work on your own industry analysis.

After you give some thought to the many forces at work in your industry, put together a written portrait. If you're stuck, imagine that someone who has no experience in your industry has come to you for advice, asking if you recommend a substantial investment in your industry. How would you respond? If you get your arguments down on paper, you've made real progress in assembling a serious industry analysis.

Coming up with supporting data

In many cases, you may need a little outside help, as well as some hard data, to support your take on how various industry forces shape your business environment. You may find it difficult, however, to get your hands on the right pieces of information to explain what makes your industry tick.

Sometimes, you may come up completely empty-handed because no one bothers to collect the data you need, or perhaps companies aren't willing to part with it because they don't want outsiders (including potential competitors) to analyze the industry too carefully.

Most of the time, however, you can find too much data, and the problem becomes knowing where to turn for the information that you need. This section gives you some details on how to dig up useful information on your industry without becoming overwhelmed.

Technology can help rescue you from information overload. You can control the recent explosion of business- and industry-related data by taking advantage of Internet-based services and online systems designed to search for information that you can actually use. You can access many of the sources that we include in the following list through your computer, and new ones appear online every day. Start by checking these out:

✔ **Resources on the Web:** A number of Internet sites focus on industry and company analysis, providing a wealth of free and easily accessed information. Check out Listings Canada (www.listingsca.com) or current industry reports available from the Winspear Canadian Industry Database (www.library.ualberta.ca/subject/business/wcid) and Statistics Canada (www.statcan.ca).

✔ **Online data providers:** A growing number of companies specialize in providing proprietary business- and industry-related data at your fingertips. Financial Post's media monitoring and company information (www.fpinfomart.ca) and Dun & Bradstreet Reports (www.dnb.ca) are available on the Internet. The information usually isn't free, but it may be worth the investment. Look for first-time-user offers or special promotions.

✔ **Government sources:** Canadian government agencies at all levels provide a wealth of data free for the asking, and you can find a good deal of it now available on the Internet. Check out Industry Canada (www.ic.gc.ca), Canadian Securities Administrators (www.csa-acvm.ca), the Department of Justice Canada (www.canada.justice.gc.ca), and other regulatory agencies.

✔ **Trade associations:** Many industries support trade groups that keep track of what goes on in their world. General business organizations, such as the chamber of commerce in your area, can also be quite useful in providing relevant information. The big voice for small and medium business is the Canadian Federation of Independent Business (www.cfib.ca).

✔ **Libraries:** Business-school libraries are the best source of info, but public libraries also house numerous business periodicals and books, as well as hard-to-find academic references, industry newsletters, and even the annual reports of large corporations. In particular, check out the *Blue Book of Canadian Business* (Canadian Newspaper Services), the *Canadian Key Business Directory* (D&B), the *Encyclopedia of Global Industries* (Grey House), the *Handbook of North American Industry* (Bernan Press), or the *Encyclopedia of Emerging Industries* (Grey House), just to name a few useful resources.

✔ **Securities firms:** Every major securities company — RBC Dominion Securities, TD Securities, Goldman Sachs Canada — has a research arm devoted to watching various industries and their players. The trick is to get your hands on the information. You may have to become a client and an investor on the side in order to have access to their information. Or do your own research through the electronic publicly traded company information sites www.sedar.com and www.csa-acvm.ca.

✔ **Colleges and universities:** In addition to offering library resources, business schools often offer flesh-and-blood business experts. These people are paid to analyze, and every once in a while they come up with a valuable insight or a really good idea. If you run across an expert in your industry, pay him or her a visit.

✔ **Direct industry contacts:** Go right to the source, if you can. Useful information can come from anywhere, including companies' Web sites, public relations departments, industry suppliers, distributors, and salespeople. You can also find information at industry conventions, trade shows, and even factory tours.

Recognizing Critical Success Factors

Time spent doing careful industry analysis rewards you with a complete picture of the major forces at work in your business: the basic structure of your industry; your core markets; key relationships with suppliers, customers, and distributors; and costs and changing profit margins. The analysis can also point out trends in your industry and show you where your company is in terms of general industry and business cycles.

This information is all well and good. But how do you go about interpreting your industry landscape so that you can use it to improve your business planning? Just for fun, think about your industry as a great whitewater river. Imagine the many forces that you can review (which we talk about in the preceding section) as being the swift currents, dangerous rapids, haystacks, and even whirlpools in that river. You're in the company canoe. You have to do more than just point out these features and paddle merrily along; you have to navigate around the hazards. As any whitewater expert can tell you, you must figure out what you need to do at every turn — what special skills, resources, and lines of communication you need to have in place to survive and conquer each stretch of river.

Back on dry land, take a fresh look at your industry analysis. Ask yourself what your company must do to succeed in the face of each powerful force that you identify. Again, what special skills, organization, and resources do you need in place to survive and conquer? In the business world, these assets are known as *critical success factors* (CSFs), also referred to as *key success factors* (KSF) — our favourite expression. Critical success factors are the fundamental conditions that you absolutely, positively have to satisfy if you want to win in the marketplace. These factors are different for every industry because they depend so directly on the particular forces that work in each industry.

The CSFs (or KSF) for your company should be rather specific — a one-of-a-kind set of conditions based on your industry analysis and the forces that you see shaping your business. You probably don't want to juggle more than three or four CSFs at any one time. But no matter how many factors you believe are important, your CSFs are likely to fall into several general categories that you can identify ahead of time. In the following sections, we provide a starting point for creating your own CSF list.

Adopting new technologies

When jet engines became available in the late 1950s, it quickly became apparent that commercial airlines had to adopt this technology if they wanted to remain competitive. Jet-engine technology became a CSF for players in the airline industry. If you (or your kids) fly jets at home by using computer simulators, you already know that the adoption of faster processors and speedier algorithms is just as important for success in the game-software industry. Even a small business can leverage new technology, such as the Internet, by creating a useful Web presence and turning it into a CSF.

Getting a handle on operations

For commodity products, such as steel or oil, large-scale mills or refineries are often the critical factors that lead to low-cost production and the capability to compete on price due to economies of scale. (For more information on economies of scale, refer to the section "Overcoming barriers," earlier in this chapter.) In high-tech industries, on the other hand, automation and efficient, clean rooms may be the critical ingredients that allow the production of competitively priced consumer electronics products: DVD players, digital cameras, PDAs, and so on.

Hiring human resources

Consulting firms usually recruit only at the top business schools because those firms sell the expertise of their consultants, and clients often equate skill with educational background. In the same way, software companies are nothing more than the sum of the talent, creativity, and expertise of their programmers. In each case, people themselves are the CSFs.

Minding your organization

The long-term success of movie companies that consistently produce hits and make money often hinges on logistics — the capability to evaluate, organize, and manage independent writers, actors, site scouts, and production companies, as well as the media and distribution outlets. In the health care industry, insurance companies are often successful because they excel at record-keeping, efficiently steering patients, suppliers, and insurance claims through the system. Even a simple bookstore that sells used books can gain an advantage by offering a quick, easy-to-use inventory of what's available and a system for reserving best sellers when they appear on the shelves.

Spicing up your services

Businesses that offer services of one kind or another sell rather abstract products that customers can't hold or touch, and those services are difficult to copyright or patent. Success often goes to service companies that enter the market first and then work hard to cultivate a following of loyal customers. Chartered Accountants (CAs), Certified General Accountants (CGAs), and accounting firms, for example, build impeccable reputations one step at a time. A major reason why clients come to them for financial advice is because of their trustworthy reputations. Because of the increasing importance of the service component in many industries, customer relationship management (CRM) software and services have become a growth industry in their own right (see Chapter 7 for a closer look at building customer relationships).

Looking for a great location

It's no coincidence that profitable mills tend to be located in agricultural areas and that brick works crop up near rock quarries; after all, transportation of the raw materials is extremely expensive. But transportation costs aren't the only reason why location matters. At the other end of the spectrum, fast-food restaurants and gas stations also live or die based on their locations. By far the most important success factor for these businesses is nabbing just the right spot along a heavily traveled route.

Moving on with marketing

Manufacturers of cosmetics, clothing, perfume, and even sneakers all sell hype as much as they do the physical products themselves. In these cases, CSFs depend on the capability of companies to create and maintain strong brands. A brand represents the image of a particular product or service in the marketplace. And in many markets, customers consider the name, the logo, or the label attached to a product before they buy the lipstick, jeans, or shoes that represent the brand.

Dealing with distribution

Packaged foods, household products, snacks, and beverages often sink or swim depending on how much shelf space the supermarkets or local grocery stores allot to them. A successful packaged-goods company works hard to create incentives for everyone in the delivery chain, from the driver to the grocer, to make sure that store shelves have plenty of room for their brands, even squeezing out competing products. Speed of delivery and logistics can also be critical success factors, especially when freshness matters.

Getting along with government regulation

Companies that contract directly with public agencies, such as waste-management firms and construction companies, often succeed because of their unique capability to deal directly with bureaucrats and elected officials. Government regulation plays a role in many industries, and the capability to navigate a regulatory sea is often the critical factor in a company's success. Pharmaceutical companies, for example, invest huge amounts of money in developing new drugs, and they stake all their potential profits and success on their skill in shepherding those drugs through Health Canada's complex regulatory approval process.

One last thing to remember before you start preparing your own CSF list: Critical success factors determine which companies are likely to succeed over the long haul in a given industry and marketplace. Unfortunately, your company's current capabilities don't always match those CSFs. Chapter 9 talks more about how you can unleash your company's specific capabilities and how you can make sure that they reflect the CSFs that you come up with here. What if your capabilities and CSFs don't match up? In that case, you may find that you need to develop new capabilities.

Preparing for Opportunities and Threats

After you have a handle on the major forces that shape your industry and you can point out the critical success factors that determine what kind of company has the best shot at coming out on top, you can begin to look ahead. Using everything that you've discovered about how your industry works (see the section "Analyzing Your Industry," earlier in this chapter, to . . . well, do some analyzing), what possibilities do you see for your company, and where do the obstacles lie?

These kinds of questions often fall under the umbrella of something called *situational analysis.* A situational analysis is a process of analysis for a company's internal and external environmental factors, successes and failures, as well as past and present resources and abilities. When you think about it, your company's situation depends partly on the structure of your organization (your strengths and weaknesses) and partly on things that happen outside (opportunities and threats).

For the moment, we want to concentrate on the opportunities and threats that you may face. (Turn to Chapter 9 to work on your company's strengths and weaknesses.) Opportunities and threats come from the forces, issues, trends, and events that exist beyond your control as a business planner and owner. Opportunities and threats represent the challenges that your company has to tackle if you want to beat the competition.

Enjoying the clear sailing ahead

Opportunities don't always knock; sometimes, you have to find the door yourself and know when to open it. Consider the following situations. They can all lead to business opportunities, so see if any of them can generate new possibilities in your industry:

- ✔ **Major shifts in technology:** When technologies change, companies are often slow to pick up on what's new because they have so much invested in what's old. New business opportunities continue to present themselves, from high-tech devices such as the BlackBerry, capable of wireless telecommunications, to virtual flea markets, Web shopping, and one-click banking by way of the Internet. Heck, we've even seen a high-level executive present a "Webinar" from his BlackBerry.

- ✔ **Availability of new materials:** New-materials science can lead to innovative products and expanded market opportunities. The DuPont Corporation, for example, developed a chemical treatment that protects fibres from discolouration; that innovation led to the creation of a new kind of carpet and the unique StainMaster line. And the 3M Company continues to develop new products based on the removable adhesive materials it develops, from Post-it Notes and easy on–easy off tape to removable hooks and picture holders.

- ✔ **New customer categories:** New market opportunities are born when you identify groups of customers who aren't satisfied with what's currently available. Toyota Motor Corporation discovered that Earth-loving drivers would flock to a part-gas, part-electric, environment-friendly automobile, and it created the hybrid-car market. In the agriculture industry, large grocery chains are jumping on the wagon as growers in all parts of the world now rush to fill the increasing demand for organic produce.

- ✔ **Sudden spurts in market growth:** When a market suddenly takes off, opportunity passes to the companies that move first to ramp up production to satisfy the growing demand. Nike, for example, sprinted out in front of the shoe industry by first understanding that marketing is a critical success factor and then meeting the phenomenal jump in demand they created for every type of athletic shoe imaginable.

- ✔ **New uses for old products:** Growth markets also spring up when people find new uses for old products. When researchers discovered that taking a small dose of aspirin a day could reduce the chance of a heart attack, aspirin became more than just an old-fashioned pain reliever. Pharmaceutical companies responded with new over-the-counter brands specifically designed for the new use and a new set of customers.

- ✔ **Access to highly skilled people:** In many industries, skills are scarce, valuable resources. Business opportunities often arise when skilled workers become available. From an abundance of biotech PhDs in the "Pill Hill" (otherwise known as Mississauga) and Vancouver areas to a growing army of programmers in India to out-of-work scientists in

Russia, companies should take advantage of any sudden expansion of the talent pool.

✔ **Additional locations:** Location means business. Although they shunned the concept of combining theatres and stores at one time, shopping malls now seek out movie theatres as important magnets to attract additional shoppers. Theatre complexes in shopping centres now represent a major percentage of the movie screens across the country.

✔ **Fresh organization models:** New ways of doing business represent business opportunities in themselves. The urge to downsize, for example, leads to the growth of outsourcing of all sorts of functions to other companies that do nothing but manage computer systems, supply training programs, or produce corporate newsletters for their clients.

✔ **New distribution channels:** You rarely come across anything more exciting in the business world than finding a new way to get to customers. Distribution creates a market, whether you're talking about a mega-discount store or a direct telephone marketing campaign. Internet business has boomed because it provides an efficient, effective way to reach customers with all sorts of products and services.

✔ **Changing laws or regulations:** The Canadian government (surprise, surprise) has had a great deal to do with the way that Canadian companies operate and make money in all sorts of industries. In particular, deregulation represents a tremendous opportunity to banks, insurance companies, airlines, media companies, and telephone companies by allowing them freer access to customers and more flexibility to compete with each other.

Watching for clouds on the horizon

Business is risky. For every big opportunity in an industry, you find an equally powerful threat to challenge the way in which you currently do business. Consider the following examples of how fundamental changes can dramatically alter the business environment and see if any of them apply to your industry:

✔ **Market slowdowns:** A shrinking market, either predicted or unforeseen, takes a toll on the industry. Excess capacity can bring a company to its knees, whether the cause is a sudden slowdown in the sales of home computers or a projected decrease in the number of passenger jets ordered by international carriers. Often, the trick is to reduce near-term production without losing the capability to react quickly when the market finally turns around.

✔ **Costly legislation:** Government programs, rules, and regulations often affect the bottom line. Canadian businesses, large and small, must plan to comply with all sorts of agency demands, from the Environmental Protection Branch (EPB) and the Workplace Safety & Insurance Board

(WSIB) to the Competition Bureau and the Canada Revenue Agency (CRA). As the saying goes, ignorance of the law is no excuse, and failure to comply can be extremely expensive in terms of both time and money.

✔ **Changing trends:** General population trends can have profound effects on certain marketplaces. The inevitable aging of the baby boomers, for example, is spurring a race to provide new products and services. Shoppers Drug Mart has increased its floor space for cosmetic counters and is filling them with age-defying remedies for the "forever young" boomers. It also provides products and services to the boomers' aging parents through Shoppers HomeHealthCare and by acquiring MediSystem Pharmacy, an innovative technology leader in multidose drug distribution.

✔ **New and aggressive competition:** Although new competitors usually have an uphill battle on their hands, they almost always come into a market with the advantages of energy, fresh talent, and a burning desire to win. Japanese car companies first came into the Canadian market with small, fuel-efficient cars, a serious marketing strategy, and a commitment to succeed over the long haul. Korean car companies were next in line, and they also succeeded in establishing a strong foothold in Canada with an emphasis on economy and value. Can Chinese cars be far behind?

✔ **Substitute products:** What happens when a gizmo comes along to replace a widget? Often, the widget company is in big trouble. The danger with substitute products is that they often seem to come out of nowhere. Digital cameras give old-fashioned vacation snapshots a run for their money, DVDs are making videocassettes extinct, CDs turned phonograph records into collectors' items, and MP3 players are now spinning CDs into techno-dinosaurs.

✔ **Exchange-rate volatility:** Today, global economic forces, including exchange rates, can affect even a local business. When the Canadian dollar rose against major currencies, including the U.S. dollar, euro, and Japanese yen, for example, Canadian companies and retailers were almost drowned in a flood of cheaper foreign imports (such as automobiles from the U.S.), and cross-border shopping was a major concern. In the past, a weakness in the Canadian dollar was a boon for exports in certain industries, but for others, the costs of imported materials and components rose sharply.

✔ **Shortages of raw materials:** From an oil crisis to a shortage of computer memory chips, supply problems can threaten a business. Companies often enter into long-term contracts with their suppliers to minimize these kinds of disruptions, but extended agreements pose their own set of risks because of limited flexibility and the need for constant executive attention.

✔ **Loss of patent protection:** Copyrights and patents usually protect creativity and intellectual property. But patents expire, and companies have to prepare for the competition that inevitably follows. Pharmaceutical firms, for example, have had to compete with the cheaper generic drugs that become available soon after successful prescription brands lose their patent protection. Schering-Plough Canada took the bold step of turning a top-selling prescription allergy drug, Claritin, into an over-the-counter brand. The move was seen as a pre-emptive strike against competitors as the company faced the inevitable loss of patent protection on the drug. The jury is still out on whether it was the right move or not.

✔ **Labour agreements:** Unions have a significant impact on the cost of doing business, and companies in various industries have figured out how to factor in their particular relationships with organized labour. Although union activity, in general, has waned for many years, companies that have no union histories may need to come to terms with organized workers in the future — especially in service industries, in which long hours and paltry benefits have become the norm.

✔ **Laziness and complacency:** Businesses tend to get lazy when the money starts rolling in, and the list of companies that have fallen into the complacency trap is much too long for comfort. General Motors, Ford, and Chrysler fell into the trap and were beaten up by Honda, Toyota, and Nissan. Likewise, The Bay, Sears, and Zellers were trapped by Wal-Mart when they failed to respond to Wal-Mart's aggressive discounting strategy. And today the big cable companies are trouncing the broadcast networks when it comes to producing daring, creative, exciting — and popular — new television shows.

✔ **Disasters, natural and otherwise:** Whether it be an earthquake, tornado, hurricane, or terrorist attack, prudent businesses prepare for the unexpected. In particular, companies in industries that rely on information technology now take elaborate steps to ensure that unforeseen disasters don't destroy irreplaceable pieces of data. This has led to the development of a new industry, with companies such as Canadian-leader Informatico Security and Iron Mountain Canada providing the data protection — and peace of mind — that their clients require.

You can find no end to the number of potential opportunities and threats in an industry. A winning business plan should include a situation analysis that points out both the biggest opportunities and the clearest threats to your company so that you can anticipate ways to deal with both the good and the bad as part of your planning process.

Chapter 6

Slicing and Dicing Markets

. . . .

In This Chapter

▶ Coming up with ways to group customers together

▶ Defining what a market segment means

▶ Creating market segments that you can use

▶ Shaping your business around the segments you serve

. . . .

*A*s you put together your business plan, it may seem nice to view each of your customers — the Tom, Dick, and Mary who regularly walk through your doors — as individuals with unique personalities and distinct likes and dislikes. You may also be tempted to make things simple: Lump everyone together and view all your customers in exactly the same way — after all, the whole world should want your products and services, right?

Unfortunately, neither of these tactics is very helpful when it comes to creating a business plan that you can use.

Luckily, you have a simple alternative. When you take a moment to think about who your customers really are, one of the first things you notice is that many of them have a great deal in common. That simple fact gives you a golden opportunity to divide customers into specific groups, based on their similarities. Eureka! By planning your business around these customer groups, you can serve each group's particular needs almost as effectively as if they were individuals. As the saying goes, you get to have your cake and eat it, too.

In this chapter, we show you how to create practical market segments that you can use in your business plan. We explore various ways to identify market segments based on who's buying, what they buy, and why they buy. Finally, we talk about things you can do to make sure that your business practices reflect who your customers are and why they come to you in the first place.

Separating Customers into Groups

What makes a good customer? The best customers that any business can hope for have these traits in common:

- ✔ They bring in a lot of business.
- ✔ They maintain loyalty.
- ✔ They make useful suggestions.
- ✔ They say nice things about you.

Good customers are satisfied, delighted customers. You provide them with exactly what they need and want. For their part, they make sure you understand their changing needs and requirements.

How do you make sure that you satisfy as many potential customers as possible? In an ideal world, you could address each customer individually. But individual attention isn't always practical in today's marketplace. Luckily, you have another way. Although each individual customer is unique, groups of customers often look a great deal alike.

When you make sense of your marketplace by grouping customers together, you create *market segments.* To be of any real use in your business planning, however, market segments should describe groups of customers that you can easily identify and that respond to your products and services in similar ways — ways that appear distinct from those of other customer groups. A successful market segment allows you to satisfy the particular needs and wants of an entire group of customers.

Good strategy not only identifies what you are and who you serve, but also what you are *not* trying to do. Similarly, identifying market segments allows you to choose those customers that are *not* a good fit with your business and that you, therefore, shouldn't spend resources on.

You may remember a time when running shoes (also known as runners or sneakers, depending on where you lived) were simple, rubber-soled canvas shoes that kids played in and maybe used for school sports. Back then, most of the buyers were parents, and most of the wearers were boys. If you wanted to play in the running-shoe market (Keds and Converse, for example, produced black high-tops that parents bought in droves), you kept your eye on what those boys needed and what those parents looked for.

Look at the market for athletic shoes today. The difference is phenomenal. Young males still wear the shoes, of course, but so do girls, toddlers, cool teenagers, serious runners, senior citizens, and everyone else — all demanding athletic shoes in various shapes and colours, with different features and options, and in a wide range of prices. Athletic shoes are designed especially for walking, running, tennis, skateboarding, and even fashion.

Extra! Extra! You now have car options!

In the early 1920s, Henry Ford and his famous Model T dominated the growing automobile industry in the United States. As Ford was fond of saying:

You can get the T in any colour you like — as long as it's black.

The key to the company's early success was its focus on just one product. Ford believed that if one size could fit all, standardized parts and mass production would lead to lower costs, lower prices, and satisfied customers. He was absolutely right . . . up to a point.

The market reached that point when American car buyers began to develop a taste for options. Some buyers wanted to be sporty; others, classy. Some wanted more leg room; others, more room for the kids. Ford continued to improve his cars, of course. The chassis became sturdier, the engine quieter, and the ride smoother. But when customers visited a Ford showroom, all that they saw was the same old Model T — still available in all shades of black.

Along came Alfred P. Sloan, Jr., the legendary head of General Motors. Sloan's genius was in recognizing that car buyers weren't all looking for the same car. He captured this vision when he said:

GM will produce a car for every purpose and a car for every purse.

Sloan soon hired a new kind of employee — the market researcher — to figure out what potential car buyers really looked for. Although he couldn't produce a unique car for each individual buyer, his market research identified five major groups of buyers with similar tastes and needs. In a bold move, he instructed his designers and engineers to come up with cars to meet those needs. The result was a new line-up of products tied directly to market segments:

- Chevrolet for entry-level buyers
- Pontiac for buyers who were moving up
- Oldsmobile for the growing middle class
- Buick for those who wanted something finer
- Cadillac for status-seekers

GM cars soon began to outsell Fords, and market segments took their rightful place as an important business-planning technique — not only for automobiles, but also for major industries across the nation and the world.

Literally dozens of athletic-shoe segments exist now, each defined in unique ways. For Nike, Adidas, or Reebok to attempt to capture the market today with one universal sneaker would be sheer folly and a financial disaster. The athletic-shoe business and the market segments that shape it have changed beyond recognition over the past 30 years.

Identifying Market Segments

Despite what the marketing gurus may tell you, you can't find one right way to divvy up your market. You need to view your customers from various angles and describe them based on several factors. The more you can apply your imagination and creativity in this area, the more successful you're likely to be in coming up with unique and effective market segments. One dimension isn't enough. As Figure 6-1 shows, you can come up with ways to create market segments by asking three basic questions:

- ✔ Who buys your product or service?
- ✔ What do they buy?
- ✔ Why do they buy?

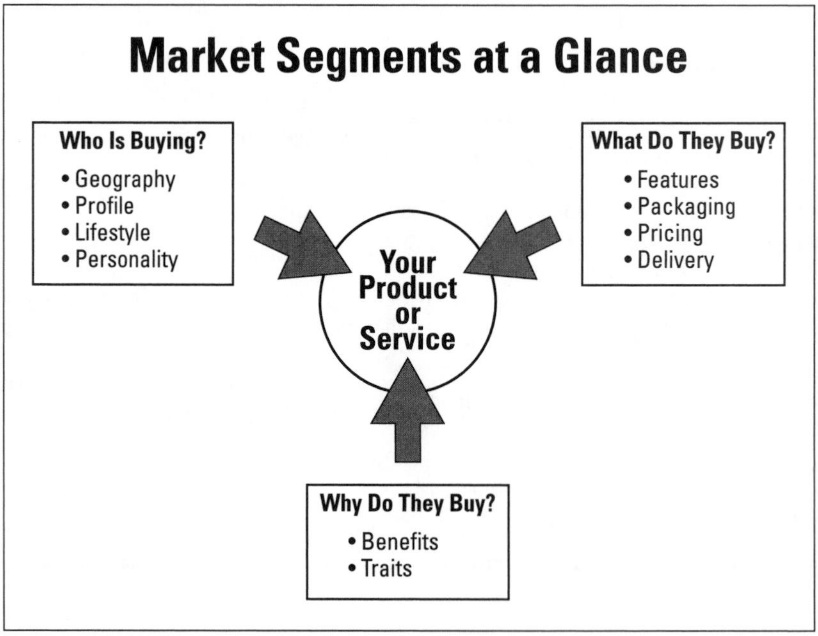

Market Segments at a Glance

Who Is Buying?
- Geography
- Profile
- Lifestyle
- Personality

Your Product or Service

What Do They Buy?
- Features
- Packaging
- Pricing
- Delivery

Why Do They Buy?
- Benefits
- Traits

Figure 6-1:
Define market segments by asking three basic questions, and then answer those questions from different market viewpoints.

Who buys

A good way to begin carving out your market segments is by researching who buys your product or service. If you focus on individual consumers, discover a bit about how they live their lives. If your customers are other companies, find out about their business operations. Think about your customers in these terms:

> ✔ **Geography:** Where do they live?
>
> ✔ **Profile:** What are they like?
>
> ✔ **Lifestyle:** What do they do?
>
> ✔ **Personality:** How do they act?

Where do they live?

Perhaps the simplest and most widely used way to describe your customers is based on where they are, beginning with a simple geographic breakdown by these factors:

> ✔ Country
>
> ✔ Region
>
> ✔ Province
>
> ✔ City
>
> ✔ Neighbourhood

But geography can also lead to more specialized groups. For example, you may find it useful to describe customers based on factors such as

> ✔ How close their nearest neighbours are
>
> ✔ How hot or cool their summers are
>
> ✔ How long their trips to the airport take

You can divide customers into groups based on geography to separate them according to regional taste — which often is a significant factor in the distribution and delivery of a product or service. Ethnic foods, for example, tend to sell better in certain regions of Canada. Indian food is hottest in the Toronto area; kosher products are most popular in central Canada; and Asian food is everywhere. Per-capita wine consumption is far higher in Montreal than it is in Edmonton.

Speaking of regions, instead of trying to sell heavy coats throughout the country, you may want to concentrate sales efforts in regions that have cold winters, taking advantage of market differences based on weather patterns. By looking at the geographic characteristics of consumers as they relate to your product or service, you begin to create market segments that you can use.

What are they like?

A profile of your customers includes all the attributes that you may expect to find in a national census. Marketing gurus call these attributes *demographic data,* which include the following:

✔ Age

✔ Gender

✔ Family size

✔ Education

✔ Occupation

✔ Income

✔ Ethnicity

✔ Nationality

✔ Religion

Company profiles, of course, are somewhat different. These profiles can include basic characteristics, such as the following:

✔ Industry

✔ Size of company

✔ Number of employees

✔ Years in business

You can often use customer profiles to spot market trends and take advantage of potential opportunities. Why is the market for health-care products booming today? Because the fabled baby boom generation — those 10 million Canadians who were born between 1946 and 1964 — is coming face to face with its own mortality. And where can you find a growing market for housing and home loans? In regions of the country with plenty of recreation, where people can enjoy their retirement years.

What do they do?

Lifestyle is an awfully tired word these days. People use it to describe anything and everything that you do in the modern world. But when applied to your customers, *lifestyle* has a particular meaning; it captures characteristics that go deeper than what's available in plain old census data. Customer lifestyle factors include:

✔ Hobbies

✔ Television viewing habits

✔ Social groups and activities

✔ Club memberships

✔ Vacation preferences

All this information is sometimes called *psychographic data* (no relation to the Psychic Friends Hotline) because you can use it to map out the psychology of the customer.

When applied to business customers, lifestyle factors include such things as what companies do when it comes to

- ✔ Protecting the environment
- ✔ Donating to charitable causes
- ✔ Investing in employee training
- ✔ Offering employee benefits
- ✔ Promoting people from inside the company

You can use these characteristics to understand how you may better serve a particular segment of your business market.

How do they act?

Your customers are individuals who have their own ways of acting and inter-acting with the world. Wouldn't it be useful, however, if you could create market segments based on general personality types? Luckily, you don't have to start from scratch. Some behavioural scientists (the spooky folks who always have their eyes on us) have come up with five basic personality types, which we describe in Table 6-1.

Table 6-1	Customer Personality Types
Type	*Description*
Innovators	Risk-takers of the world Young and well educated Comfortable with new ideas and technologies Mobile and networked Informed by outside sources
Early adopters	Opinion leaders in their communities Careful evaluators Open to well-reasoned arguments Respected by their peers
Early majority	Risk avoiders whenever possible Deliberate in their actions Unlikely to try new products until those products catch on

(continued)

Table 6-1 *(continued)*

Type	Description
Late majority	Skeptics Extremely cautious Disappointed by other products Reluctant to try new products Respond only to pressure from friends
Laggards	Hold out until the bitter end Wait until products are old-fashioned Still hesitate!

Personality type has a great deal to do with how eager people are to try new products and services. Although some people are adventurous and willing to try new things, others are quite the opposite, never using anything until it has made the rounds. In general, the laggards among us simply take longer to adopt new ideas than the innovators do. Experts make all this stuff sound like rocket science by calling it the *diffusion of innovation* (see Figure 6-3).

Over the years, marketers have accumulated plenty of data on the typical person in each of the five groups we highlight in Table 6-1. You can use this information in your planning efforts. Identify which personality types are most likely to have a positive response to your product or service. You can begin to assemble a description of your target customers and create a business plan that enables you to reach them efficiently and effectively.

What customers buy

A description of your customers in terms of their geography, profiles, lifestyles, and personalities tells you a lot about them (see the preceding sections for more information on customer research). To begin to understand how customers make choices in the marketplace that you compete in, you need to consider not only who they are but also what they buy.

A description of customers based on what they buy enables you to view them from a perspective that you're very familiar with: your own products and services. After you come up with market segments based on what your customers purchase, you can address the needs of each group by making changes in the following aspects of your product or service:

✔ Features

✔ Packaging

✔ Pricing

✔ Delivery options

What can your product do?

Features refer to all the specifications and characteristics of a product or service — things that you often find listed in a product brochure, users' manual, or the company Web site. When you group customers based on the product features that they look for, the customers themselves turn out to have a great deal in common. Their similarities include

- ✔ **How much they use the product:** Light, moderate, or heavy use
- ✔ **How well they use the product:** Novice, intermediate, or expert
- ✔ **What they do with the product:** Recreation, education, or business
- ✔ **What kind of customers they are:** Adviser, reseller, or user

WestJet Airlines is a major player in the so-called *no-frills* segment of the airline business. The company caters to price-sensitive people who travel relatively short distances and who often have to pay for travel out of their own pockets. You can usually find a cheap ticket to fly WestJet, but don't expect a seat assignment in advance (except do-it-yourself online seating 24 hours before departure) or more than a package or two of munchies after you board. You do get an easygoing, fun airline that respects you, however.

WestJet Airlines customers tend to be different from those of Air Canada, a global, full-service carrier at the opposite end of the airline spectrum. Air Canada offers service to every major airport around the globe. The company targets business customers, frequent flyers, and global travelers who expect a hot meal on a ten-hour flight, help with their international connections, and their luggage to arrive when they do, no matter where they are in the world.

How do you sell the product?

When marketing types talk about *packaging,* they refer to much more than cardboard, shrink wrapping, and plastic. Packaging means everything that surrounds a product offering, including the following:

- ✔ **Advertising:** Radio and TV, magazines, billboards, T-shirts, and the Internet
- ✔ **Promotions:** In-store sales, coupons, and sweepstakes
- ✔ **Publicity:** Book reviews, telethons, and celebrity endorsements
- ✔ **Product service:** Warranties, help lines, and service centres

The market segments that you identify based on packaging criteria often reflect customer attributes similar to the ones based on product features: frequency of use, level of sophistication, product application, and the type of user.

As we discuss in the preceding section's example, WestJet Airlines focuses on the no-frills end of the airline market, and Air Canada caters to a different market segment altogether. WestJet Airlines keeps its costs low by offering single class service and ticket offices at airports only. It doesn't offer baggage-transfer service, in-flight meals, or business-class lounges. If you want to book a ticket on Air Canada, on the other hand, you can use your favourite travel agent or travel Web site, as well as the company's representatives, and you get a lot of frills — but at a higher price, of course.

What does your product cost?

The pricing of a particular kind of product or service creates different groups of customers. Price-sensitive customers make up one camp; financially free customers who are willing to pay for a certain level of quality make up the other. If you've ever had to endure a course in microeconomics (yuck), you won't ever be able to forget two facts: Price is a major market variable, and the price/quality tradeoff is a fundamental force in every marketplace. People who buy Timex watches at their local drug store tend to be price sensitive, whereas shoppers acquiring a Rolex timepiece at a classy downtown jewellery store want luxury, craftsmanship, elegance — and the chance to make a personal statement.

In general, the *mass market* tends to be price-sensitive, and the so-called *class market* buys more on the basis of quality, high-end features, and status. But price isn't the only financial factor that can lead to different market segments. Other criteria include

- **Available financing:** Offered by home-furnishings companies
- **Leasing options:** Offered to airlines that buy airplanes
- **Money-back guarantees:** Offered regularly on TV
- **Trade-in arrangements:** Offered by automobile dealerships

Where can consumers find your product?

Distribution and delivery determine how customers actually receive your product or service. In this case, market segments are often based on where your customers shop:

- Factory outlet stores
- Discount centres
- Department stores
- Boutiques
- Catalogues
- On the Internet

Mary Kay Cosmetics reaches its customers directly at home through independent sales consultants, and its products aren't available in any store. The company believes that beauty aids are personal in nature and require highly personalized selling for its lines to be successful. With the same aim in mind, other cosmetic companies strategically place consultants (you can easily spot them by their white coats, perfect faces, and expensive aromas) in department stores.

Market segments based on delivery also may rely on additional criteria, including

- ✔ Anytime availability (convenience stores)
- ✔ Anywhere availability (gas stations)
- ✔ Guaranteed availability (video-rental stores)
- ✔ Time sensitivity (florists)

Why customers buy

When it comes to satisfying customers' needs over the long haul, you can't forget the basics. Perhaps the most difficult — and useful — questions that you can ask yourself about customers deal with *why* they buy in the first place. These include questions such as

- ✔ What do customers look for?
- ✔ What's important to them?
- ✔ What motivates them?
- ✔ How do they perceive the world?
- ✔ How do they make choices?

When you group customers by using the answers to these questions, you create market segments based on the benefits that customers look for. Because these market segments describe your customers from *their* point of view, rather than your own, these segments provide the best opportunity for you to satisfy the particular needs of an entire customer group.

What do they get?

When you try to figure out exactly why customers buy products and services in your marketplace, start a list of the benefits that you think they look for. Product benefits may sound an awful lot like product features, but in subtle, yet crucial ways, product benefits and product features are really quite different.

Features are defined in terms of products or services. A car, for example, may have a manual transmission (as opposed to an automatic) and may come with power windows, anti-theft locks, or a dashboard global positioning system (GPS). *Benefits,* on the other hand, are defined by the customer. Depending on the customer, the benefits of a manual transmission may be in handling and responsiveness, or in improved gas mileage. A dashboard computer may represent an added luxury for the weekend driver or may be an absolute necessity for the traveling sales representative. Again, the benefits are in the eyes of the customer.

Perceived benefits can change over time. Consider the newest generation of cars equipped with hybrid engines, which combine gas and electric power. A customer may buy a hybrid because it pollutes less than a regular engine, satisfying a customer's sense of social conscience. But when gasoline prices soar — like they almost always do — savings at the gas pump may begin to seem like the more important benefit.

You must understand the difference between benefits and features if you plan to use the market segments that you come up with to create an effective business plan. Take a moment to think about the business situations sketched out in Figure 6-2.

Choose The Customer Benefits

Situation	*Potential Customer Benefits*
A boutique offers upscale bath and beauty products imported from Europe, tasteful gift wrapping, and hassle-free delivery anywhere in the world.	❏ A nice place to go after lunch when you've extra time to kill ❏ The opportunity to impress relatives back in Sweden ❏ An alternative to divorce after discovering that today's the anniversary ❏ Aromatherapy after an ugly day at the office
A franchised quick-printing outlet provides—self-service copy machines; sells custom stationery and business cards; and offers two-hour rush jobs on flyers, posters, and newsletters.	❏ The ability to look like a big company—at least on paper ❏ A money-saving alternative to buying a copier ❏ A threat used to keep the printing and graphics supplier in line ❏ A job-saver when the printed brochures don't arrive at the trade show
A semiconductor manufacturer sells customized chips to high-tech companies for use in brand-name consumer products, including home-electronics gadgets, computers, and games.	❏ An extension of the in-house research and development department ❏ An easy way to expand the product line ❏ A weapon in the cost/price wars ❏ A way to reduce a new product's time to market

Figure 6-2: Consider these business situations.

The benefits of toothpaste

For many years, the toothpaste market defied successful analysis, until a team of market researchers applied the concept of customer benefits. Their research resulted in the discovery that four principal benefits — seen by toothpaste users themselves — describe the toothpaste market. Customers seek out one or more of the following benefits when they make their purchase decisions:

✔ **Dental health:** One group of customers seeks perceived dental benefits. Mothers, for example, hope to deny the dentist an opportunity to buy yet another yacht.

✔ **Taste appeal:** Another group looks for good-tasting toothpaste. Children, of course, don't particularly like to brush, unless it tastes good.

✔ **Sex appeal:** A third group desperately hopes to appeal to the opposite sex. This group, of course, includes teenagers, who struggle through the rigors of adolescence and want fresh breath.

✔ **Basic hygiene:** The final group seeks basic dental hygiene at a good price. Many men, for example, view all toothpaste as being essentially the same.

As a result of the new research, toothpaste suppliers began to market their offerings around the defined benefit categories. Crest ("recommended by 9 out of 10 dentists!") targeted mothers, for example; Aim went after kids; Close-Up targeted teenagers; and the low-price house brands appealed to men.

Which of the benefits listed represent genuine benefits to the customers of each company? A trick question, of course: *You* don't define benefits — the *customers* do.

To identify the benefits that your products offer, choose one of your products or services, and follow these steps:

1. **Draw a mental image of the product or service, based on its features, attributes, and options.**

2. **Put that picture completely aside for a moment.**

3. **Place yourself in your customers' shoes.**

4. **Now create a new description of the product or service from your customers' viewpoint that focuses on the benefits that they want.**

Grouping customers based on the particular benefits that they look for when they select a product or service in your market is the key to satisfying individual customers and keeping them happy over the long run.

How do they decide?

Different customers approach your market in different ways, and you can often identify market segments based on certain customer traits as they relate to your product or service category. Some of the conditions that guide customer buying decisions include the following:

- **Speed of the purchase decision:** The *decision-making process* (DMP) that customers go through before they purchase a product or service varies, depending on the product or service's complexity and price tag. People may buy chewing gum at a drugstore without much thought. But car dealerships and real estate agents face a completely different DMP with their customers, resulting in a slower decision to buy. (For the full scoop on the DMP, see Chapter 7, which gives you the five steps to product adoption.)

- **The actual decision-maker:** Families represent a common *decision-making unit* (DMU) that buys various consumer goods. But who in the family has the final word? If you sell clothes designed for teenagers, for example, it makes a big difference whether the kids have the final say, or Mom or Dad is always in the background, giving the thumbs-up or thumbs-down sign. This difference alone may lead to two separate market segments, each with a unique set of requirements.

- **Customer loyalty:** The way that companies relate to their customers can easily define a set of market segments. Service industries, for example, go out of their way to identify and encourage customers based on their loyalty. You've probably been asked to join more than one frequent-flyer program or to keep track of frequent-caller, frequent-diner, or frequent-you-name-it points. Companies that offer these programs promise to cater to and reward you for being a member of a loyal customer group. (For more info on customer loyalty, see Chapter 7.)

- **Level of product use:** In many industries, a small percentage of consumers account for a large percentage of sales. If you want to sell beer, for example, you may not want to ignore the heavy-beer-drinking population — an estimated 10 million Canadians. Keeping this high-consumption group of customers satisfied can be profitable indeed.

Finding Useful Market Segments

A market segment is useful only if it allows you to deliver something of value to the customers you identify — and to do so profitably. Not all the market segments that you come up with are going to be practical ones. What should you look for if you want to find a really useful market segment? In general, you want to make sure that it has the following characteristics:

✔ A size that you can manage

✔ Customers that you can identify

✔ Customers that you can reach

Is the segment the right size?

Identifying useful market segments requires a delicate balance between defining your markets so broadly that they don't offer you any guidance, and planning and defining them so narrowly that you make them impractical and unprofitable. A useful market segment has to be manageable. The right size depends on your particular business situation, including your resources, the competition, and your customers' requirements.

Choosing a manageable group of customers takes you back to the twin business goals of efficiency and effectiveness (which we cover more extensively in Chapter 4). You want to be effective in serving your market segment, but you also have to be efficient. For General Motors, Telus, or Procter & Gamble, manageable market segments are large and quite different from those of a boutique hotel; a high-tech, start-up firm; or a small, ecologically conscious manufacturing company.

The trend over the past half-century has been to slice markets into smaller and smaller pieces. Headlines in the business press tell the story:

✔ "Mass Markets Are All the Rage" (1950s)

✔ "Market Segments Come of Age" (1960s)

✔ "Niche Markets Have Arrived" (1970s)

✔ "Mass Customization Is In" (1980s)

✔ "Micromarkets Are Hot" (1990s)

✔ "Relationship Marketing Rules" (2000s)

Clearly, the notion of manageable market segments has changed over the years. Market segments are shrinking. Why? Customers continue to get more sophisticated and demanding in all markets, and companies have found new ways to become more efficient and effective at what they do. How have they done it? In a word: computers.

Don't forget, for example, that your credit-card company makes a great deal of money by selling information about you to other companies. Each time you make a purchase with your card, you reveal something highly personal and unique about yourself. Sophisticated software programs analyze your revelations (and those of your friends, neighbours, and fellow consumers), using a variety of high-tech tools to place you in a very particular consumer category. Companies — and maybe yours is one of them — pay handsomely for your name, address, and type so that they can target you directly with products and services that they tailor precisely to your identified needs.

You can bet that your customers are going to become more demanding over time and that your competitors are bound to become more adept at serving smaller markets. When you choose the manageable market segments in which you want to compete, make sure that you factor in ways to use information technology in your business. For more customer info, check out Chapter 7.

Can you identify the customers?

While you piece together a complete picture of your customers, take advantage of the many different ways to categorize them (see the section "Identifying Market Segments," earlier in this chapter, to check out the ways we describe them). In particular, market segments based on why customers buy are often the best because they define groups of customers who have similar needs. Whenever possible, come up with market segments that take into account your customers' viewpoints — the benefits that they look for, as well as their buying behaviour.

But then what? Unfortunately, you can't always detect intimate customer behaviour — motives, wants, needs, and preferences — from the outside (unless you're a psychotherapist, of course, or you're friends with a behavioural scientist). You may know what these people are really like, but how do you go about tracking them down? If you want to recognize the customers in your market segment, you have to tie their behaviour to characteristics that you can see.

Suppose that while searching for a hot new business opportunity, you discover a group of people who seem to have the same general attitude about their jobs and work. Members of this group want to be more productive on the job, yet they feel neglected and frustrated with their working conditions and office environment. You may have come up with a potential market segment. But what next? How do you identify these potential customers? Well, maybe you go on to discover that many of these workers are left-handed and would feel more comfortable with their numeric keypads on the left side of the computer keyboard and with their handsets on the right side of the telephone. Now, you've taken a major step toward defining a useful market segment because the segment is based on customer wants and needs and is made up of customers who you can describe, observe, and identify.

Given this situation, you may have the urge to take a planning shortcut and base your new market segment entirely on what you observe: left-handers, who, after all, constitute about 10 percent of the population. Bingo! You decide to design and produce office equipment exclusively for left-handed customers. But wait; control that urge. Before you identify a really useful market segment, you need to satisfy one more requirement, which we talk about in the following section.

Can you reach the market?

After you define a promising market segment based on customer wants and needs, and including customers that you can describe, you have to develop ways of communicating with those customers. You can't be satisfied just knowing that this group of customers exists somewhere out there in the consumer universe, even if you can describe and recognize them. You must be able to set up affordable ways to contact them through advertising, promotions, and the delivery of your product or service.

In the case of the left-handers market (see the preceding section for the detailed version), for example, you have to devise a plan for marketing and distribution that ties into the common behaviour of this group. Ideally, you want to get the full attention of left-handers without incurring the costs of reaching the 90 percent of folks in the right-handed world. But how do you gain the attention of, and access to, left-handed customers? An easy method would be to place ads in *Southpaw Press* or *The Gauche Gazette,* and to make your products available at all Lefties Outlet stores. The catch is that not one of these companies exists.

Maybe it's too early to give up. But, if you can't come up with creative ways to reach out to, and communicate with, left-handed customers, the group isn't a useful market segment, after all. In addition to having similar needs, common observable traits, and a manageable size, a useful market segment needs to present realistic opportunities to be reached. Perhaps that's why left-handers are always so frustrated.

Becoming Market Driven

Remember back in school when you were told to check your homework before handing it in — especially if the teacher was going to grade it? Well, the marketplace is a difficult class to tackle (as difficult as, say, calculus or physics), and the stakes are high. Before you commit to a particular market segment scheme, make sure that you look back over your homework. Pose these review questions to yourself:

- ✔ What benefits are customers in the market segment looking for?
- ✔ Will product features, options, and packaging satisfy customers' needs?
- ✔ Is the size of the segment manageable?
- ✔ Can you describe, observe, and identify your customers?
- ✔ Can you reach your customers efficiently through advertising and promotion?
- ✔ Will distribution and product service be effective?

Researching your market

At some point, you may want to use a more sophisticated approach to answer some of the questions in the preceding list. *Test marketing* tests your ideas on a carefully selected sample of potential customers in your market segment. Using a test market, you can often gauge how well your product plan is likely to work before you spend *beaucoup* bucks going forward. The bad news is that, like all market research, test marketing can be expensive and time-consuming, especially if you bring in big guns from the outside. So, you may want to start by conducting some preliminary customer interviews on your own.

Customer interviews produce a snapshot of who buys your product, as well as what they think they're buying. You can conduct interviews on an informal basis. Just follow these steps:

1. **Select customers in your market segment.**
2. **Arrange to meet with them individually or in small groups.**
3. **Get them to talk a bit about themselves.**
4. **Have them tell you what they like and don't like about your product.**
5. **Ask them why they buy your product and what they would do without it.**

One word of caution: Use common sense. These interviews aren't meant to be rigorous pieces of market research, so be careful to confirm what you see when you start drawing conclusions about customer behaviour from them.

If you feel that you need a more complete and accurate picture of your customers, you may want to consider doing a Day-In-the-Life-Of (DILO) study. Think of a DILO as a customer interview on steroids. For example, you may want to ask a group of customers to keep consumer diaries for several weeks of what they purchase, where they shop, how much time they spend shopping, and what prices they pay for products or services. Better yet, for a set period of time

- ✔ Place yourself in the role of observer

- ✔ "Handcuff" yourself to a customer

- ✔ See what your customer sees

- ✔ Do what your customer does

If you sell things to other businesses, you can also take advantage of a DILO study. Ask whether you can spend some time with some of your business customers on the job. Walk through *their* business processes. Staple yourself to one of their customer orders. See whether you can figure out anything new about how they operate their business that may help you serve them better.

DILOs often provide new and powerful insights into customer behaviour and can tell you something that you didn't know about who buys your product or service and why they buy it. Toyota, for example, sent a number of their marketing people to actually live with selected families in North America before they ever designed or built the Lexus line of automobiles. They wanted to know more about how families that buy expensive cars relate to their luxury automobiles.

Defining personality types

After you come up with a market segmentation scheme and a useful description of your customers (refer to the section "Identifying Market Segments," earlier in this chapter, for more info), you're in a good position to say something more about their buying behaviour when it comes to the products and services that you plan to offer. So, look back over your notes and review what you know about your customers and their likely personality types. (If you need help, flip to the section "How do they act?" earlier in this chapter.)

Why are personality types so important? They have a great deal to do with how eager people are to try out new products and services. Although some of us are adventurous and willing to try anything new, others are quite the opposite, never using anything until it's been around for quite a while. In general, the laggards among us simply take longer to adopt new ideas than the innovators do (see Table 6-1).

In Figure 6-3, the percentage of people who represent each personality type is just an estimate, of course. But you get a rough idea of the relative size of each personality group in your own marketplace.

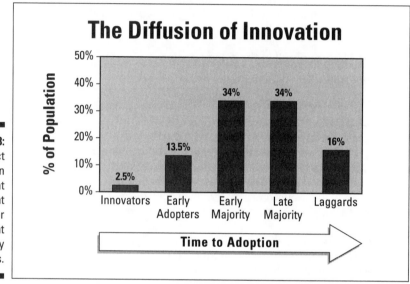

Figure 6-3:
Product
adoption
occurs at
different
times for
different
personality
types.

The important thing to remember about the diffusion of innovation is that if you bring a brand-new kind of business, product or service to the marketplace, the innovators and early adopters are going to be easier to capture than the majority of consumers out there. The longer your kind of product or service has been on the market, the more effort you must spend focusing on your customers and understanding their wants, needs, and motives. (For more on how to get acquainted with your customers, check out Chapter 7.)

Chapter 7

Getting Better Acquainted with Customers

· ·

· ·

*M*ore than almost anything else in business planning, how well you know your customers ultimately determines how successful you are.

But we're the first to admit it: Figuring out what makes customers tick can be downright frustrating. You may be tempted to throw up your hands and leave the entire mess to the so-called experts — marketing gurus, consultants, or perhaps astrologers. Don't. This chapter shows you how to acquaint yourself with your customers so that you can offer them more value and serve them more profitably than anyone else in your industry.

We compare good customers with difficult customers and try to help you gain some insights from your competitors' customers, as well. We take a closer look at why customers buy your products and services. And we examine customer perceptions and decision-making processes. We consider ways to develop loyal customers by improving customer service, and we take a quick look at other businesses that invest in your products or services.

Keeping Track of the Big Picture

Remember that old saying about not seeing the forest for the trees? Well, when you first start to think about your customers, you don't want to fall into a similar trap. Focusing on a small number of individual customers and their personal habits, likes, and dislikes is tempting. But don't! Don't view your customers and your business activities too narrowly. Look instead at the larger forest — the general customer behaviours and basic needs that define your market (see Chapter 6 for more info on defining market segments).

If you think about your business only in terms of your existing customers and current products, you risk losing sight of broader customer needs — needs that a competitor is no doubt going to satisfy at some point. You also create a short-sighted view of your strategic choices that can result in missed market opportunities and woefully inadequate business plans.

Unfortunately, companies (and even entire industries) lose sight of the big picture all the time. Companies view markets too narrowly and neglect customer needs — a classic management blunder. Keep the big picture in mind, and you can probably recognize strategic market opportunities. Charles Revson did when he revolutionized the cosmetics industry. Revson famously quipped, "In the factory, we make cosmetics; in the store, we sell hope." As the founder of Revlon, he understood that he offered his customers something far more important than simple chemistry: the prospect of youth, beauty, and sex appeal. Check out these recent examples of other companies that understand they sell customer benefits along with basic product features:

✔ Companies that make home-improvement tools often view their business in terms of product components — the making and selling of quarter-inch drill bits, for example. But when you think about it, nobody really wants or needs quarter-inch drill bits (not even your dentist). What customers *really* look for are quarter-inch holes. That basic need creates the potential opportunity for any number of possible solutions. The growing number of hardware stores that offer classes on do-it-yourself home repair techniques have found one way to seize that opportunity — and grow their businesses.

✔ Eyeglasses manufacturers, the companies that make the frames and lenses, used to be in the eye-care business. But new technologies, including laser surgery, now promise improved sight for life — no vision problems, no need for glasses, no more business. Fortunately, some of these companies were far-sighted enough to transform themselves into a fashion industry, tapping the talents of well-known designers such as Liz Claiborne and Ralph Lauren. Now, customers buy glasses not only to see better, but also to look better.

The key point here is simple: If you don't know what your customers really want, you can't possibly fulfill their needs in effective ways.

Riding basic customer needs to success

Intuit produces Quicken, a top-selling software program that helps people keep track of their financial lives. The company has been a top performer, however, because it sees itself not only as a software company, but also as a part of the personal-finance industry. This broad focus gives Intuit additional opportunities — in paper supplies (cheques, deposit slips, envelopes, and so on) and in lucrative transaction-based financial services (a credit-card provider, a bill-paying centre, even a tax advisor).

3M has developed and patented many new materials, such as a revolutionary removable glue substance. The company's Post-it division is successful, however, because it defines itself as more than simply an adhesives provider: It thrives in the reminders business. Post-its are now available for almost everything that you may ever think about forgetting. (Some of you, we hope, are using them right now to mark words of wisdom in this very book.)

Put yourself in your customers' shoes:

- ✔ Take a hard look at one of your products or services and honestly ask yourself, "Why would I need this thing?"
- ✔ Ask the same question of several people who use your product or service.
- ✔ Try to imagine a world without your product or service. What would you substitute for it?

Answering these questions can go a long way toward fostering creativity, generating new strategies, and providing expanded market opportunities.

Checking Out Your Customers

A fresh look at customers should start with the ones you enjoy seeing — those customers who regularly purchase goods or services from you. But sometimes, you need to know what a customer is *not* as much as what a customer *is*. You can find out about your business and best customers by observing the other kinds of customers shopping your industry — the difficult customers, the former customers, and the non-existent customers.

Defining your good customers

Good customers are the ones who bring a smile to your face, the ones you like serving, the ones who appreciate you, the ones who keep you in business. You want these customers to keep coming back time and again. But how do you keep them all satisfied? Success is a matter of knowing who your customers are, understanding their backgrounds, and fulfilling their needs better than the competition.

Your business can measure and describe its customers in several ways:

- Track where your customers are, breaking them down by country, region, province, city, or neighbourhood.

- Figure out who your customers are, including their age, gender, occupation, income, and nationality.

- Discover more about how they live — their hobbies, favourite sports teams, restaurant choices, and vacation destinations, for example.

If you want more details on how to separate your customers into groups, or so-called market segments, check out Chapter 6.

When it comes to understanding customers better, one strategy is to find out what other businesses are figuring out about their customers. Keep track of the questions that other companies ask you. The Source by Circuit City stores (a chain of electronics retailers), for example, routinely ask for your postal code when you step up to the register. And you often find a list of personal questions on product registration forms, warranty cards, and customer-service mailings.

Handling your bad customers

"A bad customer? Isn't that a contradiction?" you ask. Not at all. Bad customers simply cause you more trouble than they're worth and don't fit into your company's values and strategies. Bad customers do the following:

- Ask you to serve them in ways that aren't practical for your company

- Distract you, causing you to veer away from your strategy and your business plan

- Purchase in such small quantities that the cost of doing business with them far outweighs any revenue that they generate

- Require so much service and attention that you can't focus your efforts on more valuable (and profitable) customers

- Remain dissatisfied with what you do, despite all your best efforts

Bank accounts and the 80/20 principle

The retail banking division of one of the five major banks recently undertook a comprehensive study of its chequing-account customers. The results presented a classic 80/20 situation: About 19 percent of the bank's customers generated 90 percent of the total profits. What was the chief characteristic of the other 81 percent? Most of those customers had chequing accounts with average balances of less than $250, yet they wrote a lot of cheques. As a consequence, the bank lost serious money on this customer group; internal processing costs were simply greater than the revenue generated from the use of their deposited funds.

Obviously, not all small-account holders were bad customers. Some were senior citizens, for example, and a percentage of them were new and would go on to become profitable customers over time. In order to create more good customers, the bank introduced incentives to encourage customers to transfer money into related savings accounts. But the bank also knew that many of its small customers would simply remain a drain on profits. So it also created hurdles to de-market — de-marketing is activities or tactics used to reduce demand — those customers, using a new fee structure that penalized accounts when monthly average balances fell below certain levels unless the customers also maintained balances in a savings account. In other words, the bank raised its fees and in the process lost its most unprofitable customers.

The pundits have come up with a principle that you can apply here: the *80/20 principle*. In this case, the rule says that if you survey all your customers, 20 percent of them account for about 80 percent of your business. Your good customers make up that 20 percent. You obviously want to keep them — and keep them happy! But look at the remaining 80 percent of your customers, and you may discover some that you'd rather hand over to the competition.

To handle bad customers, follow these steps:

1. **Figure out who they are.**
2a. **Convert them into good customers.**

    or

2b. **Hand them over to someone else.**

Scoping out the other guy's customers

You may think that when customers take their business elsewhere, it points to a failure on your part. On the contrary, these people present an opportunity.

The fact that you haven't been able to serve this group gives you a challenge: finding out what your market really thinks is important. Your competitors' customers tell you what you lack as a company. This information is extremely useful, especially when you work on the big picture in the early stages of business planning, defining who you are and who you want to serve.

Getting to know your competitors' customers is often difficult, but not impossible. Follow these tips down the road of discovery:

- ✔ Spend some time where customers gather. Use trade shows, user groups, and industry conferences to make informal contacts and begin a dialogue with your non-customers.

- ✔ Ask pointed questions of people who choose competing products:

    - Did they take the time to see what was available on the market?

    - Have they even heard of your product or service?

    - If they have, did they actually take the time to look at it? If not, why not? If so, what were their impressions?

- ✔ Listen to what they have to say, no matter how painful. Don't get defensive if people say negative things about your company or products.

Information about your customers is valuable, if not priceless. Consultants charge you thousands of dollars for much of the same stuff, but they can often get to information you can't. How you utilize outside help depends on how much info you can gather on your own.

An acquaintance of ours used to go into supermarkets and hang out around the aisles in which the market displayed her company's goods. When a customer came along and picked out a competing product, she offered to buy that product from the startled shopper for more than the listed price! She would offer a minimal amount (a nickel over the listed price, say) and then work her way up, trying to determine the shopper's degree of loyalty to the competing brand. Finally, she asked questions to find out why. As a reward, she paid the shopper for the price of the product when the conversation was over.

Discovering the Ways Customers Behave

Perhaps the most difficult — and useful — question that you can answer about your customers has to do with their behaviour: Why do they buy what they buy? What actually compels them to seek out products or services in the marketplace? What's important to them? What are they really looking for?

Understanding customer needs

Why do people buy things in the first place? Psychologist types tell us that needs fulfillment is really at the heart of all consumer behaviour. Social psychologist, Abraham Maslow, grouped human needs into five levels from basic to highest in his famous "Hierarchy of Needs" Model (see Figure 7-1). Everybody has needs and wants. When a customer discovers a need, it creates the motivation that drives human activity:

✔ Survival, at the most basic level, results in the universal need for food, shelter, and clothing. In the modern world, these basic needs support grocery stores, carpenters, and the garment industry.

✔ The urge for safety, security, and stability generates the need for bank accounts, disability health insurance, and home alarm systems.

✔ The desire for belonging and acceptance creates the need for trendy clothes, members-only clubs, and expensive diet programs.

✔ The urge to be recognized and held in esteem establishes the need for company banquets, fast cars, and award plaques.

✔ The desire for self-achievement results in the need for adventure vacations, self-help books, and Web-based correspondence courses.

Canpar, Canada's parcel delivery specialist, is in the reliability business. Many of its customers are businesses that want the assurance — absolutely, positively — that Canpar can deliver their precious shipments within one or two days, or even early the next day. These customers are so motivated by this need that they pay a premium over other alternatives, simply for their own peace of mind. Canpar guarantees timely delivery, or customers don't pay!

Determining customer motives

Motives are needs that have been awakened and activated (see Figure 7-1). Motives send people scurrying into the marketplace to search for products or services that can fulfill a particular need, although motives aren't always what they seem to be.

The following examples illustrate that there may be more than one motive at work influencing a customer's buying behaviour:

✔ Greeting-card companies, for example, don't charge exorbitant prices just to sell cute little jingles printed on glossy paper. The prices are justified because the greeting-card companies actually sell small insurance policies against their customers' fear of feeling guilty. And perhaps that fear of guilt (over a missed birthday or anniversary), along with the desire to bring joy to loved ones, is really what propels buyers into the greeting-card market.

✔ What motivates new MBAs to take a particular job offer? Recent MBA graduates have been asked to rank what's most important to them when they decide among various job offers. When asked point-blank, a substantial majority rank quality of life, community, and public schools at the top of their list and place starting salary somewhere in the middle. A more careful survey and analysis of the MBA selection criteria, however, usually settles upon compensation as being the single most important variable in accepting a new position fresh out of school.

✔ Most people have a need to be accepted and liked by others. This powerful motivation creates great market opportunities for salons, gyms, and breath-mint companies.

Although motives obviously apply to individual consumers, they work equally well in the context of business or corporate behaviour. When a particular manufacturing company contracts with an employee assistance program (EAP) provider, for example, is the company motivated to improve the health of its employees, or is it motivated to reduce the cost of its health insurance premiums so that it can better compete (fulfilling its own need to survive)? If you run the EAP service, how you answer this question has a major impact on your internal management of costs versus the overall quality of the employee assistance that you provide.

Figure 7-1:
A basic overview of people's needs, as sketched out some 50 years ago by the social psychologist Abraham Maslow in his famous "Hierarchy of Needs" model.

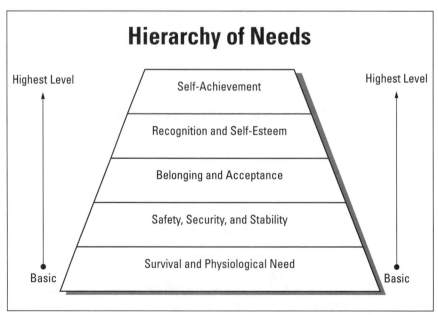

Hierarchy of Needs

Highest Level

Self-Achievement

Recognition and Self-Esteem

Belonging and Acceptance

Safety, Security, and Stability

Survival and Physiological Need

Basic

Highest Level

Basic

Your job, of course, is to dig beneath the obvious customer responses and consumption patterns to determine what the buyers' real motives are in purchasing goods and services in your market. When you understand what drives customer behaviour, you're in a much better position to talk about your product in terms that customers respond to.

Figuring Out How Customers Make Choices

How do customers make choices in the marketplace? The most important thing to remember is that customers decide to buy things based on their view of the world — their perceptions of reality. Few customers buy without thinking; instead, they bring their perceptions of the world into a decision-making process that (ideally) leads them to purchase your product or service rather than your competitors'.

Realizing perceptions are reality

Customer perceptions represent the market's world view and include not only what your customers think of your products and services, but also how they see your company and view your competitors.

As customers turn to the marketplace, they confront a mind-boggling array of products. Many variables influence your customers as they evaluate their choices: advertising, endorsements, reviews, and salesmanship, not to mention their own gut reactions. You need to know how customers respond to all these stimuli if you ultimately want to earn and keep their business.

Have you ever wondered, for example, why men's yellow sweaters are difficult to find or why women's clothes in black are everywhere? Well, it's no coincidence: Market research consistently shows that a majority of men believe that the colour yellow suggests weakness, and most women think black makes them look thin.

Or have you noticed that Daniel Craig is always wearing an Omega watch on his wrist? We know he's really *not* James Bond, of course, but the image of Agent 007 goes a long way in creating the perception of sophistication, adventure, and sex appeal around the purchase of an Omega watch.

Never lose sight of the marketer's motto:

Customer perceptions are the market reality.

People buy goods and services based on what they perceive to be true, not necessarily on what you know to be the facts. To be successful in the marketplace, you have to develop a clear insight into customers' perceptions, understanding how buyers react to products and services in your market before you complete your business plans.

Setting the five steps to adoption in motion

The decision-making process (DMP) that buyers go through often involves a series of well-defined steps leading up to the adoption of a product or service. (In this case, of course, *adoption* refers to a newly formed relationship with that product or service — not a child.)

By understanding the five major steps we describe in Table 7-1, you're better able to take advantage of customers' behaviours and build strategies that help them complete the adoption process by choosing your product or service.

Table 7-1	The Buyer's Five-Step Adoption Process	
Primary Steps	*Description of Customer*	*Your Task*
Awareness	Aware of a product or service but lacking detailed knowledge	Develop a strategy that educates and excites potential customers
Interest	Curious because of publicity and seeking more information	Provide more detailed product information and continue to build momentum
Evaluation	Deciding whether or not to test the product or service	Make the product-evaluation process as easy and rewarding as possible
Trial	Using the product or service on a test basis	Make the trial as simple and risk-free as you can
Adoption	Deciding to become a regular user	Develop strategies to retain good customers

Suppose that you own a software company with a brand-new, business-productivity program. You fear, however, that customers will be reluctant to give the program a try if they assume the software is difficult to figure out or incompatible with their computer systems. (Keep in mind that people act on their perceptions of reality rather than on the reality itself!) To move potential customers past the evaluation step of the adoption process, you may want to consider creating a trial version of the program and making it available over the Internet — along with a simple purchase option after the trial period ends. Some software makers have gone even further by sponsoring hands-on workshops to demonstrate their fancy programs, which gives potential buyers a chance to evaluate, try, get comfortable with, and then buy the product.

Serving Your Customers Better

The more you discover about your customers, the better you can serve them. And, in competitive markets, that can mean the difference between a successful business and a failure. Remember, your competitors can always try to copy the products you offer; copying the services you provide to support those products is a lot more difficult.

Often, the difference between a customer and a *satisfied* customer is based entirely on the service you provide. Satisfied customers become loyal customers. And loyal customers are one of the keys to growth and profit.

Taking a look at the lost customer

You can often gain a better understanding of your most loyal customers by taking a look at the customers you've lost. Your former customers may paint a rather grim picture for you, highlighting where and how you fall short of their expectations. But their insights are worth the discomfort.

Although lost customers may represent a series of disappointments to you, you may find their individual experiences invaluable when you focus on your business-planning efforts. So, take the initiative and contact some of the customers who walked to find out why. Employ the following tips to contact the missing:

- ✔ **Use mailing lists or old customer registration data.** Ask lost customers why they left and what you can do to get them back.

- ✔ **Hang around places where people buy similar products or services.** Engage these customers in conversation. A few of these people were probably your customers at one time, and they can tell you something

> important about why they aren't your customers any longer. Be sure to make them feel comfortable about giving you honest criticism.
>
> ✔ **Advertise a toll-free number or an e-mail address.** Encourage current customers to contact you with any complaints — real or imagined, big or small — 24 hours a day.

Coca-Cola found that only 2 percent of its dissatisfied customers publicly complained when they became unhappy with the company or its products. The remaining 98 percent simply switched to a rival brand. In far too many cases, the reasons for customer defection are often fixable — if you follow up and ask! The direct approach not only brings customers back, but also generates precisely the kind of information you need to adjust your strategy and business plan.

Catering to the loyalty effect

When profitable companies are asked to explain their success, they often take special care to mention their loyal customer base. This observation shouldn't surprise you: Loyal customers aren't only cost-effective, they also tend to attract other loyal customers.

Take a look at the flip side of the coin: Lost customers are expensive. Research shows that most of your customers probably aren't profitable for you until they use your product or service for about three years. Why? Because in the beginning, you have to shoulder hidden costs, including such expenses as advertising, promotions, customer training, and perhaps help lines or Web sites to acquire and keep a new customer — costs that you add to those directly associated with providing your product or service.

A typical company loses 15 to 20 percent of its customer base annually. Even more striking, the customers who leave were often good customers in the past, patronizing the firm for more than three years. Many companies maintain an attitude that borders on the cavalier: "Look, customers come and go. Such is life. That's why we advertise, do promotions, and hire sales people — to attract new customers and continue to expand our markets."

But what kind of customers come in? New ones, of course. Expensive ones. Customers who have yet to pay off their acquisition costs. And who leaves? To a large extent, customers who have already paid for themselves — the profitable ones. Studies across industries indicate that it costs about five times as much to attract a new customer as it does to keep an existing one. And it can cost up to 16 times as much to bring a new customer up to the level of profitability that a loyal customer represents.

The lessons here are obvious. When planning where to spend your time and money, use more of your resources to keep the customers you already have — and keep them happy.

Managing relationships

Customer relationship management (CRM) systems are all the rage in the business world today because of their promise to transform every customer into a loyal customer. What exactly are they? The systems are complex software programs designed to capture all sorts of information about your customers and then organize it, analyze it, and provide you with a current and complete picture of all your customer relationships. They sound too good to be true.

Here's the rub: Successful CRMs have to extend way beyond cool new technologies that make

them seem so simple. Effective customer relationship management often requires a completely new way of thinking about customers: seeing them as central to the entire business operation. It means that all your business functions must come together around the customer — not just the marketing and sales staff. It also means that you must centre all business strategy and planning on customers. Planning around customers is a wise thing to do, but if your business isn't already set up that way, CRM may require a good deal of effort and investment on your part.

Looking at a Special Case: Business Customers

Many of the business examples we include in this book have to do with companies that sell products and services primarily to individual consumers. But we don't want to neglect the other companies out there in the business-to-business markets. In the following sections, you can find details on how companies, institutions, and government agencies behave when they act as the customers.

Filling second-hand demand

Demand for goods and services in business-to-business markets is almost always *derived demand*. In other words, businesses purchase only the goods and services that they can use to better serve their own customers.

Steel is typically a product that individual consumers don't shop for. Steel purchasers tend to be automobile manufacturers, construction firms, appliance companies, and so on. After these businesses use the steel to make their products (cars, office towers, and refrigerators), you come into the picture as a potential customer.

What are the implications for the steel sellers? If a steel maker cuts prices across the board, for example, should it expect a huge increase in orders? Not necessarily. The steel buyers increase their purchases only if they think that they can sell more of their own product or service, and many factors beyond the underlying price of steel may affect sales. How many of us dashed out to buy a new car the last time Algoma Steel reduced its steel prices by 10 percent?

If you offer products or services in the business-to-business market, make sure you think through what your planning decisions mean to business buyers. You need to consider your business customers' customers, too:

- ✔ Will a price reduction on your part result in increased sales for your business customers — and your company?
- ✔ Will your customers (and their customers) benefit if you offer them additional bells and whistles with a raise in costs?
- ✔ Are your business customers looking for continuity and price stability?

Decision-making as a formal affair

Purchase decisions in the business-to-business marketplace tend to be more formal, rational, and professional than in most consumer markets. Many people from different parts of the target company may be involved in the decision-making process (DMP). One division in the company may recommend your product or service, another may acquire it, yet another may pay for it, and all the divisions do the work for a separate customer centre that actually uses the product. Taken together, these groups form the *decision-making unit* (DMU).

Table 7-2 describes three ways in which a business DMU may behave when it thinks about buying a product or service. Businesses often change their buying behaviour over time, so knowing where your business customers are in their DMP can help you plan when and how to make the sale.

Table 7-2	How Businesses Behave When They Buy
Buying Behaviour	*Description of the Customer's DMP*
Business as usual	Continues to order more of the product or service, perhaps even automating the process so that inventories don't fall below certain levels
Yes, but . . .	Asks for changes in the existing sales arrangement, modifying one or more purchase terms (such as pricing, financing, quantities, and options) and including various people who are part of the DMU
Opportunity knocks	Purchases a product or service for the first time, perhaps after putting out a request for proposal (RFP) to several possible suppliers and making a deliberate, complete decision involving all parties in the DMU

Knowing the forces to be reckoned with

When you work with business customers, you have to deal with several powerful customer forces that you rarely encounter in consumer markets. If you want your business-to-business strategies to succeed over time, you must factor these forces into your business plans. Consider the following questions:

✔ What's the state of your customer's business?

- Is your customer's business booming, maturing, or dying?
- Is it facing increased competition or enjoying record profits?
- Is it outsourcing business and creating new opportunities?
- Is it threatening to become a competitor?

✔ How does your customer's company operate?

- Does your customer purchase from you centrally, or does it have buyers scattered around the company?
- Does the purchase require several levels of approval before your customer makes a decision?
- Do senior executives (who may or may not know much about the product) make the ultimate purchase decisions?

✔ Who's important to whom?

- Do your customer's key decision-makers tend to be engineers or marketing people?
- Does your customer use both small and large suppliers?
- Does your customer have a policy of requiring more than one supplier in critical areas?

As you develop strategies for managing your business customers, take the time to investigate the unique forces of business-to-business markets:

✔ Go out into the field and talk to potential business buyers.

✔ Read about your business customers' organizations and their industries.

✔ Attend conferences and conventions that your business customers attend and find out about critical events and forces that shape their thinking.

All these activities take time and resources, of course, but your investment is rewarded many times over when you incorporate what you discover into your business-to-business planning.

Chapter 8

Checking Out Your Competition

. . . .

In This Chapter

▶ Seeing the value in competition

▶ Unveiling your real competitors

▶ Keeping tabs on your competitors' actions

▶ Predicting what your competitors are going to do next

▶ Putting together competitive data

. . . .

S pending time with the competition isn't anyone's idea of fun. Think they're out to get you? You bet they are. But the more you know about the competition, the better off you are when it comes to figuring out their next move — and setting a strategy to stay one step ahead.

If you haven't gotten around to thinking about the competition yet, you're in bad company; many businesses fail to take this part of planning seriously. Typical excuses at both extremes include

> *We have no way of knowing who all our competitors really are or what they're up to, anyway.*

or

> *We already know everything about them. We compete with them every day.*

Business owners or managers in the first group wring their hands because trying to find out about the competition is tough. Those in the second group cover their eyes, assuming that if they don't look too hard, nothing bad can happen. Both groups are making a big mistake. The competitor you're familiar with is much less dangerous than an unknown enemy.

When the Japanese decided to become global players in the automobile industry in the late 1960s, their car manufacturers planned very carefully. They knew what they had to do because the Western business experts had taught them. First, they needed to understand the consumer markets in Canada, the United States, and Europe; second, they needed to know everything about the worldwide competition.

So, Japanese car-makers came to Canada and the United States to analyze and learn from their competitors-to-be. They visited General Motors, Ford, and Chrysler. They asked questions, taped meetings, took pictures, measured, sketched, and studied. While they did all their research, the Japanese were amazed by the Canadian and American hospitality. When they got back home, of course, they hatched their plans. By finding out as much as possible about their marketplace and the competition in advance, Japanese auto firms were able to successfully penetrate the North American market and other world markets.

North American car companies never knew what hit them, even though the blow was a decade or more in coming. They simply failed to track their competition and take their competitors seriously. Over the last 35 years, the automobile industry has dealt with waves of competition, not only from the Japanese, but also from European and Korean car makers. And who knows, your next sedan may just be made in China or India.

In this chapter, we show you why you need to have competitors in the first place. We help you identify your current competitors and your potential competitors. We look at competition from the viewpoint of customers and the choices they make in the marketplace. And we examine your competitors in relation to their strategies and company structure, introducing the idea of strategic groups. After identifying your competitors, we help you understand them better by looking at what they do; by forecasting their future plans; and by checking out their capabilities, strategies, goals, and assumptions.

Understanding the Value of Competitors

Competitors are almost always portrayed as the bad guys. At best, they annoy. At worst, they steal customers away and bank the cash — your cash. In short, they make your business life miserable. Is this picture unfair? You bet.

Look up from the fray, and we can point out another way to look at your competitors: They invent new technologies, expand market opportunities, and sometimes create entire industries . . . and believe it or not, they also bring out the best in you. Competitors force you to sharpen your strategies, hone your business plans, and go that extra mile when it comes to satisfying customers. After all, your real goal is satisfying customers and developing long-term, rewarding relationships with them.

The power of competition as a force for good has persuaded regulators around the world to loosen their grip on one major industry after another, including

- ✔ Airlines
- ✔ Banks and insurance companies
- ✔ Postal services
- ✔ Telecommunications
- ✔ Utilities

In each of these industries, a newly competitive marketplace has led to more products, services, and customers — along with more choices and lower prices for customers. Well-run companies have grown stronger, and market expansion has made room for many new players. The biggest beneficiaries of all are people who travel, use ATMs, buy insurance, send express mail, call home from the road, and turn on the lights at night.

Competition is a force to be reckoned with because of the power of customers. (If you need a refresher on customer needs, benefits, and buying behaviours, turn back to Chapters 6 and 7.) Customers are always out there making market choices, deciding what to buy and where to spend money based on their needs and willingness to pay. How do they do it? The process is based on the *value equation,* which looks like this:

Customer value = Benefits ÷ Price

Figure 8-1 illustrates this equation.

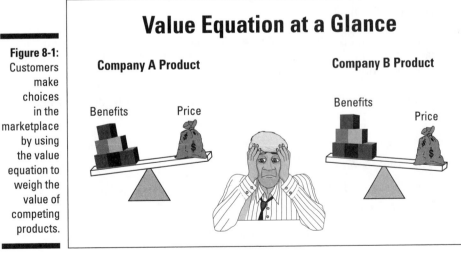

Value Equation at a Glance

Figure 8-1:
Customers make choices in the marketplace by using the value equation to weigh the value of competing products.

Company A Product

Company B Product

Benefits   Price

Benefits   Price

The equation may look complicated, but it points to a simple truth: Today's consumers are awfully good at making complex choices. Think about the last time you went out to run errands. You probably stopped by the grocery store, where you used the value equation to make all sorts of tradeoffs. Maybe you chose a certain cut of meat, weighing what you were in the mood for and what looked fresh against the price per kilogram. Maybe you decided that you didn't have time to drive to the warehouse store, so you bought cereal in the more expensive 375-gram box. On your way out, you picked up organic tomatoes for your salad at three times the conventional price. Driving home, you put fuel in the car. You opted for the most conveniently located station, even though its fuel prices were a little higher.

Competition encourages each player in your industry to figure out how to provide customers with the best value possible. Competition can often create a win-win situation, so don't try to avoid it by ignoring your competitors. Don't ever think that you're immune to it, either. Instead, take advantage of competition and what it can do for your company.

Identifying Your Real Competitors

Two boys go hiking in the woods. They suddenly come across a bear. One of the boys immediately sits down and tightens his shoelaces. The other kid looks down at him and says, "There's no way we can outrun that bear." The first kid replies, "I'm not interested in outrunning the bear. I just want to outrun you!" Like the boy in the story, you need to know who you're really competing against.

You can come up with a list of possible competitors based on any number of factors. The problem is finding the method that most successfully identifies the competitors who impact your company.

To really understand your competition, you need to know the following things:

- ✔ How customers make choices
- ✔ How customers use products
- ✔ The capabilities of your competitors
- ✔ Your competitors' strategies
- ✔ Where future competition may come from

Clearly Canadian

Clearly Canadian Beverage Corporation (CCBEF), based in British Columbia, is a leading producer of alternative beverages. You know — those premium drinks that contain natural ingredients, little sugar and few calories, and little or no carbonation. Its flagship brand, Clearly Canadian Sparkling Flavoured Waters, has sold more than 2 billion bottles worldwide, but it has serious competition. You could safely say, for example, that most Clearly Canadian drinkers have tried a Coke at least once. Coca-Cola accounts for almost half the soft drinks consumed in the world today. But which other beverages compete with Clearly Canadian? The following list of competitors starts with the most obvious:

✔ Colas

✔ Other soft drinks

✔ Juices and juice drinks

✔ Isotonic drinks

✔ Flavoured iced teas

✔ Iced coffees

✔ Seltzers and mineral waters

✔ Beer and wine

And, of course, tap water. Does Clearly Canadian really compete with tap water? As it turns out, yes. Water is the most common substitute drink in place of a non-alcoholic beverage. But CCBEF has to draw the line somewhere when it comes to identifying its major competitors — the ones that have a real impact on its business over time. Knowing where and how it should draw that line largely depends on understanding what customers look for. For CCBEF, that understanding involves customer choices based on the following factors:

✔ All-natural versus preservatives

✔ Diet versus non-diet

✔ Low-calorie versus high-calorie

✔ Caffeine-free versus caffeinated

✔ Low-carbonation versus high-carbonation

✔ Non-alcoholic versus alcoholic

The importance of these criteria differs in different markets and may change over time. Accordingly, CCBEF has to continually assess and reassess its competition.

Considering competition based on customer choice

Customers choose to buy certain products based on a value equation, weighing the benefits of several products against their relative prices (refer to Figure 8-1 for more equation info). But which products do customers actually compare? If you want to know who your real competitors are, you need to know how many products — and which products — your customers typically look at before they decide to buy.

If you identify your customers and their *selection criteria* — that is, what they look for in a product or service — you can divide a list of competitors into groups based on how intensely they compete with you:

- **Head-to-head competitors:** Together, these companies represent your most intense competition. Their products always seem to be on customers' *short lists* (those three or four competing products that they plan to compare very carefully), and customers may ask you to compare your features, benefits, and pricing with these competitors' products. You want to know as much as you can about these competitors. In the world of magazines, for instance, health publications such as *Canadian Health & Lifestyle, glow,* and *alive* compete head-to-head for readers — and for advertising dollars.

- **First-tier competitors:** These companies are direct competitors, but perhaps not quite as fierce as the head-to-head kind. You may run up against one of these companies only in certain areas and among particular kinds of customers. You don't want to ignore this group too long, however, because any of these companies may have the desire and capability to become a head-to-head competitor. Women's magazines, for example, represent first-tier competitors to health-related publications because women's magazines include a lot of health-issue coverage.

- **Indirect competitors:** These competitors are the ones that you don't often think about. Their products surface as alternatives to yours only occasionally, and you usually have more important competition to worry about. Again, this group deserves a periodic review because indirect competitors always have the potential to surprise you with competing products that come out of the blue. Many health-related magazines find themselves competing indirectly with sites on the Internet that can provide much of the same updated medical information.

You should be able to count your head-to-head competitors on one hand. You may have twice as many first-tier competitors to track and an equal number of indirect competitors. Be careful to keep the number of competitors that you track manageable. Your head-to-head competition deserves much more attention than your indirect competitors, obviously, but you should set up a schedule for reviewing companies in each of the three competitor groups. Start with a weekly analysis of your head-to-head competition, a monthly review of first-tier competitors, and a quarterly review of your indirect competitors, adjusting the schedule to fit the pace of change in your industry.

One way to come up with levels of competition in your business is to ask potential customers to consider playing their product-selection process backward for you, as we describe in the following list. (For more detailed information on how customers make choices, check out Chapters 6 and 7.) Sometimes, you can also get this kind of information through your salespeople or customer-service representatives (if you have them). Follow these steps to get a handle on how your customers think:

1. **Ask customers for the short list of products that they seriously evaluated for purchase.**

    Your head-to-head competitors probably offer these products.

2. **Ask customers for the larger list that they came up with when they started investigating what was available in the market.**

    Your first-tier competitors are likely to offer these products.

3. **Ask customers for the names of products that popped into their heads when they first decided to go shopping.**

    These products may include those your indirect competitors offer.

Paying attention to product usage and competition

Looking at products and services in the context of how customers use them gives you another viewpoint from which to eye the competition. In this case, follow these steps:

1. **Ask customers to think about situations, applications, or occasions in which they may use your product.**

2. **Ask customers to come up with other kinds of products or services they think are appropriate and may be just as satisfying in the same situations.**

3. **Ask customers to identify two things they would change about the product that they use.**

Clearly Canadian Beverage drinkers, for example, may associate weekend outdoor activities (such as baseball and soccer games) with enjoying a dailyEnergy. They also may single out beer and maybe even mineral water as other possibilities to help them cool off and relax after a game. In this context, dailyEnergy has a well-defined set of competitors that may be quite different from its competition in other settings.

By viewing your competitors from a marketplace perspective — how customers choose and then use alternative products — you're rewarded with a fairly complete picture of the competitive landscape that you face.

Parable of the Corvette and the Sundancer

The Corvette is still a car with an image. General Motors has made the two-seater since 1953, and even today the 'Vette conjures up fond memories of the muscle cars of the '50s and '60s. But, in the last two decades, the Corvette has faced increasing competition, so General Motors decided to find out exactly what it was up against.

Now, you may assume that the typical 'Vette buyer is a young, restless male longing for a cool, fast car — and if he could afford it, you'd probably be right. But GM discovered that the profile of the typical Corvette buyer is actually a man reaching middle age. This typical buyer, who grew up in the '60s and '70s, now has some disposable income, a few grey hairs, and an empty nest, and is approaching retirement.

When the company asked these Corvette buyers about other ways that they could have spent their money, customers came up with the usual suspects: a BMW Z4, an Audi TT, maybe a low-end Porsche. But something else appeared on the radar screen: the Sea Ray Sundancer. What? Isn't that a boat? In fact, the Sundancer is a fast, sporty cabin cruiser that sleeps six. How in the world did a boat get into the running with the Corvette, BMW, Audi, and Porsche?

To find out, GM asked customers how they plan to use their Corvettes — in what kinds of situations and for what purposes. The answers made it clear that a Corvette was worth the big bucks because it offered these buyers a ticket back to their youth — a way to cope with getting older. And they could punch that ticket just as easily on a Sundancer as in a Corvette. Either vehicle seemed to fit the bill when it came to showing off, getting away for a weekend escape, or just feeling young again. By asking the right questions about the context of this purchase, GM identified an indirect competitor — one that also had some muscle.

Spotting strategic groups

If you step back and look at the competitors around you, their differing appearances may amaze you. In certain industries, for example, companies that have a full product line compete with companies that offer a single product. In other industries, companies that gain recognition for their innovative R&D (research and development) compete with companies that don't develop anything on their own.

How can competitors in the same industry be so different? Over time, doesn't every company figure out the best strategies, as well as the most efficient and effective ways to do business? Shouldn't all companies end up looking pretty much alike? These good questions have two possible answers:

- ✔ Companies don't always discover a best way to do things. Markets and industries are complex, and different ways of doing business can exist side by side and be equally successful.

- ✔ Companies that do business one way can't always easily change and start doing business another way.

Identifying competitors based on their unique capabilities and strategies has a great deal in common with some of the industry analysis discussed in Chapter 5. Sometimes, you can take that analysis one step further and divide companies in your industry into groups based on what they do and how they operate — sort of like the market segments that we talk about in Chapter 6, but this time applied to companies rather than individual customers.

A *strategic group* is a set of companies in a particular industry that look alike and tend to behave in similar ways. In particular, firms in the same strategic group have the following traits:

- They display similar characteristics (size, geography, rate of growth).
- They operate in similar ways (degree of risk-taking, level of aggressiveness).
- They demonstrate similar capabilities (people, skills, image, money in the bank).
- They pursue related strategies (customer segments, distribution, marketing, and product-line decisions).

You can apply all sorts of business criteria to identify the most useful strategic groups. Although every industry is different, you need to consider these general variables:

- Companies that manufacture most of their product components versus those that assemble or resell products
- Companies that produce name-brand products versus those that produce generic or private-label brands
- Companies that rely on their own R&D versus those that license or buy technology
- Companies that have a full product line versus those that have limited or specialized products
- Companies that emphasize marketing versus those that focus on production
- Companies with diverse endeavours versus those that thrive in only one industry

Strategic groups fall somewhere between an individual company and the entire industry. Lumping your competition into groups is helpful because all the companies in a strategic group tend to be affected by, and react to, changes in the marketplace in the same ways. But grouping works only if those companies stay put in their assigned groups long enough to be analyzed. Fortunately, they usually do.

A strategic circle of friends

The Canadian communication sector is so complex that keeping track of competitors would be tough without the help of strategic groups. Fortunately, players can use several criteria to break the communication world into more manageable industry segments.

When Rogers Communications Inc. looks out over the competitive landscape, the competitors that loom the largest are Bell and Telus. The following traits, which these companies have in common, place them in the same strategic group:

✔ They're extremely large companies.

✔ They have a hand in many aspects of the telecommunication process.

✔ They boast a full line of offerings with many services, bundles, and prices.

✔ They distribute services on a national scale.

These companies need to know about one another in terms of resources, capabilities, goals, and strategies. Although Rogers keeps a close eye on CTVglobemedia and CanWest Communications (after all, Rogers has broadcasting, content, and publishing holdings), the company tracks those media with different criteria and intensity of effort than it tracks BCE and Telus. By identifying the members of its own strategic group, Rogers focuses on the competitors that have the greatest impact on its strategic business units.

As part of your industry analysis, you may have already discovered a few *entry barriers* — factors that make it tough to get into your business, such as high capital costs, expensive distribution systems, new technology, and regulation. You also may have come up with some *exit barriers* — factors that keep competitors from getting out of the business, such as expensive factories, specialized equipment, and long-term agreements. Strategic groups can have the same kind of *mobility barriers,* which tend to keep competitors where they are, in one group or another.

Strategic groups can be a great timesaver in business planning because, when you put all your competitors in strategic groups, you know where to focus your energies. You can spend most of your time analyzing the companies in your strategic group and deal with the rest of the companies in clusters instead of tracking each company separately.

To divide your list of competitors into strategic groups, follow these steps:

1. **Put your competitors in a small number of groups, based on their similarities.**

2. **Add your company to one of the groups.**

3. **Looking at each group carefully, try to come up with the basic criteria that you used to make your selections.**

4. **Take a hard look at the group in which you put your company.**

   Are these competitors really closest to you in terms of their characteristics and the criteria that you identify?

5. **Ask a few trusted customers to look over your groups and see whether they agree.**

   Viewing the world through your customers' eyes is always worthwhile and can sometimes be a real eye-opener.

6. **Adjust the groups, if necessary, and work on additional criteria that may point to other strategic groupings.**

Strategic groups are relevant and useful in many industries; they often provide a means of organizing competitors in ways that can simplify the competitive landscape. But keep in mind that all industries don't play by the same rules. If the mobility barriers aren't very high, for example, companies are free to adjust their capabilities and change strategies quickly, limiting the usefulness of long-term strategic groups. In addition, acquisitions and alliances between companies can change the composition of groups very rapidly. Make sure that the groups you identify in your industry are real and won't dissolve before you have a chance to analyze them.

Focusing on future competition

Always remember that new competition can come from anywhere. So keep an eye out for emerging competitors. Determine who they are and how seriously you should worry about them. The following are the most likely sources of new competition:

- ✔ **Market expansion:** A company that operated successfully for years outside your geographic region decides to expand into your territory, making it an overnight competitor. Think about Japanese car companies successfully entering the North American market in the 1970s. Alternatively, a company that makes a product that dominates another market segment sees an opportunity to target your customers, as well.

- ✔ **Product expansion:** A company decides to take advantage of its brand name, technology, or distribution system and creates a new product line in direct competition with yours. Remember Microsoft's success when it took on the Netscape Internet browser and created Internet Explorer.

✔ **Backward integration:** One of your major customers decides that it can do what you do — and do it faster, better, and cheaper. So the former customer sets up shop and hands the business that it used to give you to its in-house group. Suddenly, your old customer is a new competitor. In-house grocery store brands, such as President's Choice, are a perfect example of a packaged goods customer becoming a direct competitor.

✔ **Forward integration:** Your company buys many products from many suppliers. One day, one of those suppliers decides that it can bring all the pieces together as well as you can. So, it creates a new business and a product line that competes with yours. Dell goes directly to the consumer through the Internet, cutting out traditional computer stores. Other computer manufacturers are doing the same in addition to their retail channel.

✔ **Change in fortune:** Out of the blue, a major company purchases a minor competitor. With access to new resources (financing, marketing, and distribution), the minor competitor becomes a major player. You really have to watch out for these competitors; when they appear, they may catch you off guard and be all the more dangerous.

Keeping track of your future competitors is as important as tracking your current ones. So, keep your eyes and ears open, and don't be shy about asking your customers and suppliers about competitors on a regular basis.

Tracking Your Competitors' Actions

Suppose that you're armed with a fresh, up-to-date list of competitors. You rank which of those competitors you have to watch most carefully and tag them as head-to-head competitors, first-tier competitors, or indirect competitors. (We discuss separating companies into groups in the section "Identifying Your Real Competitors," earlier in this chapter.) Maybe you even put them into strategic groups, singling out the competitors in your group for special attention.

So, what's next? First, you should decide which of the competitors on your list you want to spend more time with. Remember — you probably can't find out all there is to know about each competitor. Keeping track of competitors' actions involves looking at both what the companies are capable of doing and what they plan to do.

Determining competitors' capabilities

You need to ask the same kinds of questions about your competitors that you ask yourself when you complete a company checkup in Chapters 9 and 10. We introduce the basics here, but turn to those chapters for all the nitty-gritty details.

The capabilities that you're most interested in tell you something about your competitors' ability to react when your industry changes. How quickly they can react — and how much they can do to change themselves — says a great deal about the competitive danger they pose.

To determine your competitors' capabilities, start with this list of important business functions and areas. The following questions should get you going, but check out Chapter 9 if you need more help, along with the section "Organizing facts and figures," later in this chapter:

- **Management:** What do you know about the background and experience of the company's chief bigwigs? What functional areas (marketing, finance, engineering, and so on) do they come out of? What about the board of directors? How many talented, qualified, and accomplished people are at or near the top? Do any managers hail from another industry? If so, what are their past track records?

- **Organization:** How structured and centralized is the company's organization? Does it have tight controls in place, or does it delegate authority down through the organizational levels? Does it promote from within or hire from the outside? How would you describe the corporate culture?

- **Customer base:** What's the company's share of the market? Is it growing? How loyal are its customers? Are customers concentrated in one segment, or do the company's products appeal to several segments?

- **Research and development:** Is the company known for innovation and technology? Is it even involved in R&D (research and development)? How often does it come out with new products? Does it have patents and copyrights to rely on? How stable and committed are the members of its technical staff? Does the company have sources of outside expertise to draw on?

- **Operations:** How modern are the company's facilities? How has automation affected operations? If the company is a manufacturer, does it have flexible production facilities? What about capacity? Can the company count on its suppliers? What's the general attitude of the workforce? Does the company have a history of labour disputes?

- **Marketing and sales:** How strong are the company's products? How broad is the product line? Does the company have a reputation for quality? How about brand-name recognition? Does the company put a large amount of its resources into advertising and promotion? Is it known for its customer service? Are the salespeople aggressive and well trained?

- **Distribution and delivery:** How many distribution channels does the company sell through? Does it have a good relationship with its distributors? Is it quick to take advantage of new distribution opportunities?

- **Financial condition:** Is the company's revenue growing? How about profits? Does the company manage costs well? Are profit margins steady or growing? What's the cash-flow situation? Is its long-term debt manageable? Does the company have ready access to cash?

Jot down a half-page corporate bio on each competitor. Each bio should capture the company's defining traits, including the following:

- ✔ Capability to respond quickly
- ✔ Willingness to change
- ✔ Determination to compete
- ✔ Capacity to grow

Assessing competitors' strategies

Your competitors' capabilities tell you something important about their capacity to get things done right now in your business. But what are they planning to do for the future?

To answer that question, you need to assess their capabilities strategically. (We talk a lot more about how to think strategically in Chapter 14, so turn there for the details.) The following three strategies are sometimes called generic strategies because they've been tried many times before and because they work well in almost any market or industry:

- ✔ **Low cost:** The first generic strategy comes from a basic economic principle: If you can offer a product or service at the lowest price in the market, customers are naturally going to buy from you. In the retail food industry, Thrifty Foods, Real Canadian Superstore, Price Choppers, and other discount chains compete almost exclusively on low cost. This strategy assumes, of course, that you can also produce your product at a low-enough cost so that the company makes a profit over time. The strategy also assumes that your product or service is similar enough to the competition's that a lower price can entice customers and clinch the sale.

- ✔ **Something different:** This strategy is based on the simple notion that if you can come up with something different or unique in the products you offer or the services you provide, customers will beat a path to your company door. These customers are likely to become good customers, loyal customers, and customers that aren't terribly sensitive to price because you offer them special benefits that they can't find anywhere else. Almost every big city has specialty markets such as Longos or Choice Markets, which compete with the big food chains by offering items you can't find at regular grocery stores.

- ✔ **Focus:** The last generic strategy is about the kinds of customers you decide to serve. Instead of positioning yourself everywhere in the market and trying to sell products and services to everyone, carefully choose your customers. You win these customers over as a group by focusing on understanding their needs better than the competition does and by providing them with the benefits that they look for, be it price savings or something unique. In the retail food arena, ethnic markets, such as Asian or East Indian grocery stores, compete by focusing on a very specific market.

A competitor doesn't have to go with just one of these generic strategies; Chapter 14 shows that you can often combine strategies. A company that follows a focused strategy may find success in serving a particular market segment simply because its products or services are different from those of the competition.

Put together a short summary of what strategies you think your competitors may be coming up with. Review their capabilities and past actions, considering the following questions:

✔ What generic strategies has each competitor adopted in the past?

✔ Have the strategies generally been successful?

✔ Are changes in the industry forcing competitors to change their strategies?

✔ What kinds of change is each competitor capable of making?

✔ How fast can each competitor change?

Usually, you find that a long-term strategy requires time and the total commitment of the company. So, it turns out that knowing a little about your competitors' history is very useful in understanding their strategies. It also helps you keep in mind what you think your competitors are capable of in the future. Remember, you can use the concept of strategic groups to simplify this process. (See the section "Spotting strategic groups," earlier in this chapter, to find out more about this concept.)

Predicting Your Competitors' Moves

Trying to predict where your competitors are headed isn't easy, of course; looking into the future never is. But where your competitors plan to be in the months and years to come certainly depends on where they are today, as well as on their capabilities and the strategies that they've set in motion.

Many companies intentionally (or accidentally) send market signals about how they may behave. Some companies, for example, always lower their prices in response to a competitor. Looking at the past actions of competitors can provide you with an indication of what they may do next. Predicting your competitors' actions also requires a little insight into what they think and how they think — the goals that they aim for, as well as the assumptions that they make about the industry.

Winner's circle of stocks

When Frank Stronach first dabbled in horse racing, business leaders and racing pundits thought the results-oriented entrepreneur would give up after a number of disappointing outcomes. However, Stronach had something else in mind — owning the winner's circle. He was pretty clear about his goals in media interviews. Under Magna Entertainment Corp. (MEC), he had his senior people move quickly to expand his herd of thoroughbred horses, buy up a number of racetracks in the United States, and branch out into breeding.

MEC's competitors should have paid attention. If past performance is an indicator of future performance, then surely it was clear that Stronach's passion for taking risks and capturing market leadership would mean swift and aggressive action. Competitors who saw the early warning signs had the opportunity to adjust their strategies to meet a changing landscape.

Figuring out competitors' goals

Your competitors' mission, vision, and values statements tell you a great deal about what they expect of themselves in the future. (Chapters 3 and 4 talk about these statements.) These documents aren't top-secret; they communicate a company's intentions to all its stakeholders, and you should take advantage of them. You don't have to read your competitors' minds. All you have to do is read what they say about themselves and what they plan to do. (See the section "Organizing facts and figures," later in this chapter, for places to find such info.)

To discover the details about your competitors' plans, take the following steps:

1. **Select a short list of competitors.**

2. **Dig up as much information as you can find on each competitor's values, vision, and mission statements, as well as any stated business goals and objectives.**

   The Internet is always a good place to start. And, if the company is publicly traded, check out its annual report to shareholders (usually posted on the Internet, as well).

3. **Ask customers, suppliers, your sales force, and maybe even your competitors' former employees for information about each of your competitor's long-term plans.**

   This isn't spying — you're not looking for patent data, trade secrets, or other proprietary information, but a sense of the company's direction.

4. **Write down your educated estimation of your competitors' financial and strategic goals.**

   Don't forget to read between the lines. In particular, look for the following:

   - Market-share goals
   - Revenue targets
   - Profitability targets
   - Technology milestones
   - Customer-service goals
   - Distribution targets
   - Changes in leadership or senior management

Uncovering competitors' assumptions

What your competitors plan to do is usually related to their assumptions about themselves, about you and other companies like you, and about your industry — how they think and the way in which they see the world. Sometimes, you can get important clues about your competitors' assumptions by going back over their goals and objectives. Companies can't easily make a statement about where they want to go without giving something away about where they think they are today. You can often come up with valuable insights by comparing your competitors' assumptions about the industry with what you know (and think) to be true.

When Martin Cooper, an inventor and general manager at Motorola, placed the first cellphone call to his rival at AT&T Bell Labs in 1973, neither of these two men, nor their companies, could have imagined that an obscure little company in Canada would eventually challenge them for worldwide dominance in the mobile telecommunications marketplace. By the time these American companies realized the large gap in their assumptions, the competitive damage had already been done. (For a heads-up, see the section "Focusing on future competition," earlier in this chapter.) Through a series of innovative product introductions with its flagship BlackBerry, Research In Motion (RIM) laid the strategic groundwork to capture the world market. And by 2007, RIM was the largest producer of smart phones in the world, leaving its pastoral past far behind.

Assumptions aren't always true — which is what makes them assumptions in the first place. As the preceding RIM example suggests, false assumptions can be very dangerous for companies, especially when they lead to so-called conventional wisdom or result in competitive blind spots:

✔ **Conventional wisdom:** Prevailing assumptions in an industry often become so ingrained that companies mistake them for the gospel truth. In the 1970s, for example, conventional wisdom said that cutting-edge telecommunications technologies would naturally emerge and prosper in the United States. RIM proved otherwise. Conventional wisdom is almost always proved wrong when an unconventional competitor comes along. Watch your competitors for signs that they take their assumptions too seriously and have forgotten the importance of asking, "Why?"

✔ **Blind spots:** Missing the significance of events or trends in an industry is all too easy, especially if they run counter to prevailing notions and conventional wisdom. A competitor's worldview often dictates what that company sees and doesn't see. RIM's product introductions, for example, didn't appear high on Motorola's radar screens because, in the beginning, RIM had a shortage of good software applications. While you track your competitors, look closely for actions and reactions that may point to blind spots and a misreading of what's happening in the marketplace.

Competing to Win

The more you get to know your competitors, the better off you are when it comes to understanding their actions and anticipating their moves.

But remember — the more you discover about your competitors, the more they probably discover about you. You can bet that you probably put out as much information about your company and its intentions as your competitors do, so listening to yourself is just as important as listening to your competition. Put yourself on your list of competitors. Interpret your actions from a competitor's point of view. That way, you understand the implications of your competitive behaviour in the industry as well as you understand your competitors' behaviours.

If you're serious about the competition, you can't do all this analysis one time, wash your hands, and be finished with it. You have to monitor your competitors in a systematic way. If you're good at observing your competitors, you can choose the competitive battles that you want to win. You don't get ambushed in competitive situations where you're bound to lose.

Organizing facts and figures

To find out what really makes your competitors tick, take advantage of data from all sorts of places. (Refer to Chapter 5 for a list of resources.) Start your search by using the power of the Internet. You can usually find facts and figures on the competition included in the following resources:

✔ Business, trade, and technical publications

✔ Trade shows

✔ Company documents

✔ Stock-market analyses

✔ Management speeches

✔ Suppliers and distributors

✔ Customer feedback

✔ Your employees

The last item in the preceding list deserves a special note. Your employees are an invaluable source of data when it comes to the competition. When you look inside your company, start with your salespeople, who are smack-dab in the middle of the information stream. They talk with customers, deal with distributors, and occasionally run into competitors. They hear all the gossip, rumours, and news flashes that flow through your industry. Take advantage of their position and figure out how to capture what they know — and how to use it to your advantage.

You have to be a little careful about gathering information from employees other than your salespeople. In many industries, people move from job to job and company to company. Brainstorming about what a competitor may be up to is harmless, but warning flags should go up if someone pulls out documents marked Top Secret. Such behaviour isn't only wrong, it's also illegal. You can't use certain pieces of information that a former employee may have about a competitor — anything that may be construed as proprietary information or trade secrets. High-tech companies are forever exchanging threats and lawsuits over alleged violations of trade secrets laws. If you feel that you're standing on shaky ground, check out Chapter 3 and your company's values statement — and talk to your company's lawyer.

You need a way to organize the facts and figures that you collect from your many sources so that you can turn the pieces into useful competitive information. Long ago, filing cabinets and file folders did the trick nicely. Now, however, it probably makes more sense to set up a computer-based system to keep track of the data. When you set up the system, keep in mind that information about your competitors won't fall in your lap in the next two days — instead, it trickles in over weeks, months, and years.

More than likely, you already have bits and pieces of data about your key competitors stashed away. You just need to develop a procedure that keeps the bits and pieces coming in and brings them together to create a useful, up-to-date profile of the competition. The following steps should help you develop such a procedure:

1. **Start with a pilot procedure for tracking competitors.**

   Beginning with your sales force (or yourself, if you're self-employed), set up a trial system to capture competitive data from the sales channel. Create periodic paper reports in a standard format or computerize the process, if you can.

2. **Set up a company-wide system for tracking competitors.**

   Bring other people and parts of your company into the process of identifying and tracking competitors so that you have as much accurate information on the competition as you can get, when and where you need it. Competitor analysis is too important to do haphazardly or only when a crisis hits. Remember to be careful when dealing with employees outside the sales force.

3. **Make someone responsible for competitor analysis.**

   Put a manager (or yourself) in charge of competitor analysis for your company. That way, everyone understands that competitor analysis is important. Your employees also have someone to turn to when they need to give or get information on the competition.

4. **Make it your priority to see that the system is carried out.**

   Make sure that everyone in your company takes competitor analysis seriously by including it in your business plan. Become an advocate, insisting that the competition be addressed in any planning document that comes across your desk. Periodically update and validate your competitor analysis with outside resources, such as customers, suppliers, or perhaps even an outside consultant.

Choosing your battles

The more thoroughly you understand your competitors — what they did in the past, what they do now, and what they may do in the future — the better you can plan for and choose the competitive battles that you want to take part in.

Naturally, you want to go after markets in which you have a strategy and the capability to succeed. But you have to keep your eyes wide open because you're never alone in any marketplace for long. By embracing the competition, rather than ignoring it, you have the added advantage of knowing where the competition is weakest. Choose each battleground by pitting your strengths against areas where the competition has weaknesses so that you win half the battle before the contest even begins.

Part III
Weighing Your Company's Prospects

The 5th Wave — By Rich Tennant

SWIM WITH THE GIANT SQUID

SWIM WITH THE MORAY EELS

SWIM WITH THE JELLYFISH

SWIM WITH OCTOPI

"Since we lost the dolphins, business hasn't been quite the same."

In this part . . .

*W*henever you take on something big and new, whether you change jobs, buy a house, go back to school, or start a business, doubting questions come up. Are you really up for the challenge? Is this the right decision? Is it too risky? Will things work out in the end? These are good questions because they force you to take a good, hard look at the capabilities and talent that you bring to the table.

In this part, we help you look at who and where you are and show you how to make an honest assessment about what you discover. We set out to discover all the abilities and resources that you have. We help you determine which of them are strengths and which are weaknesses by comparing them to what you need to succeed in your industry — and what opportunities and threats you face. We help you focus on the real, added value you can bring to your customers by finding out what they want and what your company does best. We also help you figure out how to develop a workable business model so that you can extend and maintain the competitive advantages you already have in the market. Finally, we turn to your finances and help you create a clear picture of your company, based on your revenue, profits, assets, and cash position, and then we help you use that picture to create a financial forecast and budget.

Chapter 9

Assessing Where You Stand Today

● ●

In This Chapter

▶ Discovering your capabilities and resources

▶ Spotting company strengths and weaknesses

▶ Reviewing critical success factors

▶ Recognizing opportunities and threats

▶ Using SWOT to analyze your business landscape

● ●

*W*e've all looked at a snapshot of ourselves or listened to our voices on the outgoing voicemail messages and said

> *That sure doesn't look like me.*

or

> *Is that what I really sound like?*

In fact, we don't know exactly what we look or sound like to other people. Which explains the difficulty most people have creating an honest self-portrait — whether they try to recognize their appearance or voice, or make objective statements about their strengths and weaknesses.

Assessing yourself isn't an easy task. You have to measure strengths and weaknesses relative to the situations at hand; a strength in one circumstance may prove to be a weakness in another. Leadership and snap decision-making, for example, may serve you extremely well in an emergency. But the same temperament may be a liability when you're a part of a team that must navigate delicate give-and-take negotiations.

If your business is already up and running, you face similar problems of seeing clearly and objectively when you take on the task of measuring your company's internal strengths and weaknesses. If you're just starting up a business, this chapter shows you what you need to think about soon enough because successful business planning absolutely requires that you always know where you currently stand.

In this chapter, we help you get a handle on your company's strengths and weaknesses in relation to the opportunities and threats that you face. We look at ways that you can spot potential strengths and weaknesses by making a list of your capabilities and resources. We show you how the critical success factors in your industry come into play to determine which of those capabilities and resources are strengths and which aren't. We help you pull all the pieces of the puzzle together — your company's strengths, weakness, opportunities, and threats (SWOT) — to create a complete picture. And we also create a strategic balance sheet that helps you keep track of where you stand, what you should do, and when you should do it.

Doing Situation Analysis

It shouldn't surprise you that many businesses fail miserably at the job of objective self-analysis. They cling to a distorted image of the resources that they command and the capabilities that they bring to the marketplace. To avoid this trap, examine your company's situation by using a tried-and-true approach known as SWOT. Don't worry about guns or sharpshooters here *SWOT* is simply an acronym for *strengths, weaknesses, opportunities,* and *threats.*

You can't measure your company's strengths and weaknesses in a vacuum, of course. Your situation depends not only on your capabilities and resources, but also on the opportunities and threats that arise from situations beyond your control. (Check out Chapter 5 to review opportunities and threats.) Depending on the situations that you face, opportunities and threats appear, disappear, and change all the time, and your company's strengths and weaknesses change with them.

Because knowing where your company stands today is such an important part of a business plan, a thorough SWOT analysis is something that you should complete more than once. In fact, you should carry out a SWOT review on a regular basis, depending on how fast your business environment, the industry, and your company change. (To complete the full SWOT analysis, turn to the section "Completing your SWOT analysis," later in this chapter.)

Identifying Strengths and Weaknesses

Your company's *strengths* are the capabilities, resources, and skills that you can draw upon to carry out strategies, implement plans, and achieve the goals that you set for the company. Your company's *weaknesses* are any lack of skills or a deficiency in your capabilities and resources relative to the competition that may stop you from acting on strategies and plans or from accomplishing your goals.

To capture your first impressions of your company, complete the Company Strengths and Weaknesses Questionnaire (see Figure 9-1). On the right side of the questionnaire, assess your capabilities and resources in each area. On the left side, rate the importance of these elements to your industry.

Keeping frames of reference

After you complete the questionnaire shown in Figure 9-1, you should have a beginning list of your company's strengths and weaknesses. To be objective, however, you need to go beyond first impressions and look at your business assets from more than one point of view. Different frames of reference offer the advantage of smoothing out biases that creep into a single viewpoint. They also offer the best chance of making your list as complete as it can be. Consider these three independent viewpoints:

Cognos: Brains are its brawn

In the early 1980s, Ottawa software company Cognos shifted from IT consulting and custom software to packaged software solutions — no easy feat! The strength of Cognos's management and its committed team of employees pulled it off — one of the first demonstrations of its ability to adapt and manage change. These strengths would carry Cognos from a small Canadian software firm to the world's leading firm in business intelligence software. Over the next decade, it adapted its software and services to the frequent technology changes in hardware, from mainframes to LANs to networks, and remained a leader.

When the Internet and intranets started to threaten Cognos's leadership, it once again changed its business model. Rather than relying on its own research and development (R&D) to introduce new software, it began buying companies that had the current technology. It was successful in managing the change and integrating the new acquisitions into its existing corporate structure. The result: Cognos maintained its leadership position.

The strength of competent management, committed employees, and the ability to adapt and manage change in the volatile high-tech industry are hallmarks of Cognos's success.

Company Strengths and Weaknesses Questionnaire

Importance to Industry			Business Area	Your Capabilities and Resources			
Low	Moderate	High		Poor	Fair	Good	Excellent
❏	❏	❏	Management	❏	❏	❏	❏
❏	❏	❏	Organization	❏	❏	❏	❏
❏	❏	❏	Customer base	❏	❏	❏	❏
❏	❏	❏	Research and development ❏	❏	❏	❏	❏
❏	❏	❏	Operations	❏	❏	❏	❏
❏	❏	❏	Marketing and sales	❏	❏	❏	❏
❏	❏	❏	Distribution and delivery	❏	❏	❏	❏
❏	❏	❏	Financial condition	❏	❏	❏	❏

Figure 9-1: Fill out the questionnaire to get a quick take on your company's strengths and weaknesses in major business areas.

✔ **Internal view:** Draw on the managerial experience inside your company (use your own experience or that of your friends and former co-workers if you're self-employed) to come up with a consensus on your business strengths and weaknesses. You may want to use the same people to get a sense of what happened in the recent past, as well. A little corporate history can show you how your company's strengths and weaknesses have changed over time — and how easily the organization can shift gears.

✔ **Outside view:** Perhaps you identify company strengths as assets only because your competitors haven't reacted yet, or maybe you ignore real weaknesses because everybody else has them, too. You need an objective outside assessment of what's happening in your business, and consultants can actually be of some use. If you can't afford that kind of advice, make sure that you at least monitor the business media to get an outside view of what the experts say about your industry's key players.

✔ **Competitive view:** Beware of becoming too self-absorbed in this analysis. Step back and look around, using your competitors as yardsticks, if you can. Your competitors do business in the same industry and marketplace, and they show strength or weakness in all the key areas that interest you. If your list is going to mean anything when the time comes to apply it to your business situation, you have to measure your strengths and weaknesses against your competitors'. (Flip to Chapter 8 for more information on the competition.)

If you don't have a management team that can conduct a situation analysis, bring together one of the informal groups that you rely on for some of your other planning tasks. Ask the group members to spend some time analyzing strengths and weaknesses. Make sure that the group looks at your company's situation from various perspectives, using the different frames of reference in the preceding list.

Defining capabilities and resources

In putting together a list of your company's capabilities and resources, cast your net as widely as possible. Start by reviewing all the business areas we introduce in the Company Strengths and Weaknesses Questionnaire (refer to Figure 9-1). In each area, try to identify as many capabilities and resources as possible by using different frames of reference (refer to the bulleted list in the preceding section). At the same time, assess how relevant each capability or resource is in helping you carry out your plans and achieve your business goals. You use this master list as raw material when the time comes to identify your company's strengths and weaknesses.

Management: Setting direction from the top

Your company's management team brings together skills, talent, and commitment. You want team members to find their direction from your company's mission, values, and vision statements, as well as from the business goals and objectives that you plan to achieve. Top-notch managers and owners are particularly important in industries that face increasing competition or fast-changing technologies. Try to think of an industry that doesn't fit into one of these two categories.

Management determines what your company does in the future. Senior managers are officially charged with setting the direction and strategy for your company and laying the foundation for a new company, but all managers indirectly set a tone that encourages certain activities and discourages others. Frank Stronach, the founder of automotive-parts giant Magna International, has always believed employees should own a piece of the company, share in its profits, and receive excellent benefits without the help of a labour union. Therefore, Magna International employees receive this vested involvement in the company, and the company has the speed and flexibility of much smaller rivals. Edmonton-based BioWare Corp, a world leader in video-game design, ranks close to the top of the Best Employer list when it comes to providing a healthy workplace and recognizing good performance. Because of this culture, the company attracts highly qualified men and women who want to work in a business environment that values both personal and corporate responsibility. These capabilities point to great strengths of both companies.

The following list gives you some key questions to ask about the management and/or ownership of your company:

- ✔ How long have managers been around at various levels in your company? (Alternatively, what variety of experiences do you have as an owner?)

- ✔ Does your company plan to hire from the outside or promote from within?

- ✔ What's the general tone set by you and your company's management?

- ✔ Do you have a management-development program in place? (Alternatively, how do you plan to develop your own skills, if you're a sole proprietor?)

✔ What background do you or your managers have?

✔ How do you measure management performance in your company?

✔ How would you rate the general quality of your skills or those of your management team?

Organization: Bringing people together

The people who make up your company and its workforce represent a key resource, both in terms of who they are and how you organize them. Although human resources are important to all companies, they play an especially key role for companies in service industries, in which people are closely tied to the product. (We take a closer look at your organization in Chapter 16.)

Your organization starts with who your employees are, and that characteristic depends first on how well you select and train them. Beyond that, the work environment and your company's incentive systems determine who goes on to become a dedicated, hard-working employee and who gets frustrated and finally gives up. The setup of your organization (its structure and how it adapts) can be just as important as who your employees are when it comes to creating a company team — even a small one — that performs at the highest levels, year in and year out.

Many industries, such as financial services, experience high employee turnover at a cost of millions of dollars a year. So, it's no wonder that the key expressions of employee engagement and retention dance on the lips of Human Resources managers. The National Quality Institute (NQI) knows this and not only provides a menu of solutions for its members, but also recognizes outstanding results through its Canada Awards of Excellence (CAE). By implementing healthy workplace programs, some award winners have reduced employee turnover by an outstanding 99 percent — obviously becoming "employers of choice." A recent NQI study showed CAE recipients experienced a whopping 143-percent total growth between 1990 and 2005, outperforming the TSX Composite index by 55 percent for the same period.

The following list includes some key questions about your organization that you may want to consider:

✔ What words best describe the overall structure of your organization?

✔ How many reporting levels do you have between a front-line employee and your CEO?

✔ How often does your company reorganize?

✔ What are your employees' general attitudes about their jobs and responsibilities?

✔ How long does the average employee stay with your company?

> ✔ Does your company have ways to measure and track employees' attitudes and morale?
>
> ✔ What does your company do to maintain morale and positive job performance?

Customer base: Pleasing the crowds

Your business success depends, to a great extent, on the satisfaction and loyalty of your customers. In Chapters 6 and 7, you discover who those customers are and what makes them tick. Understanding your customers and satisfying their wants and needs are critical to the future of your company.

Nordstrom is a Seattle, Washington–based department store chain that appeals to upscale shoppers. The company bases its reputation on the simple idea that the customer is always right. And the company means it. As one story goes, some time ago, a disgruntled customer stormed into the back loading dock of a Nordstrom store, demanding the immediate replacement of defective tires that he recently purchased. The store managers were extremely polite. They quickly discovered that the man was indeed one of their best customers, and they arranged an immediate reimbursement for the full price of the tires. In a better mood, the customer decided that he'd rather have a new set installed. When he asked where he should take the car, the managers informed him that Nordstrom doesn't sell tires. Obviously, this man became a satisfied customer — and a Nordstrom advocate for life.

Is the story true? Maybe, maybe not. The point is that this often-repeated account highlights the customer-focused mentality of the department store chain. Nordstrom customers receive thank you cards for shopping. Unusual requests are handled with aplomb by a knowledgeable sales staff. Employees have hand-delivered special orders to customers' homes and even obtained specialty merchandise from competing stores to satisfy customer requests. And merchandise returns are never challenged when the items clearly have not come from Nordstrom stock.

The following list gives you some key questions to consider when you study your customer base:

> ✔ What does your company do to create loyal customers?
>
> ✔ How much effort do you put into tracking customers' attitudes, satisfaction, and loyalty?
>
> ✔ What do you offer customers that keeps them coming back?
>
> ✔ How easy and economical is it for your company to acquire new customers?
>
> ✔ How many years does a typical customer stay with you?
>
> ✔ How many markets does your company serve?
>
> ✔ Are you either number one or number two in the markets in which you compete?

Research and development: Inventing the future

Research and development (R&D) often plays an important role in the long-term success of a company. R&D is particularly critical in industries where new and better products come along all the time. But your research and product-development efforts must align with your business strategy and planning to make the investments pay off.

The makers of communications equipment and infrastructure — the highways of electronics — have little choice but to commit themselves to aggressive R&D efforts. Nortel and Cygnal each have world-class R&D organizations because continuous product innovation drives their industry. These companies continually push for greater processing speed and power in ever-leaner packages. Failure to maintain leadership in research could result in catastrophe for either company. The same holds true for a variety of industries, from automotive to pharmaceuticals.

The following key questions can help you examine the role of R&D in your company:

- ✔ To what extent does technology drive your industry?

- ✔ Can you get enough bang for your buck to bother with R&D?

- ✔ Does your company have a consistent, long-term commitment to R&D?

- ✔ How many dollars do you spend on basic research, as opposed to applied research?

- ✔ How long have the key people on your research team been with you?

- ✔ Does your company protect what it owns with copyrights and patents?

- ✔ Have you set up partnerships with universities or outside research labs?

- ✔ Do you have technology agreements with other companies in your industry?

Operations: Making things work

The operations side of your business is obviously critical if you're a manufacturing company. The products that you make (and the way that they work, how long they last, and what they cost) depend entirely on the capabilities and resources of your production facilities and workforce. But you can easily forget that operations are equally important to companies in the service sector. Customers demand value in all markets today, and they simply won't pay for inefficiencies in any business. Whether you make autos or anoraks, produce cereal boxes or serial ports, run a bank or manage a hotel, operations are at the heart of your enterprise.

Operations in your company are driven, to some extent, by costs on one side and product or service quality on the other. The tension between controlling costs and improving quality has led many companies to explore new ways to reduce costs and increase quality at the same time. One way is to involve outside suppliers in certain aspects of your operations, if those suppliers have resources that you can't match. Another way to achieve both goals is to streamline parts of your operations (through automation, for example).

Automation can also be a source of growth and may even create new business opportunities for your company. The airline industry is as big as it is today because of the computer revolution: Computers enable airlines to track millions of passenger reservations and itineraries at the same time. Imagine the lines at airports if airlines still issued tickets by hand and completed passenger flight lists by using carbon paper.

Business operations are often at the heart of major corporate success stories. Wal-Mart's relentless rise to become the world's largest company is based largely on its continuously improving ability to handle, move, and track merchandise. Wal-Mart uses its operations efficiency for one strategic goal: to bring the lowest possible prices to its customers. And the company now does more business than HBC, Sears, Zellers, and a number of major U.S. retailers combined.

Airlines have tried to streamline their business operations by offering online reservations systems and installing do-it-yourself check-in kiosks at major airports. They even want to do away with the hassle and expense of paper tickets, so they now offer electronic tickets, which customers can print out themselves.

The following list gives you some questions to mull over about the operations side of your business:

- ✔ Does your company have programs for controlling costs and improving quality?
- ✔ Has your company taken full advantage of new technologies?
- ✔ Are your production costs in line with those of the rest of the industry?
- ✔ How quickly can you boost production or expand services to meet new demand?
- ✔ Does your company use outside suppliers?
- ✔ Is your operations workforce flexible, well trained, and prepared for change?
- ✔ Can you apply your operations expertise to other parts of the business?

Sales and marketing: Telling a good story

The best product or service in the world won't take your company far if you don't successfully market and sell it to all the potential customers out there. Your sales and marketing people are your eyes and ears, giving you feedback on what customers think about and look for. They're also your voice, telling your company's story and putting your products in context, offering solutions, satisfying needs, and fulfilling wants in the marketplace.

What could a marketing department possibly do to package and promote a boring old chemical such as sodium bicarbonate? It turns out that such a department can do quite a bit, if it happens to be part of Arm & Hammer, which markets sodium bicarbonate as Arm & Hammer baking soda. Their marketing strategy created an indispensable product for baking, cleaning, bathing, and even medicinal purposes. The familiar yellow box finds its way into thousands of refrigerators, open and ready to remove unpleasant odours. The company also created a successful market for baking soda–based toothpaste. And in another pitch, Arm & Hammer now touts baking soda as the best way to ensure that your fresh fruits and vegetables are as clean as they can possibly be. All this from a common, readily available chemical salt.

Lately, drug makers have also begun to tell good stories about their products to polish up their images and to encourage patients to ask their doctors about specific drugs. Some tell the inspirational stories of patients whose lives have been saved by cancer treatment and support programs, such as *Canada AM's* Beverly Thomson, whose photograph was included in the global Breast Friends initiative that was sponsored by a pharmaceutical company. Others show happy families enjoying a summer picnic, thanks to new allergy medicines.

The following list includes a few key questions to ask about the marketing of your product line:

- ✔ How broad is your company's product or service line?
- ✔ Do consumers identify with your company's brand names?
- ✔ Are you investing in market research and receiving continuous customer feedback?
- ✔ Are you using all the marketing resources you have at your disposal? (Check out Chapters 6 and 7 for more info on markets and customers.)
- ✔ Is your company's sales force knowledgeable, energetic, and persuasive?

Distribution and delivery: Completing the cycle

To be successful, you have to make sure that your products and services actually get to their final destinations and into your customers' hands. Distribution and delivery systems must come into play. No matter how good your products are, your customers have to be able to get them when and where they want them.

Your company most likely distributes its products and services through *traditional channels* — time-tested ways in which you and your competitors have always reached customers. On top of that, your distribution and delivery costs may represent a significant part of your total expenses. The standard costs often include warehouse operations, transportation, and product returns. If you operate in retail, you can end up paying for expensive shelf space, as well. Supermarkets routinely ask for money up front before they stock a new item, and you pay more for the best locations. After all, supermarkets control what customers see — and buy — as harried shoppers troop down the aisles with kids and carts in tow.

How — and where — customers shop is often just as important as what they buy, so when a different way to deliver products and services comes along, the new system revolutionizes a marketplace or even an entire economy. The Internet offers companies a new and powerful way to reach out to their customers more directly, increasing company clout and, at the same time, lowering distribution costs. So, you should consider *alternate channels* and *multichannels (more than one type of channel)* as you plan your distribution and delivery strategy going forward.

Many innovative products and companies succeed because of their novel approaches to the costs and other hurdles associated with traditional distribution networks. In the '80s, Canada Post was mandated by the federal government to improve its operations, reduce losses, and perhaps (just perhaps) make a profit, despite being a crown corporation. Canada Post revisited its mission and values, and claimed its vision prepared it to be a world leader in providing innovative, physical and electronic delivery systems, creating value for customers, employees, and all Canadians. One approach was to cut cost and improve service. It accomplished that by franchising some of its postal outlets, increasing their number, and making them more accessible to customers through new locations, such as in convenience stores. These privately owned outlets have longer hours and a wider range of services than government-owned locations. Canada Post also increased the number of stamp retailers by 75 percent and provided electronic postage service through its Web site. Along with implementing other changes, Canada Post now boasts 11 years of profits and a spot on Canada's Top 100 Employers list.

Not all promising new distribution methods pan out. Even the latest technologies can go belly-up if they don't take into account what people really want (refer to Chapter 7 to find out more about your customers). E-books, for instance, looked as if they would be the hot new way to deliver reading material right into the hands of customers by bypassing bookstores and even doing away with the costs of printing and distributing books. Trouble is, many people don't like reading long passages of text on computer screens.

The lonely shopping cart

Imagine going into a store, taking the time to fill a shopping cart with all sorts of things, and then abruptly walking away, abandoning the cart and leaving the store without purchasing a single item. Strange? Well, it happens from time to time at almost every grocery or department store. And it happens too many times at Internet stores. At Chapters.indigo.ca, for example, customers routinely prowl around the online aisles, select this and that, fill up their shopping carts — and then suddenly vanish. Poof.

Believe it or not, this phenomenon has wheeled out more than one research study by global firms trying to understand why online shopping carts get abandoned between 25 and 75 percent of the time. It turns out that researchers don't really know much about how people interact with Web sites while they surf around the Net, but those researchers are figuring it out quickly. Some have identified that a multiple-page checkout process is too complicated; shoppers don't want to pay shipping costs, especially if shipping costs more than the item itself; and if the total cost of the purchase is more than expected, the shopper gets cold feet. Some shoppers just look.

Companies noticed the lonely shopping cart phenomenon and are finding ways to turn it into an asset. Many of the biggest Internet retailers now set up their systems so that if you fill your cart and then log off without buying anything, you get an e-mail within five minutes asking what's wrong. Weeks later, you might receive an e-mail stating that your filled cart is still waiting for you if you want to log in again. Some retailers (or e-tailers) allow you to manage your cart, deleting items, saving others, or setting up wish-list carts filled with items you want to buy — or have someone buy for you — at a later date. The smart e-tailers calculate the total price as a continuous process and have streamlined checkout to one page for you.

And when it comes to beach reading, a laptop just doesn't cut it. Old-fashioned books, sold in old-fashioned bookstores and through e-tailing, give customers what they really want — convenience, rather than bells and whistles.

The following list gives you some questions about the distribution and delivery of your product or service:

- ✔ What are the costs associated with your company's inventory system?
- ✔ Can you reduce inventories by changing the way that you process orders?
- ✔ How much time does it take you to fill a customer order, and can you reduce the time?
- ✔ How many distribution channels does your company use?
- ✔ What are the relative costs in various channels, and which are most effective?
- ✔ How much control do your distributors have over your company?
- ✔ Can you use any new channels to reach your customers more directly?

Financial condition: Keeping track of money

The long-term financial health of your company determines the overall health of your company, period. You simply can't survive in business for long without having your financial house in order. Come to think of it, the expenses that you have to track when looking at company finances aren't all that different from the issues that you face in running your own household.

If you're just starting in business, for example, how much money your company can get its hands on up front (your *initial capital*) is a key to survival. (Does this sound like trying to buy and furnish your first house?) When your company is up and running, you need to make sure that more money comes in than goes out (a *positive cash flow*) so that you can pay all your bills. (Remember those times when the mortgage and utility bills were due, but payday hadn't come yet?)

Figuring out how to keep your company financially fit is critical to planning your business. When you take the time to look over your important financial statements periodically, you give your company the benefit of a regular financial checkup. The checkup is usually routine, but every once in a while, you uncover an early-warning symptom — lower-than-expected profits, for example, or an out-of-line promotional expense. Now, all your financial vigilance is worth it.

The following list includes questions to ask about your company's financial health:

- ✔ Are your revenue and profits growing?
- ✔ Are you carefully monitoring your company's cash flow?
- ✔ Does your company have ready access to cash reserves?
- ✔ Does your company — and every business unit or area — have a budget for the coming year?
- ✔ Do you consistently track key financial ratios for the company?
- ✔ How does your company's financial picture compare with that of the competition?

If you don't know how to answer the questions in the preceding list, carve out some time to spend with Chapters 11 and 12.

Monitoring critical success factors

Not all your capabilities are equally important. Some may be critical to success. Others may be nice to have but not especially relevant to your business. You must decide whether your capabilities and resources represent company strengths that you can leverage or weaknesses you have to correct as you plan for the future. To make those decisions, you have to be clear about what's important to your industry and the marketplace. The *critical success factors* (CSFs) are the general capabilities and resources that absolutely have to be in place for any company in your industry to succeed over the long haul.

You may have already prepared a list of CSFs (if you haven't, take a look at Chapter 5). Along with a CSF list, you need a list of your company's capabilities and resources. You can use the two lists to construct a grid, which in turn allows you to compare your capabilities and resources with those that your industry thinks are important. In a perfect world, the lists match up exactly, but that seldom occurs. The completed grid helps you identify your company's current strengths and weaknesses (see Figure 9-2).

Figure 9-2:
Compare your capabilities and resources with the critical success factors (CSFs) in your industry.

To complete a grid similar to the one in Figure 9-2, remember the following:

- ✔ The capabilities and resources that you place on the left side of the grid are in your industry's must-have category. They represent critical success factors.

- ✔ The capabilities and resources that you place in the top-left corner of the grid are critical success factors in which your company is good or excellent. They represent your company's strengths.

- ✔ The capabilities and resources that you place in the bottom-left corner of the grid are critical success factors in which your company is only fair or even poor. They represent your company's weaknesses.

You can easily find some value in the capabilities that your company already excels in, and you can just as easily underestimate the importance of things that your company doesn't do very well. Admitting that you devote valuable resources to areas that don't affect you as much is a hard pill to swallow, as is admitting that you may neglect key business areas. Try to be as objective as you can here.

Analyzing Your Situation in 3-D

You must be prepared to take advantage of your company's strengths and minimize its weaknesses, which means that you have to know how to recognize opportunities when they arise and prepare for threats before they overtake you. Timing is everything here, and it represents another major dimension that you need to think about.

Chapter 5 discusses where major opportunities and serious threats may arise. These bolts of lightning can strike from almost any source and from all directions. They often change the rules of the game and can even alter critical success factors (CSFs) that you assume are mainstays of your industry. Many opportunities and threats are the direct result of change (check out Chapter 13 if you don't believe us); others come directly from your competitors and the uncertainty that they introduce.

Getting a glance at competitors

Create strengths-and-weaknesses grids for two or three of your most intense competitors. (Turn to Figures 9-1 and 9-2 for grid info and Chapter 8 for a refresher on exactly who your competitors are and what information you have about them.) You don't know as much about your competitors as you know about yourself, of course, so the grids can't be as complete as they may be for your company. But what you *do* know tells you a great deal.

Comparing the strengths and weaknesses of competitors with your own can help you see where competitive opportunities and threats to your business may come from. Opportunities often arise when your company has a strength that you can exploit in a critical area in which your competition is weak. And you can sometimes anticipate a threat when you see the reverse situation — when a competitor takes advantage of a key strength by making a move in an area where you're weak. Because the competitive landscape always changes, plan to monitor these grids on a regular basis.

Completing your SWOT analysis

A *SWOT* analysis (an analysis of your strengths, weaknesses, opportunities, and threats) allows you to construct a strategic balance sheet for your company. In the analysis, you bring together all the internal factors, including your company's strengths and weaknesses. You weigh these factors against the external forces that you identify, such as the opportunities and threats that your company faces due to competitive forces or trends in your business environment. How these factors balance out determines what your company should do and when it should do it. Follow these steps to complete the SWOT analysis grid (and check out Figures 9-1 and 9-2 for info on coming up with a strength/weakness grid):

1. **Divide all the strengths that you identify into two groups, based on whether you associate them with potential opportunities in your industry or with latent threats.**

2. **Divide all the weaknesses the same way — one group associated with opportunities and the other with threats.**

3. **Construct a grid with four quadrants.**

4. **Place your company's strengths and weaknesses, paired with industry opportunities or threats, in one of the four boxes (see Figure 9-3).**

SWOT analysis provides useful strategic guidance, mostly through common sense. First, fix what's broken and address imminent threats. Next, make the most of the business opportunities that you see out there. Only then do you have the luxury of tending to other business issues and areas. Be sure to address each of the following steps in your business plan:

1. **Eliminate any company weaknesses that you identify in areas in which you face serious threats from your competitors or unfavourable trends in a changing business environment.**

2. **Capitalize on any business opportunities that you discover where your company has real strengths and your competitors may have weaknesses.**

3. **Work on improving any weaknesses that you identify in areas that may contain potential business opportunities.**

4. **Monitor business areas in which you're strong today so that you aren't surprised by any latent threats that may appear.**

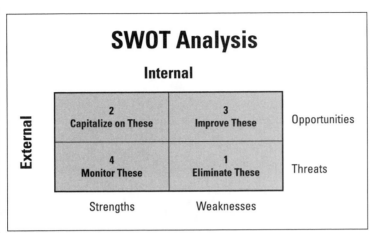

Change is the only constant in your business, your industry, and your marketplace. Constant change means that you can't complete your SWOT analysis only one time; you have to revise the grid regularly while your company grows and the environment around you changes. Think of your SWOT analysis as a continuous process — something that you do repeatedly as an important part of your business-planning cycle.

Chapter 10

Making Money Doing What You Do Best

Chances are, when you leave the house to go shopping, you don't give it much thought. But, in fact, you're about to make a complex set of choices. You may decide to go to one grocery store to buy bulk items and to another to pick up produce. If you have to stop for gasoline, you may weigh the convenience of a station on your route with the cheaper prices at a station farther away. If you go shopping during holiday season, your decision-making process becomes even more complex — simply because you have so much more to buy. Think back on what's involved in a typical day of holiday shopping. While you look down the shopping list over morning coffee, the decisions begin:

> *Downtown stores or the shopping mall*
>
> *Specialty shops or a department store*
>
> *Clothes, gadgets, toys, or kitchenware*
>
> *Designer brands or store labels*
>
> *$25, $50, or $100 limit*

If you happen to own a retail business, what the customer chooses can make or break your company. Your survival depends on knowing the answers to some critical questions. How do shoppers make their choices? Why do they go into one store and not the next? What determines where they stop to browse and what they take a second look at? What gets them to open their wallets and grab their credit cards? No matter what industry you're in, the same kinds of questions are just as crucial. (For the complete lowdown on customers, flip back to Chapters 6 and 7.)

When customers go about making decisions on what to buy and where to shop, they continually weigh various combinations of product or service benefits against price. This calculation is referred to as the *value equation.* (Check out Chapter 8 if you want to know more about this equation.) But what does it actually mean to have the best value? If you want to be successful in your marketplace, you need to know exactly where and how your products add value in the eyes of your customers. In the customers' mind, their perception is reality.

In this chapter, we take a look at creating customer value around products and services. The approach is called the *value chain,* and you use it to identify which parts of your business are responsible for adding the greatest value for customers. We look at how to put together a value proposition for your customers and how you can use it as the basis for your *business model,* or plan for making money. We also show you how to use your value chain to help explain why you may have a competitive advantage in the marketplace, and we talk about how you can maintain that competitive advantage over the long term. Finally, we show you how to make the most of your company's human and financial resources while you put your business plan and business model to work.

Describing What You Do Best

Describing what your company does best — summarizing your key business activities in a few well-chosen sentences or in a clear diagram — should be easy, shouldn't it? It's not. (Refer to Chapter 4 for help in capturing your business in 50 words or less.) From the inside of your company looking out, you may have difficulty pushing away the everyday details and getting at the core of what actually keeps you in business from one day to the next.

Due to this difficulty, business consultants do a bang-up business. They may have fancy names for the services they offer, but the essence of what they do is simple: They help you describe what you do. Their little secret, of course, is that they don't really possess more valuable knowledge than you. Consultants seem to have a clearer view of your business simply because they view it from the outside looking in.

You have a built-in understanding of your business and what really makes your company successful — you just need to unlock what you already know.

Looking at the links in a value chain

A business constructs its *value chain* from the sequence of activities that it engages in to increase the value of its products and services in the eyes of its customers (see Figure 10-1). The chain shows where a business may have an advantage over its competitors, and it connects a company to the marketplace, making sure that it doesn't stray too far from the customers it plans to serve.

The links in a value chain help you better understand your business activities.

Primary links in the value chain are the business functions representing the heart of what your company does (see Chapter 9). Primary links are usually sequential. They're the essential stages that your company goes through in developing, producing, and getting products to market, and they often involve the following:

- ✔ Research and development
- ✔ Operations
- ✔ Marketing and sales
- ✔ Distribution and delivery
- ✔ Service

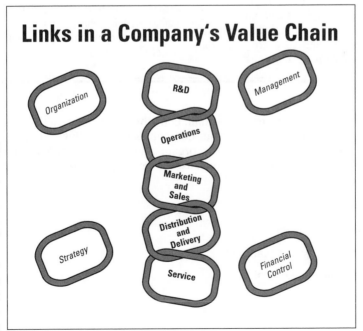

Figure 10-1:
A company's value chain has two types of links: primary activities and support activities.

The great U.S. Steel conundrum

Created in 1901 out of the combined steel holdings of J. P. Morgan and Andrew Carnegie, U.S. Steel was a giant corporation on the day it was born. The firm started with 70 percent of the U.S. basic steel-making capacity and became the world's first billion-dollar company. For the next half-century, however, U.S. Steel saw its share of the market erode until it fell down to 20 percent by the mid-1960s. Thus, the riddle of U.S. Steel: How did the company manage to keep its profits consistently high over this 60-year period while losing almost three-quarters of its market share?

The answer: U.S. Steel's share of the market didn't really matter.

You may be shaking your head and asking how that could possibly be the case. Well, the first head of U.S. Steel, Judge Elbert Gary, started out worrying about his company's market share, too — but he worried that it was too big. He feared that Teddy Roosevelt and the U.S. government would think that U.S. Steel looked a lot like a monopoly and would break the company up into much smaller pieces.

Judge Gary turned out to be one smart capitalist. Although he didn't have a name for it at the time, he created a value chain for U.S. Steel. He discovered that one of the most important links in the steel-making value chain was the mining of its basic ingredients: iron ore, coal, and limestone. Coincidentally, U.S. Steel owned vast land holdings and pretty much controlled the source of all these raw materials. So, the good judge decided to invite competitors to join him in making steel — the more, the merrier. In fact, he demanded competition, and the industry recognized him as an industrial statesman for his efforts at the time. He never stopped making tons of money for U.S. Steel, of course. He knew that the real value in his business was in the sale of raw materials to any and all competitors on an equally profitable basis.

Even U.S. Steel's recent purchase of Canada's largest steel producer, Stelco Inc., is consistent with Gary's strategy. Along with the acquisition came part ownership in three Canadian iron ore mines that supply domestic, as well as international, competitors.

Supporting links in the value chain contribute to the overall success of the business by strengthening your company's primary links. Supporting links are often spread throughout an organization. They assist and tie together all the primary business functions, as well as support one another. The activities often involve the following:

- ✔ Management
- ✔ Organization
- ✔ Strategy and planning
- ✔ Financial control

Forging your value chain

To develop your company's value chain — the sequence of activities that you go through in the process of adding value to your products and services — you need a list of your company's capabilities and resources. Take a look at Chapter 9 if you need help.

You can construct a framework for your value chain by creating a grid that divides your business into value-creating areas (see Figure 10-2). You place activities in the grid based on whether they act as part of your primary business functions or you associate them with supporting areas.

Follow these steps to create the grid that shapes your value chain:

1. **List all the key business areas that work to put together your company's products and services and get the products and services out to customers.**

   Include such departments as R&D (research and development), operations, marketing, sales, distribution, delivery, and service. (See Chapter 9 for more details on these areas.)

2. **Arrange a list of key business areas in order, from the first good idea R&D produces to the finished product or service.**

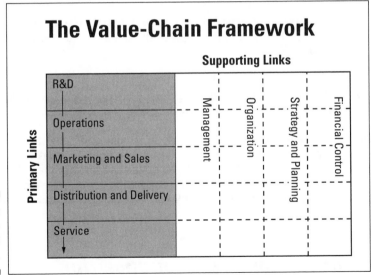

Figure 10-2:
The value-chain framework.

3. **List the general business areas in your company that support the primary business functions.**

   Include such supporting areas as management, organization and human resources, strategy and planning, and financial control.

4. **Construct a grid similar to the one you see in Figure 10-2, using your lists of primary and supporting business areas.**

Your value chain may not look exactly like all those organization charts you see floating around your company. The primary and supporting business functions that add customer value may be framed differently, depending on whom you ask, so you should talk to customers and co-workers. Ask your customers to describe your business as they see it — they may have a better vantage point.

To fill in the value-chain grid, you have to fill in all the specific value-adding activities — the capabilities and resources that your company uses to increase the value of your products and services. Follow these steps:

1. **Go through the lists of capabilities and resources, and make a first pass at placing them in the value-chain grid.**

2. **In the boxes on the left side of the value-chain grid, place value-adding activities that directly contribute to your primary business functions.**

   These activities make up the primary links in your value chain.

3. **Place value-adding activities that you associate with supporting functions in grid boxes to the right of the primary functions that they support.**

   These activities make up the supporting links in the value chain.

4. **On the grid, include a description of the customer value that the various links add, as well as how they add that value.**

The value chain offers you a unique look at your company through your customers' eyes. Every link in the value chain is something that you do as a company. Every link is an activity that you spend money on. The value chain allows you to see exactly what value customers get out of each link. It gives you a relatively clear picture of why you stay in business, as well as where you could do a better job.

Creating your value proposition

During a recent business trip, a colleague of ours pulled into a small town to look for a gas station. She had two choices, and the gas prices were exactly the same. One station had several cars at the pumps; the other was empty. When she asked the manager of the busy station whether he could explain the popularity of his station compared with the one across the street, the man didn't miss a beat:

> *Oh, they're in a different business. They're a filling station; we're a service station.*

This canny businessman had a real feeling for why his station is successful. You can develop that same feeling by taking the value chain that you put together for your company (see the preceding section) and boiling it down into a clear statement of what benefits you provide your customers and what real value your customers place on those benefits.

Business people refer to the preceding statement as the *value proposition* — fancy jargon for a simple idea. A value proposition may be similar to your company's mission statement (flip to Chapter 4 for the details on mission statements), but the proposition is more narrowly focused on customers — what you provide them and what they take away. At first glance, a company's value proposition seems pretty obvious:

- ✔ Giant Tiger Discount Stores offer the cheapest prices around on a wide range of merchandise.

- ✔ Canadian Tundra Diamonds offers unparalleled luxury and the ultimate in snob appeal in the world of jewellery.

- ✔ Canadian Automobile Association (CAA) offers travel and motoring services at home and around the world.

But companies often provide their customers with more value than first meets the eye — even more value than the businesses themselves may realize.

Consider Chapters.indigo.ca. The Internet company sells its books and other merchandise at a substantial discount, so the company clearly bases part of its value proposition on low prices. But shoppers come to the site for much more than a good deal. Chapters.indigo.ca also happens to stock one of the largest inventories of books and music anywhere in the world, as well as DVDs and toys; thus, having a wide selection is also part of its value proposition. And Chapters.indigo.ca's appeal to book and music lovers doesn't stop there. The online retailer invites shoppers to review and rate books and recordings — a feature that many customers like so much that they don't dream of shopping anywhere else. They can usually look over the first chapter of many of the books on sale or listen to audio clips from recordings. The site also offers expert opinions on many topics through its Trusted Advisor Program. Each of these features represents additional customer value. And as Chapters.indigo.ca expands its offerings, it expands its value. Now, from the comfort of your den, you can fill your shopping cart with a wide variety of items — from books and movies to games and iPods.

Putting Together a Business Model

Back when you were a kid, you may have gone through a phase when you enjoyed nothing better than assembling a plastic airplane, boat, or car from a model kit that you got for your birthday. Well, putting together a workable business model is completely different from the models you constructed as a kid. And it doesn't come in a kit.

Business models don't have to be complex or elaborate, however. In fact, when management types talk about them — as in, "So what's your business model?" — they intend to ask a very direct and basic question: How do you plan to make money? Your answer should be at the very heart of your business plan and reflected in each of its sections.

Where's the money?

Whether you like it or not, at some point, you have to get down into the nitty-gritty details of your company's finances — income statements, balance sheets, cash flow, budgeting, and all that stuff. We try to make it as painless as possible in Chapters 11 and 12. In this chapter, you need to ponder something much more basic: coming up with the money. Not literally, of course (just yet). But you need to know how you expect to make money in your business.

Simple, you say. Your customers give you money in exchange for the valuable products and services you provide, right? Well, much like the value chains that support them (refer to the section "Describing What You Do Best," earlier in this chapter, for more on value chains), business models aren't always that obvious or straightforward. Businesses often make a profit on areas outside the main product or service — areas that customers don't focus on. These areas can bring great success. Here are some surprising examples:

- ✔ Given the price of a good meal out, you may think that successful restaurants rake in the dough. And many of them do. But they make the bulk of their profits not on those delicious appetizers and entrees, but on the mixed drinks and wine that they serve before, during, and after the meal.

- ✔ Luxury vacation fractional ownership is all the rage for the about-to-be-retired set. The prices sound reasonable, and who wouldn't enjoy owning a piece of a condo or villa overlooking the Rockies, the ocean, or a pristine Muskoka lake? It turns out that fractional-ownership real estate companies make their profits not on that primo real estate, but on all the maintenance fees they tack on to the contract — fees that every fractional owner must pay on an ongoing basis.

✔ Some companies happily sell their products at break-even prices — and then make their real money on the so-called *consumables* (products you use up). Hewlett-Packard, for example, doesn't mind selling its printers at close to cost, knowing that the company makes its real profits on ink and toner cartridges. As long as HP can keep customers satisfied with their total printing experience, the money flows in month after month, year after year.

How's your timing?

How you expect to make your money is only one part of your business model. An equally important piece relates to *when* you get the cash. You may like the idea that the loonies are going to start pouring in tomorrow; however, reality suggests that your company may begin incurring costs and spending money months (or maybe even years) before a revenue stream begins to flow. In the case of pharmaceuticals, for instance, a company can spend years and millions of dollars developing and testing a drug before the first patient — or insurance company — pays a penny to buy it. If your business must spend money before it starts sending out those invoices, your business model must include a timeline that takes the following factors into account:

✔ The up-front costs you expect when you set up your business. (Refer to Chapter 12 for more information on how to make a budget.)

✔ The source of funds to pay for your up-front costs. (See Chapter 2 for good ideas on how to fund a new business venture.)

✔ A schedule showing when you expect cash to pour in. (Check out the section on projected cash flow in Chapter 12.)

The question of timing is as important for small companies as it is for big ones. Many retail businesses that operate year-round actually take in most of their revenue during one season — the Christmas holiday rush, for example. In some cases, retailers rake in half of their annual revenues during late November and December. Timing for these establishments is quite literally a make-or-break affair.

At Harris Hatch Inn, a bed and breakfast in St. Andrews-by-the-Sea, New Brunswick, the tourist season begins on May 24 and ends in September. Except for a few hardy souls who make their way there for holiday weekends — Thanksgiving, Christmas, and New Year's — virtually all Harris Hatch's revenue comes in during those three summer months. The inn's business model must ensure that the money coming in during that short period is enough to pay for fixed costs — mortgage, utilities, taxes, salaries, and upkeep — throughout the entire year. If not, the innkeeper could wake up one morning to the sound of creditors knocking on the door.

Making Your Business Model Work

Companies don't stay in business year after year by accident. Oh, maybe a manager somewhere gets lucky occasionally, making a brilliant move without knowing its significance. But that kind of luck never lasts long, especially when the competition is intense. Companies succeed over the long haul because they understand what their customers value the most, and they figure out how to make money by providing products and services that consistently meet or exceed customer expectation, often at the expense of unsuspecting competitors. By capturing this information in your business plan, you improve the odds of your business model continuing to work in the future.

A downtown video rental store may focus on the value of its convenient location and a membership club that offers one free video for every ten rentals. A competitor located on the outskirts of town may create value by offering a large selection that features hard-to-find videos. In the same way, large chain bookstores compete on the basis of savings, whereas customers value local or specialized booksellers for their knowledgeable staff, personal service, and friendly atmosphere.

Seeing things differently

Fast-forward a few years: You may not have to slog to the neighbourhood video store to catch your favourite movie. While technology improves — and gets cheaper — huge numbers of film aficionados are going to pick up flicks in new ways:

- Pay monthly fees to rent movies that arrive and return by mail.

- Download movies over wireless connections to your smart phone or handheld player.

- Buy DVDs that self-destruct after you view them three times.

- Download movies onto your computer and watch them in 3D format.

Each of these cutting-edge delivery systems seems easier than a trip to the video store. So a revolution is undoubtedly coming. How soon? Netflix.com is already here. The company stocks only DVDs and offers them through a subscription program over the Internet. For a monthly fee (similar to a premium cable channel), customers can rent as many movies as they want. The only limitation: They can keep a maximum of three titles at any one time. When customers finish viewing a DVD, they just pop it in the mail, using a handy prepaid envelope. Netflix.com automatically sends out the next title in the customer's online rental queue.

Obviously, this business model offers customers new benefits, but it also creates a challenge for the company. Netflix.com must continuously analyze the rates at which customers rent DVDs so that they can set an appropriate subscription fee and make sure that the business model works, which means the company continues to enjoy a profit. Video store companies, such as Rogers, have countered with monthly plans of their own and lowered prices.

Take a close look at what it means to have an advantage over the competition in your marketplace, where you gain the advantage, and how you can factor that advantage into your business model.

Searching for a competitive advantage

Most people who take car trips have a special produce stand, a favourite diner, or a certain ice-cream place along the way that they never miss. Why do these travelers develop such affection for specific stops on their route when hundreds of other places are available? What makes particular establishments so unique?

These travelers could come up with all sorts of reasons. They may tell you that they've stopped at the same places for years, they love the food, they like the atmosphere, they know the owners, they can count on the service . . . whatever. No doubt, all these things are true. But if you take a careful look at the value chain for many of these businesses, one important link likely jumps right out at you: location. (Refer to "Describing What You Do Best" for more about the value chain.) Distances and driving times likely are the major reasons why many customers find these businesses in the first place; the storefronts literally happen to be in the right place at the right time. Customers choose the business based on location and stay for the value added in other business areas. Location provides a significant competitive advantage in this on-the-move marketplace.

Competitive advantage means exactly what it says; a company has some sort of advantage over the competition. Where does it come from? Usually, out of the distinct and special value that the company can offer its customers — and from the premium that customers place on that value. Ask yourself this basic question:

> *Why do customers choose my company and its products when other competitors in the industry have more-or-less similar offerings?*

You can find the answer in the strongest links of your value chain — the links that produce the bulk of your customer value. Location, service, image, and product features are some of the links that create a competitive advantage in the marketplace.

In 1975, Microsoft was a partnership of two: Bill Gates and Paul Allen. They started out competing against a host of bright young entrepreneurs like themselves and eventually had to go head-to-head with IBM. Today, Microsoft has 79,000 employees and $51 billion in revenue, and it offers a wide array of software products, ranging from word processing programs and spreadsheet applications, to language tools and operating systems, to games and smart-phone applications. You can find Microsoft's competitive advantage in these areas:

✔ **Standards:** Microsoft's programs pretty much set standards in the PC world. Microsoft offers the standard operating system and the standard suite of office applications. Although other companies sell better products here and there, customers see Microsoft as the safe and sensible choice across the board, a distinctive image advantage over the competition.

✔ **Compatibility:** Microsoft programs promise to work with one another and with the operating system. You don't have to worry about your favourite application becoming an outcast or somehow misbehaving on your computer.

✔ **Product range:** You name it, and Microsoft probably has a product that can do it — from word processing to picture editing, from managing your money to keeping track of your e-mail. The company continues to aggressively develop new software to meet the needs of rapidly changing markets. Most recently, the company targeted Internet users with a host of new products, including its flagship Internet site, www.msn.com.

✔ **Service and support:** With Microsoft, you know what you're getting. If a product doesn't work, the company tries hard to fix it quickly. Microsoft devotes tremendous resources to product support and provides a wide range of service options, including online knowledge bases, news groups, chat rooms, e-mail, and (of course) telephone support.

Discount Car & Truck Rentals is by far Canada's largest privately owned international car-rental agency. The company has more than 300 rental locations in Canada and Australia. But Discount faces competition at all levels, from the mom-and-pop rental outlets at popular vacation spots to regional agencies and global companies, including Avis, Hertz, and National. Here's how Discount finds a competitive advantage:

✔ **Free pickup and return:** When you call Discount to book a vehicle, a representative picks you up at your home, office, or travel location. Discount also takes you where you need to go after you return the rental unit.

✔ **National presence:** No matter which major Canadian city you visit, Discount can rent you what you need.

✔ **Peace of mind:** With Discount, you don't have to worry about the car not being there, the rate doubling, or that you'll end up paying for an old rent-a-dent.

✔ **Rewards for loyalty:** As a loyal Discount customer, the company rewards you with membership in a club that provides notification of low-rate specials; a rent two weekends, get one free deal; and frequent-user points that you can redeem toward free rental days.

Focusing on core competence

You create your competitive advantage in the marketplace. Your advantages have everything to do with your customers — with the relative value that they place on your products and services, and with the purchase decisions that they finally make. What internal capabilities and resources do you have, and what business activities do you engage in that lead directly to your competitive advantage? You must make sure to capture these in your business plan.

Go back to your company's value chain (which we discuss in the section "Describing What You Do Best," earlier in this chapter) and focus on the links that provide your competitive advantage. When you do, you come face to face with something that the gurus call your core competence. Simply defined, *core competence* is your company's special capability to create a competitive advantage in the marketplace. In almost all cases, this gift is specific to your company. Think of core competence as being corporate DNA. Unlike your personal genetic code, however, your company's core competence is something you can build on — or lose, depending on how attentive you are to your marketplace and your business.

The preceding section examines two well-known companies: Microsoft and Discount.

Microsoft's core competence consists of

- ✔ **Visionary executives:** The executive team has a broad vision of the future, enabling the company to forge today's software standards and shape tomorrow's.

- ✔ **Top-notch development team:** The company supports a dream-team corps of developers and programmers who create and maintain a state-of-the-art product line.

- ✔ **Management of complexity:** Microsoft manages a complex related set of software products that all have to behave and work together.

- ✔ **Capability to change direction:** The company has the capacity to redirect resources and energies when the fast-moving marketplace shifts course and the rules of the game suddenly change.

Microsoft's first two core competence factors lead to the others because success and profit allow for more capabilities and value.

Discount's core competence includes

- ✔ **Information systems:** A sophisticated computer database allows the company to keep track of customer profiles and match them against an ever-changing supply of rental cars and special rates.

✔ **National logistics:** The company has the capability to track, distribute, arrange, and rearrange a huge fleet of vehicles in all shapes and sizes on a regional and national basis.

✔ **Scale of operations:** The company uses its sheer size and business volume to negotiate favourable terms when it comes to new-car purchases and even insurance premiums.

✔ **Relationships and tie-ins:** Discount has the resources to work closely with corporate clients, travel agencies, and the travel industry to create new business by expanding car-rental options and opportunities.

A company's core competence can point the way toward new market opportunities. Honda, for example, used a core competence in designing engines to expand its markets. The company created product lines in lawn mowers, snow throwers, snowmobiles, motorcycles, and all-terrain vehicles, to name just a few of its motor-based businesses. Honda benefits from a related competitive advantage (state-of-the-art engines) in each of these distinct markets. Take another look at your company's core competence to see if you can come up with any new business directions based on your already successful business areas.

Sustaining an advantage over time

Every company that manages to stay in business has some sort of competitive advantage and core competence to draw upon; otherwise, it simply can't exist. But here comes the million-dollar question: How can you renew and sustain that competitive advantage over years and even decades? Customers and their needs shift over time, competition gets more intense, and industries evolve, so your competitive advantage and the core competence that supports it aren't guaranteed to stay around. You rent them; you don't own them. You want to make sure that you keep a long-term lease on both.

Sustained competitive advantage — the business world's Holy Grail — is a company's capability to renew competitive advantages over and over again in the face of a constantly changing business environment and marketplace. But, if you want to sustain competitive advantages over time, you need to have a long-term strategy in place. Chapter 8 introduces three common alternatives called generic strategies and gives you a handle on what your competitors may be up to. Chapter 14 takes a much closer look at your strategic options.

Spend some time thinking about strategies that your company can use on an ongoing basis to see that you preserve your core competence. How can you sustain the competitive advantage that your company already has? Get a blank sheet of paper and jot down answers to these key questions:

> ✔ Where will changes in your business most likely come from?
>
> ✔ How will those changes likely affect your company's competitive advantage?
>
> ✔ What can your company do to maintain core competence in the face of change? Is it consistent with your values and mission statements? (Refer to Chapter 3 for more about values and Chapter 4 for information about your mission statement.)

Focus on each of the major forces that fuel change in your industry:

> ✔ Your customers and their changing needs and requirements
>
> ✔ Your competitors and their changing capabilities, strategies, and goals
>
> ✔ Your company, its value chain, and its shifting strengths and weaknesses

When you create your business plan, make sure that you continue to track these forces so that they don't threaten the core competence that you work so hard to achieve.

Earmarking Resources

The value chain paints a portrait of your company as your customers see it. (We talk about the value chain in the section "Describing What You Do Best.") Links in the chain reflect the value that customers place on aspects of your products and services. The strongest links capture your competitive advantage in the market and define your core competence as a business.

Because the value chain is so good at helping you weigh the importance of your business decisions, it comes in handy when you put together your business plan. In particular, the value chain is invaluable when it comes time to earmark scarce resources toward specific business activities.

At almost any major racetrack, a group of regulars hangs around the stands or clusters at the fence. These people are serious about horse racing. They spend time poring over track sheets and newspapers — circling this, checking that, and pacing back and forth.

When they finally place bets, they don't rely on Lady Luck alone. They use all the information available — the condition of the track, the horse's racing history and bloodlines, the jockey's record, and the betting odds — to place their cash on the wagers most likely to result in the best payoffs and the biggest winnings.

Betting on the horses is a serious business for these committed professionals. And they can show you something about how to divvy up your working
assets. Is it sensible to spread your company's limited resources equally
among all the areas that make up your business? Probably not. Each time you
set aside time and money for a particular business activity, you place a bet
on your business plan. You bet that the resources you commit are going to
contribute to your business, add value to what you do, and eventually come
back around to generate revenue and profits.

Chapters 11 and 12 help you pore over the numbers (financial statements,
ratios, and budgets) that keep track of where you spend money, and then tell
you if you're winning. In short, your financial statements tell you a great deal
about how you manage your cash, what bets you place, and how well you do
at the track. But your financial statements alone don't tell you *what* to do.

So, how do you know where to place your bets? You guessed it: You go back
to your company's value chain. Follow these simple steps to check your
resource allocation based on your value chain:

1. **Look at where your company currently spends money.**

   Make a quick-and-dirty estimate of how you divvy up yearly expenses
   among business activities — from R&D (research and development) to
   delivery and service — and jot the numbers down on your value-chain
   grid (refer to Figure 10-2). To keep things simple, use percentages. Make
   sure that the numbers add up to 100 percent.

2. **Look at where your customers think that you provide them value.**

   Take the total value that customers think you provide and divvy it up
   among your business activities. If customers pay $100 to buy your
   widget, for example, how much of that do they pay for features, how
   much for service, and how much for convenience? Again, use percentages and jot the numbers on the same value-chain grid. Make sure that
   the numbers add up to 100 percent.

3. **As a reminder, highlight the boxes on the value-chain grid that
   represent your core competence and account for your competitive
   advantage in the marketplace.**

4. **Analyze the completed grid.**

   If the percentages line up and are concentrated in the highlighted boxes,
   you're in good shape. But if you find a glaring mismatch in terms of
   where you spend money, what your core competence is, and where your
   customers think that your products give them value, you need to
   reassess where you direct your company's resources.

Chapter 11

Figuring Out the Financial Details

· ·

In This Chapter

▶ Understanding how you calculate profits

▶ Balancing assets against your liabilities

▶ Keeping track of your cash

▶ Looking at your company's financial ratios

· ·

*N*umbers. Some people love them; others are bored by them; some begin to stammer, shake, and exhibit other physical signs of distress around them. But almost everyone agrees that — love 'em or hate 'em — numbers are the way that you keep track of things. Think baseball, cholesterol, the stock market, and (of course) your very own business venture. Numbers tell you more than simply the score at the end of the game or the final TSX closing, however. When you put them together in the right ways, numbers paint a detailed picture of everything from the career of a hockey player to the state of the global economy.

You're probably familiar with the financial forms that a bank requires when you want to borrow money for a new car, a bigger house, or your dream cottage at the lake. Those tedious documents include an income statement, as well as some sort of balance sheet. The income statement tells the bank where you get your money and where you spend it. The balance sheet lists the value of all the assets you own and balances the value against the money that you owe, including your car loans, mortgages, credit cards, and even personal I-owe-yous.

Financial statements tell the bank a great deal about you, and the bank discovers even more by taking numbers from the statements and calculating a bunch of ratios. The bank totals your monthly loan payments and divides that number by your monthly income, for example, and then compares this ratio with the average for other borrowers. The result gives the bank a good measure of your ability to repay the loan. Taken together, the statements and ratios create a financial portrait that the bank uses to get to know you better.

And the better your bankers know you, the more comfortable they are with the decision to loan you money. The same goes for when you try to obtain money to start a business.

In this chapter, we introduce the basic financial statements and ratios that professionals widely use in business planning. In fact, these numbers look almost identical to those that paint a picture of your personal finances, only a little more complicated. We show you how an income statement and a balance sheet are put together. We explain cash-flow statements, which do pretty much what the name implies (they detail where the money comes from, where it goes, and how much is left over). Finally, we explore simple financial ratios that you can use to evaluate your business.

Reading Income Statements

An *income statement* presents the proverbial bottom line. By adding all the revenue that you receive from selling goods or services and then subtracting the total cost of operating your company, the income statement shows *net profit* — how much money your company makes or loses over a given period. Here's how to think of net profit:

Net profit = revenue – costs

The most important thing to remember here is the fact that the income statement captures a very simple idea. No matter what your accountants call it — an income statement, earnings report, or a statement of profit and loss — or how complicated they make it look, the income statement still uses the same basic principle of subtracting cost from revenue to come up with your profit.

Your income statement should cover a period that makes the most sense for your business planning: monthly, quarterly, or yearly. (The CRA, of course, always wants to see your income statement once a year.) You get a better financial picture of your company and its direction if you look at income statements over several periods and even over several years. In Chapter 12, you develop a *projected income statement* — a forecast of your future profits based on projected revenue and costs.

Look at the various parts of an income statement for Global Gizmos Company in Figure 11-1. Notice that Global Gizmos includes a two-year comparison to show how revenue, costs, and profits have changed. Global Gizmos is a small company; if you want to make it a big company, add three zeros after all the numbers. In either case, the income statement works exactly the same way.

Income Statement at a Glance

Global Gizmos Company

INCOME STATEMENT AS OF DECEMBER 31

	This Year	Last Year
① ▷ Gross Revenue on Sales	$810,000	$750,000
② ▷ Cost of goods sold	-560,000	-520,000
Gross Profit	250,000	230,000
③ ▷ Sales, general, and administration	-140,000	-140,000
Depreciation expense	-30,000	- 25,000
Operating Profit	80,000	65,000
④ ▷ Dividend and interest income	+ 3,000	+ 2,000
Interest expense	- 13,000	- 14,000
Profit Before Taxes	70,000	53,000
⑤ ▷ Taxes	- 20,000	- 18,000
NET PROFIT FOR YEAR	**$ 50,000**	**$ 35,000**

Rendering revenue

Revenue refers to all the money that a company receives as a result of being
in business. The most important source of revenue (usually the sale of goods
or services) always appears as the first item on the income statement — in
the case of Global Gizmos (refer to Figure 11-1), you see gross revenue on
sales. In this context, *gross* doesn't mean anything unpleasant; it indicates the
total revenue without costs subtracted. Revenue from sources other than
sales, such as interest earned or other payments not related to product revenue, usually shows up a bit later on the income statement.

Gross revenue on sales

▷ *Gross revenue on sales* is based on the number of units sold during a particular period multiplied by the prices paid. Global Gizmos sold 32,400 widgets at a price of $25 each, for a gross revenue of $810,000. You can find more
complicated examples than this one, of course; your company may have several products or kinds of services, or your prices may change over time.

Maybe you have to make an allowance for items that customers return. All these considerations contribute to your calculation of gross revenue on sales.

Dividend and interest income

Your company may have sources of revenue besides sales — the income from savings accounts and other securities, for example. Because you must have money to operate the company, you probably want your securities to make money while they sit around. You should keep this investment income separate from your revenue on sales, however, so that you always know how much money the company itself generates. On your income statement, your dividends and interest income should appear separately from your other revenue.

Calculating costs

Typically, most businesses have to spend money to make money. You can divide the cost of doing business into general categories that reflect the separate activities that your company is involved in and the different kinds of expenses that you incur. Major cost categories include cost of goods sold, sales and administration expenses, depreciation, interest expense, and — don't forget — taxes. Each item deserves its own entry on the income statement.

Cost of goods sold

The *cost of goods sold* (COGS) combines all the direct costs of putting together your product or service. Raw materials, supplies, and the labour involved in assembling a product are all part of the COGS; as are the electricity, water, and fuel that you use in manufacturing and the costs of maintaining production facilities. If you offer a dog-walking service for vacationing pet owners, for example, the costs associated with delivering that service — leashes, doggy-do-do bags, and time spent — go into the COGS.

You may have to make a judgment call here and there about what is or isn't part of the COGS. Just remember to be consistent over time.

Sales, general, and administration expenses

Sales, general, and administration (SG&A) expenses combine all the costs associated with supporting your product or service. If the company consists of you, a telephone, and a tiny rented office above the hardware store, the costs don't amount to much. But for larger companies, these costs seem to go on and on. SG&A expenses include salaries and overhead for the sales staff, as well as the receptionist, secretary, and the boss. SG&A expenses can also include advertising and promotion, travel, telephone calls, accounting fees, office supplies, dues and subscriptions, and everyone's favourite: miscellaneous expenses.

You track SG&A costs separately because they don't have a direct tie-in to revenue. Make sure that you keep an eye on this particular entry because these costs can sometimes grow too large without generating additional revenue for the company.

Depreciation expenses

▷ *Depreciation expense* is a standard way to spread both the cost and usefulness of big-ticket items out over time. Whether you buy a building, a truck, or a computer, almost any durable item slowly declines in value due to simple wear and tear, or because new technology makes the item obsolete. CRA bean counters have come up with various ways to calculate that depreciation. All the methods allow you to allocate a portion of the purchase price as a business expense each year to reflect a decrease in value. (You can't depreciate land, by the way.)

Interest expenses

▷ *Interest expense* includes all the money that you pay out to the parties that loan you funds to operate your business. You don't want to overlook this cost. You may enter into agreements with banks or other investors, for example, in which you have to pay back interest on a fixed schedule. You isolate an interest expense (often called a *fixed charge*) on the income statement because you absolutely, positively have to pay it, year after year.

Taxes

▷ Even Albert Einstein stopped short of trying to figure his own taxes. But taxes are a fact of life and represent another cost of doing business. You can minimize your company's taxes by keeping careful track of all your other expenses — expenses that lower your profit and, therefore, lower your taxes.

Pondering profits

Profit is the pot of gold at the end of the business rainbow. When you run your business well, the total costs flowing out are less than all the revenue coming in. Your *profit,* of course, represents the difference. But you should consider different kinds of profit at various stages along the way. In particular, you can keep track of gross profit, operating profit, and profit before taxes, as well as your overall net profit. Comparing profit at different stages gives you a clearer picture of where your company is most efficient and where you can improve your resource allocation (see Chapter 10 for more resource info).

Gross profit

▷ *Gross profit* measures how much money your company still has after you subtract all the direct costs of putting together your product or service *(cost of goods sold)* from the total revenue generated by sales. This profit doesn't include the many indirect expenses you incur while running the company or any revenue sources other than sales.

Operating profit

▷ *Operating profit* accounts for all the additional sales, general, and administration (SG&A) costs that you incur as part of operating your business; it also subtracts the depreciation expense of your big-ticket purchases and reflects the money that you make from your overall business operations.

Profit before taxes

▷ *Profit before taxes* takes everything else into account, including any financial transactions that you make. Your income from other sources (such as investment dividends and interest) is included here, as well as your interest payments to creditors.

Net profit

▷ *Net profit,* of course, represents the bottom line after the government subtracts the company's tax bite. Global Gizmos (refer to Figure 11-1) made money in its most recent period (yeah!).

Interpreting Balance Sheets

An income statement reports on the financial results of your business over a given period; a *balance sheet* is more like a snapshot of your financial condition at a particular time (although a balance sheet can cover an extended period, if you want). The income statement lists your revenue, your costs, and the profit that you make. The balance sheet, on the other hand, captures what your company owns, what it owes, and, therefore, what it's worth at a given moment. Ideally, the balance sheet tells you how much money you'd have left over if you sold absolutely everything and then paid every last one of your debts. Your investors, and particularly your bankers, are interested in your balance sheet because it gives them some idea of what their investment in your company is worth.

The things that your company owns are called *assets*. The amounts that you owe make up your *liabilities*. The difference between the two represents the *equity* in your business. Think of equity in terms of the following equation:

Equity = Assets – Liabilities

The equation couldn't be simpler. So, naturally, accountants dreamed up another, less-straightforward way of looking at this equation — and, of course, you find this one on most balance sheets. It looks like this:

Assets = Liabilities + Equity

You always find a balance sheet divided into two parts. The top half deals with all the company's assets; the bottom half lists liabilities and equity. Because of the second equation, the top and bottom halves are always in balance, adding up to exactly the same amount. Although the two totals always match, the entries along the way say a great deal about the overall financial health of your business.

With the preparation of tax returns in mind, you often compile the balance sheet for the last day of the year (although you can generate these statements quarterly if you want, depending on your business — some stores generate almost all income during the holiday season, for example, so they need to generate a balance sheet only once a year). Figure 11-2 shows Global Gizmos's balance sheet. In this case, we provide figures for two years so that you can make a comparison.

Ascertaining assets

Your company's *assets* include anything and everything you own that has any monetary value. When you think about your assets in terms of the balance sheet, all that should concern you is how much each asset is worth and how quickly you can sell it. So, you separate assets into categories, depending on how *liquid* they are — how quickly and easily you can liquidate (or sell) them into cold, hard cash. You can dispose of *current assets* within a year if you have to, whereas *fixed assets* often take much longer to get rid of. You can't convert *intangibles* into cash.

Balance Sheet at a Glance

Global Gizmos Company

BALANCE SHEET ON DECEMBER 31		
ASSETS	**This Year**	**Last Year**
Current Assets		
Cash	30,000	15,000
Investment portfolio	35,000	20,000
Accounts receivable	135,000	150,000
Inventories	115,000	120,000
Prepaid expenses	5,000	5,000
Total Current Assets	$ 320,000	$ 310,000
Fixed Assets		
Land	60,000	60,000
Buildings, equipment, machinery	355,000	315,000
Minus accumulated depreciation	-125,000	-95,000
Total Net Fixed Assets	$ 290,000	$ 280,000
Intangibles (goodwill, patents)	$ 5,000	$ 5,000
TOTAL ASSETS	**$ 615,000**	**$ 595,000**
LIABILITIES & OWNERS' EQUITY	**This Year**	**Last Year**
Current Liabilities		
Accounts payable	60,000	70,000
Accrued expenses payable	80,000	90,000
Total Current Liabilities	$ 140,000	$ 160,000
Long-term Liabilities	$ 90,000	$ 100,000
Owners' Equity		
Invested capital	155,000	150,000
Accumulated retained earnings	230,000	185,000
Total Owners' Equity	$ 385,000	$ 335,000
TOTAL LIABILITIES & OWNERS' EQUITY	**$ 615,000**	**$ 595,000**

Indicators in the left margin: 1, 2, 3, 4, 5, 6

Figure 11-2:
The balance sheet captures what the company owns, what it owes, and what it's worth.

Current assets

▷ *Current assets* represent your company's readily available reserves. You draw on these assets to fund your day-to-day business operations; you may have to turn to them in a financial emergency, as well. Current assets include the following:

- ✔ **Cash:** You can't get any more liquid than cash, which is just what you expect: bills and coins in the till, the petty-cash fund, and money deposited in the bank.

- ✔ **Investment portfolio:** Investments are usually liquid assets. Your investment portfolio includes savings accounts, short-term government bonds, and other safe securities that you invest in to watch your cash earn a bit of money while you wait to use it.

- ✔ **Accounts receivable:** *Accounts receivable* represents the money that customers owe you for goods and services that you previously delivered. Maybe you give customers 30, 60, or 90 days to pay. Keep tabs on this particular asset and reduce it by some percentage if you run into deadbeat customers who refuse to pay up.

- ✔ **Inventories:** The cash value of your inventories can be a bit tricky to calculate. The cash value should reflect the costs of the raw materials and supplies that you have on hand, as well as the value of partially finished products and products that your shipping department is ready to transport.

- ✔ **Prepaid expenses:** If you pay any of your business expenses ahead of time, you should treat them as current assets. These expenses may include insurance premiums or retainers for unused accounting or advertising services.

Fixed assets

▷ *Fixed assets* are fixed in the sense that you can't readily convert them into cash. These assets are the big-ticket items that usually cost a great deal of money up front and are meant to last for several years.

On the balance sheet, the value of a fixed asset is based on its original cost minus its accumulated depreciation over time, so the figure doesn't necessarily reflect the true market value of the asset or how much it may actually cost to replace it. Fixed assets can include the following:

- ✔ **Land:** You list the land that your company owns separately on the balance sheet because it doesn't depreciate over time; its value on the books remains the same from year to year.

- ✔ **Buildings, equipment, and machinery:** This asset class represents the original cost of all the big-ticket items that you invest in to operate your company. The entry should include anything you purchase that you expect to last more than a year.

- ✔ **Minus accumulated depreciation:** Depreciation measures the decline in the useful value of a big-ticket item over time, so the original cost of all your fixed assets (excluding any land) is reduced by an amount equal to the total depreciation accumulated over the years. Global Gizmos (in Figure 11-2) shows accumulated depreciation increasing by $30,000 in its most recent year. Because its fixed assets are now worth $30,000 less on paper, Global Gizmos also takes a $30,000 depreciation expense on its income statement (refer to Figure 11-1).

Intangibles

You can't hold them in your hand or store them in a warehouse, but intangibles can be extremely important to your company. *Intangibles* include such things as your rights to a manufacturing patent, a long-term contract, or an exclusive service franchise. How important is the "swoosh" to Nike, for example? Intangibles also cover something called goodwill. Although not obvious from the name, *goodwill* represents the extra money that you may spend for an asset above and beyond its fair market value — maybe because the asset is worth more to your company than to any others.

By definition, intangibles are hard to describe and difficult to put a real value on. Some companies don't even try. Instead, they place a nominal value of one dollar on all their intangibles to indicate that although these assets exist, the companies don't have a way to measure their actual worth.

Categorizing liabilities and owners' equity

Your company's *liabilities* cover all the debts and obligations that you enter into when you run your business. In the same way that you divide your assets up, your liabilities come in categories based on how soon you must pay. *Current liabilities* are those that you have to pay off within a year; *long-term liabilities* may stay on the books much longer. When you subtract these liabilities from total assets, you come up with *owners' equity*, which is a measure of how much the company is worth.

Current liabilities

Current liabilities are the debts that your company agrees to pay in the short term (say, within a year), so you have to be able to cover them from your current assets. What you have left over (the difference between your current assets and current liabilities) is so important that it has a name: *working capital,* or the chunk of money that you actually have to work with in the short term. Here are some standard types of current liabilities:

- ✔ **Accounts payable:** *Accounts payable* represents the amounts that you owe your regular business creditors as part of your ongoing operations. At any given time, you may have accounts payable to many outside suppliers and service people, including the suppliers, professionals, and even utility companies that you deal with every day.

- ✔ **Accrued expenses payable:** Your company also owes salaries and wages to its employees, interest on bank loans, and maybe insurance premiums — not to mention the taxes that you haven't sent in. To the extent that any of the obligations are unpaid on the date of the balance sheet, you total these liabilities as *accrued expenses payable.*

Long-term liabilities

Long-term liabilities usually represent large chunks of money that you pay back over several years. These liabilities are often at the centre of your company's financing. You may have issued bonds to investors, for example, or you may have gone directly to the bank and secured a loan against your company's assets. In any case, you probably use the money to invest in the long-term growth of your business — acquiring new equipment, building a new manufacturing facility, developing additional products, or expanding into new markets.

Owners' equity

A company's owners come in various shapes and sizes. Their investments and equity in the company are arranged and distributed in all sorts of ways and can become incredibly complicated, especially if the company is a publicly traded corporation. But don't be confused. All this complexity boils down to two major sources of equity: money and resources that flow in from outside the company, and profits that the owners keep and pump back into the company. Owners' equity can be any of the following:

- ✔ **Invested capital:** The money that people invest in your company can take various forms, from the direct infusion of cash by inside owners who manage the business to the buying and selling of stocks that represent small chunks of the company owned by outside investors. *Invested capital* represents the total of all this money, no matter where it comes from or how you describe it.

- ✔ **Accumulated retained earnings:** After your company starts making a profit each year (and we hope it does), you choose what to do with that excess cash. You can distribute it to the owners (that arrangement is where dividends come from) or keep part of it to reinvest in the business. If you put profits back into the company, your business can grow. And if the business grows, you can increase the company's net worth and owners' equity (at least, we hope you do). *Accumulated retained earnings* represent the profits that you put back into the company year after year.

Examining Cash-Flow Statements

If you know what your company is worth and how much it makes every year, can't you just relax and assume that your financial plan is in reasonably good order? After all, what else do you need to know?

As it turns out, you have to keep close track of one other absolutely indispensable resource: cash. No matter how good your situation looks on paper — no matter how bright the balance sheet and how rosy the income statement — you still need cash on hand to pay the bills. The fact that you retain assets and make a profit doesn't automatically mean that you have money in the bank. Cold, hard cash can turn out to be much more important than income, profits, assets, and liabilities put together, especially in the early stages of your business.

The *cash-flow statement* monitors changes in your cash position over a set period. The top half of the statement tracks the flow of cash into and out of your company; the bottom half reports where the funds end up. Just like on a balance sheet (see the section "Interpreting Balance Sheets," earlier in this chapter), the amounts represented on the top and bottom halves of a cash-flow statement match. Given the importance of ready cash, you want to look at cash-flow statements on a regular basis — quarterly, monthly, or maybe even weekly.

Figure 11-3 shows a cash-flow statement for Global Gizmos Company. The cash-flow statement contains many of the same elements as an income statement, with a few critical adjustments.

Moving money: Cash in and cash out

The top half of the cash-flow statement deals with the inflow and outflow of cash, tracking where your company gets funds and how you use them. The cash-flow statement is a little more telling than an income statement because the cash-flow statement shows money coming in only when you actually deposit it, and money going out only when you actually write a cheque.

Cash Flow at a Glance

Global Gizmos Company

CASH FLOW AS OF DECEMBER 31		
INFLOW AND OUTFLOW	This Year	Last Year
Funds Provided By:		
Gross receipts on sales	825,000	760,000
Dividend and interest income	3,000	2,000
Invested capital	5,000	10,000
Total Funds In	$ 833,000	$ 772,000
Funds Used For:		
Cost of goods produced	555,000	515,000
Sales, general, and administration	160,000	150,000
Interest expense	13,000	14,000
Taxes	20,000	18,000
Buildings, equipment, machinery	40,000	50,000
Long-term debt reduction	10,000	5,000
Dividend distribution to owners	5,000	5,000
Total Funds Out	$ 803,000	$ 757,000
NET CHANGE IN CASH POSITION	$ 30,000	$ 15,000
CHANGES BY ACCOUNT	This Year	Last Year
Changes In Liquid Assets		
Cash	15,000	5,000
Investment portfolio	15,000	10,000
Total Changes	$ 30,000	$ 15,000
NET CHANGE IN CASH POSITION	$ 30,000	$ 15,000

Figure 11-3:
A cash-flow statement monitors changes in a company's cash position over time.

Knowing where your funds come from

▷ Where does all your money originate? Because the cash-flow statement reflects the actual receipt of cash, no matter where it comes from, the entries are a bit different from the revenue shown on a company's income statement. Your funds are usually made up of the following:

✔ **Gross receipts on sales:** This entry represents the total money that you take in on sales during the period. Gross receipts are based on your gross revenue, of course, but they also take into account when you actually receive payment. Global Gizmos, as Figure 11-3 shows, received all $810,000 in gross revenue this year, plus $15,000 in accounts receivable that customers owed the company from last year, for a total of $825,000.

✔ **Dividend and interest income:** Your income from savings accounts and other securities is also reported on your income statement. The amounts should be the same, as long as you actually receive the money during the period your cash-flow statement covers.

✔ **Invested capital:** The money invested in your company shows up as part of the owners' equity on your balance sheet. Invested capital doesn't represent revenue from your business operations, of course, so it never appears on the income statement, but it can be a source of cash for your company. As Figure 11-3 shows, Global Gizmos received an additional $5,000 in invested capital this year.

Gauging how you use your funds

▷ Where does all your money go? The cash-flow statement keeps track of the costs and expenses that you incur for anything and everything. Some of the expenses appear on the income statement; others don't because they don't directly relate to your costs of doing business. These funds usually consist of the following:

✔ **Cost of goods produced:** This entry represents the total cost of producing your product or service during the period. The cost of goods produced often differs from the cost of goods sold shown on your income statement because the cost of goods sold also includes sales out of inventory (items that your company already produced and paid for) and doesn't include the cost of products that you add to inventory. Global Gizmos, as shown in Figure 11-3, reduced its overall inventory by $5,000 this period, so the company's cost of goods produced was $5,000 less than its cost of goods sold from the income statement.

✔ **Sales, general, and administration (SG&A):** These expenses are the same SG&A expenses that appear on an income statement (see the "Sales, general, and administration expenses" section, earlier in this chapter), except that paying off bills that you owe or postponing payments may change the SG&A amount. Global Gizmos, as shown in Figure 11-3, paid down $10,000 in both its accounts payable and expenses payable this year, increasing its SG&A cash outflow by $20,000, for a total of $160,000.

✔ **Interest expense:** Interest expense shows up on the income statement, as well. The number reflects the amount that you actually pay out during the period.

✔ **Taxes:** Taxes also appear on the income statement, but you actually pay out the taxes on the cash-flow statement during the period it covers.

✔ **Buildings, equipment, and machinery:** When your company buys a big-ticket item, it doesn't appear on your income statement as an expense because you're really just trading cash for another asset. Instead, you take a depreciation expense each year to reflect the slow decline in the value of that asset. When you buy the building, truck, or computer, however, you have to pay for it. The cash-flow statement reflects the costs. Global Gizmos, as shown in Figure 11-3, shelled out $40,000 this year for new equipment.

✔ **Long-term debt reduction:** It costs you money to pay down any long-term debt that your company may have, and that expense doesn't appear on the income statement. Global Gizmos reduced its long-term debt by $5,000 last year and $10,000 this year.

✔ **Dividend distribution to owners:** The portion of your company's profits that you decide to give back to the owners comes directly out of your cash box. Again, this entry isn't a business expense that appears on the income statement, but it costs you, nonetheless. Global Gizmos distributed $5,000 to its owners this year.

Watching cash levels rise and fall

The flow of cash into and out of your business is like water flowing in and out of a reservoir. If more water comes in than goes out, the water level goes up. When your company's cash reserves rise, the money flows into one or more of your liquid-asset accounts. The bottom half of your cash-flow statement keeps track of what happens to those accounts.

Changes in liquid assets

▷ With cash flowing in and out of the company, your liquid assets (see the section "Ascertaining assets," earlier in this chapter) change in quantity during the period your cash-flow statement covers. The items listed on the bottom portion of the cash-flow statement are the same ones that appear on the balance sheet. This year, for example, Global Gizmos improved its cash reserves and investment portfolio by $15,000 each (see Figure 11-3).

Net change in cash position

▷ Raising the balance of your liquid-asset accounts has the happy effect of strengthening your cash position. Global Gizmos increased its liquid assets and cash position by $30,000 this year (see Figure 11-3). Not coincidentally, this $30,000 is the difference between the $833,000 that Global Gizmos took in during the year (total funds in) and the $803,000 that it spent (total funds out).

Making a profit and going broke at the same time

Meet poor Floyd Finance, a classic example of the manager and company owner who falls into a common financial trap. Floyd used to work for Global Gizmos. But one night, after working late on widget sales, he decided that it was high time to start a small business of his own. Floyd developed a business plan to make and sell a little doohickey that he invented in high school. He figured that he could produce it for 75 cents and sell it for one dollar. To test his concept, Floyd withdrew some money from his savings and produced 2,000 doohickeys. He sold 1,000 right off the bat.

Armed with a product, a market, and a plan, he opened his doors for business on January 1. His total assets were $1,000 in cash left over from

his savings, 1,000 doohickeys in inventory, and $1,000 in accounts receivable from his first customers.

Floyd's business plan was relatively straightforward. He gave his doohickey customers 30 days to pay, he always maintained a 30-day supply of doohickeys in inventory, and he paid his own bills promptly. And business was great. He sold another 1,000 doohickeys in January. After that, sales steadily climbed by 500 a month, and all his customers paid within their 30-day limit. Within six months, his profits hit $2,500.

But none of that really matters now because Floyd Finance went broke.

How did that happen? Take a look at his books:

Income Statement

	January	February	March	April	May
Revenue on sales	$1,000	$1,500	$2,000	$2,500	$3,000
Cost of goods sold	$750	$1,125	$1,500	$1,875	$2,250
Monthly profit	$250	$375	$500	$625	$750
Yearly profit to date	$250	$625	$1,125	$1,750	$2,500

Cash-Flow Statement

	January	February	March	April	May
Funds in	$1,000	$1,000	$1,500	$2,000	$2,500
Funds out	$1,125	$1,500	$1,875	$2,250	$2,625
Change in cash position	$–125	$–500	$–375	$–250	$–125
Total cash on hand	$875	$375	$0	$–125	$–375

Poor Floyd just didn't understand that a growing company can eat up capital, even while it makes a profit. Each month that he did business, Floyd took the preceding month's revenue (his accounts receivable) and paid out the next month's costs (his inventory). The difference between the two grew while his business expanded. Floyd's business plan simply didn't include the money he needed up front to support his company's growth.

Whatever you do, don't be like Floyd Finance. Don't assume that as long as you make a profit every month, you always have money in the bank. It isn't necessarily so.

Evaluating Financial Ratios

Armed with an income statement, a balance sheet, and a cash-flow statement, you have a relatively complete financial picture of your company in front of you (if you don't have these financial statements, check out the preceding sections in this chapter). But when you look everything over, what does that financial picture actually tell you? Is it good news or bad news? What should you plan to do differently as you go forward?

Your financial picture may tell you that you pay your bills on time, keep a cash cushion, and make some money. But could your company do better down the road? Ideally, you could look at the picture year after year and compare it against a competitor, several competitors, or even your entire industry. But companies come in all shapes and sizes, and comparing numbers from any two companies and making sense of them is a hard task.

As a result, companies use *financial ratios.* When you divide one number by another, you create a ratio and eliminate many of the problems you encounter when comparing numbers on different scales.

Take your personal finances as an example. Maybe you want some help on investments. One friend boasts that he made $5,000 in the stock market last month; another made only $1,000. Who do you ask for advice? It depends. If the first friend invests $500,000 and the second friend invests only $20,000, who's the savvy investor?

A ratio gives you the answer. The first friend saw a return of only 1 percent (5,000 ÷ 500,000), whereas the second friend realized a better return of 5 percent (1,000 ÷ 20,000).

Comparing two companies of different sizes works the same way. If you want to compare your company's financial ratios with those of major competitors or with an industry average, you need to get your hands on some outside data. You can always start by asking your banker, accountant, or investment adviser, because financial institutions keep close track of standard ratios across industries. But you should also check out financial-data services, such as Industry Canada (www.ic.gc.ca), and Statistics Canada's publication *Financial Performance Indicators for Canadian Business*. Dun & Bradstreet also offers a publication called *Industry Norms and Key Business Ratios*.

With all the data in hand, you can see how your company measures up. You can bet that your investors, creditors, and competitors want to look into it, even if you don't.

Financial ratios fall into three categories. The first two categories take your company's vital signs to gauge your chances of pulling through (remaining solvent, that is). One set of ratios measures your company's capability to meet its obligations in the short term; the other looks at the long term. The final set of ratios indicates just how strong and vigorous your company really is, measuring its relative profitability from several points of view.

Meeting short-term obligations

The overriding importance of promptly paying your bills every month is the major reason why current assets and current liabilities receive special attention on a company's balance sheet (see Figure 11-2). The difference between the two — your working capital — represents a safety net that protects you from financial catastrophe.

How much working capital do you need to ensure survival? Having liquid assets available when you absolutely need them to meet short-term obligations is called *liquidity*. You can use several financial ratios to test your company's liquidity. You should monitor the following ratios year by year and measure them against your competitors' ratios and the industry averages.

Current ratio = Current assets ÷ Current liabilities

You determine your company's current ratio by looking at your balance sheet and dividing your total current assets by your total current liabilities. Global Gizmos Company, for example, has a current ratio of $320,000 ÷ $140,000, or 2.3 (refer to Figure 11-2). You can also express this ratio as 2.3 to 1 or 2.3:1.

Like most financial ratios, the current ratio isn't an especially precise measurement, so you don't need to calculate it to more than one or two decimal places.

What magic number should you aim for? If your company falls below a current ratio of 1.0, you face serious financial danger. In most cases, you want the number to stay above 2.0, which means that you have more than twice the current assets that you need to cover current liabilities. But again, the answer depends on your industry. Companies that move inventories quickly can often operate with somewhat lower current ratios because the inventories are a little more liquid. You don't want your current ratio to get too high, either, by sitting on excess cash that you should put to work and invest back into the company.

Quick ratio = (Cash + Investments + Receivables) ÷ Current liabilities

You sometimes hear the quick ratio called the *acid test* because it's more stringent than the current ratio. The quick ratio doesn't allow you to count inventories and prepaid expenses as part of your current assets because of the difficulty in turning them back into cash quickly, especially in an emergency. This situation holds particularly true in industries in which products go out of fashion rapidly or become quickly outdated by new technology.

Global Gizmos has a quick ratio for this year of $200,000 ÷ $140,000, or 1.4 (refer to Figure 11-2). You want to keep your company's quick ratio above 1.0 by a comfortable margin or measure it by standards in your industry.

Inventory turnover = Cost of goods sold ÷ Inventories

Inventory turnover (sometimes shortened to inventory turn) tells you something about the liquidity of your inventories. This ratio divides the cost of goods sold, as shown on your yearly income statement, by the average value of your inventories. If you don't know the average, you can estimate it by using the inventories listed on the balance sheet at the end of the year.

Global Gizmos has an inventory turnover of $560,000 ÷ $115,000, or 4.9. (Refer to Figures 11-1 and 11-2 for the company's income statement and balance sheet, respectively.) This ratio means that Global Gizmos turns over its inventory almost five times each year. Expressed in days, Global Gizmos carries a 75-day (365 ÷ 4.9) supply of inventory.

Is a 75-day supply of inventory good or bad? It depends on the industry and the time of year. An auto dealer that carries a 75-day supply of cars at the height of the season may be in a strong inventory position, but the same inventory position at the end of the season can represent a real weakness. Because automation, computers, and information systems are making business operations more efficient across all industries, inventory turnover is on the rise, and the average number of days that inventory of any kind hangs around continues to shrink. The bottom line is this: You want to understand how quickly you sell your inventory versus the competition so that you can make sure you don't make more product sooner than you need to.

Receivables turnover = Sales on credit ÷ Accounts receivable

Receivables turnover gives you information about how fast customers pay you by dividing the sales that you make on credit by the average accounts receivable. If an average isn't available, you can use the accounts receivable from the balance sheet.

If Global Gizmos makes 80 percent of its sales on credit, its receivables turnover is ($810,000 × .8) ÷ $135,000, or 4.8. (Refer to Figures 11-1 and 11-2 for Global Gizmos's income statement and balance sheet, respectively.) In other words, the company turns over its receivables 4.8 times per year, or once every 76 days on average — not a good turnover if Global Gizmos's payment terms are 30 or 60 days. Unlike fine wine, receivables don't improve with age.

Remembering long-term responsibilities

Your company's liquidity keeps you solvent from day to day and month to month, but what about your ability to pay back long-term debt year after year? Two financial ratios indicate what kind of shape you're in over the long haul. The first ratio gauges how easily your company can continue to make interest payments on the debt; the second determines if the principal amount of your debt is in any danger.

If you've read this chapter from the beginning, you may be getting really bored with financial ratios by now, but your lenders — bankers and bond-holders, if you have them — find these long-term ratios incredibly fascinating, due to your possession of their money.

Times interest earned = Earnings before interest and taxes ÷ Interest expense

Earnings before you pay any interest expense and taxes (EBIT) represents the profit that you have available to make your interest payments. Global Gizmos, for example, has an EBIT of $83,000 divided by an interest expense of $13,000 this year for a times-interest-earned ratio of 6.4. (Refer to Figure 11-1 for the company's income statement.) In other words, Global Gizmos has 6.4 times as much profit as it needs to pay off its interest expense obligation.

You may also hear the same number called an *interest coverage*. Lenders get mighty nervous if this ratio ever gets anywhere close to 1.0 because, at that point, you must use every last cent of profit to pay interest on the long-term debt.

Debt to equity = Long-term liabilities ÷ Owners' equity

The debt-to-equity ratio says a great deal about the general financial struc-ture of your company. After all, you can raise money to support your com-pany in only two ways: borrow it and promise to pay it back with interest, or sell pieces of the company and promise to share all the rewards of owner-ship. The first method is debt; the second, equity.

Global Gizmos has a debt-to-equity ratio of $90,000 ÷ $385,000, or .23. (Refer to Figure 11-2 for Global Gizmos's balance sheet.) This ratio means that the company has more than four times as much equity financing as it does long-term debt.

Lenders love to see plenty of equity supporting a company's debt because they know that the money they loan out is safer. If something goes wrong with the company, they can go after the owners' money. Equity investors, on the other hand, actually want to take on some risk. They like to see relatively high debt-to-equity ratios because that situation increases their leverage (see the section "Return on equity = Net profit ÷ Owners' equity," later in this chapter) and can substantially boost their profits (as the following section points out). So, the debt-to-equity ratio best suited for your company depends not only on the stability of your industry, but also on whom you ask.

Reading relative profitability

If profit is the bottom line for your business, profitability is the finish line. *Profitability* shows you how well you measure up when it comes to creating financial value out of your company. Profitability ratios allow you to keep track of your performance year by year. They also allow you to compare your profitability against the performance of other competitors, other industries, and even other ways of investing resources.

You can easily invest the money that flows into your company into other businesses, for example, or put the money into bank accounts, real estate, or government bonds. Each investment involves a certain level of risk. By com-paring profitability ratios, you begin to see whether your company measures up, generating the kinds of financial rewards that justify the risks involved.

Profitability ratios come in three flavours. The first type of ratio examines profit relative to your company sales. The second type examines profit rela-tive to total assets. The final type examines profit relative to owners' equity. Each of the ratios reflects how attractive your company is to an investor.

Net profit margin = Net profit ÷ Gross revenue on sales

The net profit margin ratio says more about your costs in relation to the prices that you charge than about net profit divided by gross revenue. If your net profit margin is low compared with the margins of other companies in your industry, your prices are generally lower or your costs are too high. Lower margins are acceptable if they lead to greater sales, larger market share, and bigger profits down the road, but you want to monitor the ratio carefully. On the other hand, no one quibbles with high net profit margins, although the high number is an awfully good way to attract new competitors.

Global Gizmos Company has a net profit margin this year of $50,000 ÷ $810,000, or 6.2 percent. (To examine Global Gizmos's income statement, refer to Figure 11-1.) That result shows a substantial increase from the 4.6 percent of the year before. The company not only grew in terms of revenue, but it also got more profitable.

When you calculate your net profit margin, you should also think about calculating margins based on your operating profit and gross profit. Together, these ratios give you a better idea of where your company's profitability comes from.

Return on Investment = Net profit ÷ Total assets

Net profit divided by total assets gives you the overall return that you can make on your company's assets — sometimes referred to as *return on assets* (ROA). Because these assets are equal to all your debt and equity combined (refer to the section "Interpreting Balance Sheets," earlier in this chapter), the ratio measures an average return on the total investment in your company. What does the ratio mean? You see similarities in the yield on Grandma's savings bonds or in the return on that hot new mutual fund you discovered. *Return on investment* (ROI) is widely used as a test of company profitability because you can compare it to other types of investments that an investor can put money into.

The value of the total assets that you use in the calculation of ROI is taken from your company's balance sheet, and those numbers may be way off base. If the assets have been around for a while, the numbers on the page may not reflect real replacement costs, and if the assets are undervalued, the ROI is bound to be a bit exaggerated.

Global Gizmos has an ROI this year of $50,000 ÷ $615,000, or 8.1 percent. (Refer to Figures 11-1 and 11-2 for the company's income statement and balance sheet, respectively.) That figure is up from 5.9 percent the year before, and the increase certainly represents good news.

Whether your company's ROI calculates to what you expect it to be depends to a large extent on your industry, as well as on where the economy stands at the moment.

Return on equity = Net profit ÷ Owners' equity

Net profit divided by the owners' equity in your company gives you the return on the equity portion of the investment (ROE). Keep in mind that you already took care of all your bankers and bondholders first by paying their return — the interest expense on your debt — out of your profits. Whatever remains goes to the owners and represents their return on equity.

You always pay your creditors first, and you pay them a fixed amount; everything else goes to the owners. Now, you find out where leverage comes in. The more you finance your company by building debt, the more *leveraged* you are; and the more leveraged you are, the more you use other people's money to make money. Leverage works beautifully as long as you successfully put that money to work — creating returns that measure higher than your interest costs. Otherwise, your lenders may end up owning your company.

Global Gizmos, for example, has an ROE of $50,000 ÷ $385,000, or 13.0 percent. (The income statement and balance sheet shown in Figures 11-1 and 11-2, respectively, shed some light on where these figures come from.) Without any leverage, that ROE is the same as the company's return on investment (ROI), only 8.1 percent (see the preceding section). More leverage may raise the ROE even higher, upping your risk of losing your company if your revenues fall too far too fast. In short, leverage makes the good years better for the owners and the bad years much worse.

Chapter 12

Forecasting and Budgeting

· ·

In This Chapter

▶ Forecasting your financial picture

▶ Looking at financial alternatives

▶ Forming your company's budget

· ·

*Y*ou've most likely sat down at the kitchen table at some point in your life to put together a household budget — when money was tight and you had to pinch every penny to cover all your bills. Everybody knows what a *budget* is, of course: A way to figure out how much you need to spend on essentials (rent, utilities, car payments) and incidentals (all the frills that you don't exactly *need,* such as that new golf club). By its very nature, a budget looks ahead and combines a forecast and a set of guidelines for spending money.

As you may know from experience, putting together a budget is much easier if you have some basic financial information to work with. You can take comfort in knowing how much money is going to come in, for example, and when you expect it to arrive. You also need to keep track of the essentials that you have to take care of immediately, such as the mortgage and the car payment. Only then can you find out what you have left over. In your business, what's left over is your *working capital.*

For your company, your financial picture resides in the financial statements you put together. Take a look at Chapter 11 for more statement information. These financial statements — income statements, balance sheets, and cash-flow statements — are fairly straightforward because you base them on how your company has performed in the prior years. Unfortunately, financial information isn't quite as easy to put together and use when you have to plan for next year, three years from now, or even five years down the road.

Why go to all the trouble of predicting your finances in the first place? The answer is simple: Although the financial estimates and forecasts aren't your business plan by themselves, they support your business plan in critical ways. Without them, you face the real danger of allowing your financial condition — money (or the lack of it) — to take control of, or even replace, your business plan.

In this chapter, we help you construct a financial forecast for your company, including a projected income statement, an estimated balance sheet, and a projected cash-flow statement. Because nothing in the future is certain, we also introduce *sensitivity testing* — scenario planning and what-if analysis that help you consider several financial alternatives. Finally, we show you how you can use your financial forecast to create a budget.

Constructing a Financial Forecast

So far, no one has found a way to accurately predict every detail of the future. The only thing that you can know for certain is that you face an uncertain future.

You make decisions every day based on your personal views of what lies ahead. Although situations may often end up surprising you, your assumptions about the future at least give you the basic framework to plan your life. Your expectations, no matter how outlandish, encourage you to set objectives, to move forward, and to achieve your goals somewhere down the road.

You can think about the future of your company in much the same way. Assumptions about your industry and marketplace — that you'll have no new competitors, that a new technology will catch on, or that customers will remain loyal, for example — provide a framework to plan around. Your expectations of what lies ahead influence your business objectives and the long-term goals that you set for the company.

You need to know what your business assumptions are and where they come from because your assumptions are as critical as your numbers when it comes to making financial predictions. If you make the assumption that no new competitors will enter the market, say why. If you see a period of rapid technological change ahead, explain your reasons. Don't try to hide your business assumptions in a footnote somewhere. State them clearly in the Financial Review section of your business plan. (For a recap of the important pieces of a business plan, see Chapter 1, and for an example of a business plan, see the Appendix.) If you keep all your assumptions out in the open, you make your financial forecast as honest, adaptable, and useful as it can be, in the following ways:

- Everybody who looks at your forecast knows exactly what's behind it.
- You know exactly where to go when you need to change your assumptions.

As you may have experienced elsewhere in life, coming up with predictions that you really believe in isn't always easy. You may trust some numbers (next year's sales figures) more than you do others (the size of a brand-new market). Your best estimates form the basis of some of your financial predictions, and you may use sophisticated number-crunching techniques to arrive at others. After you get the hang of it, you begin to see what a powerful and useful planning tool a financial forecast can be. You find yourself turning to it to help answer all sorts of important questions, such as

✔ What cash demands does your business face in the coming year?

✔ Can your company cover its debt obligations over the next three years?

✔ Does your business plan lead to profitability this year?

✔ Is your company meeting its overall financial objectives?

✔ Do investors find your company to be an attractive business proposition?

With so many important questions at stake, a financial forecast is worth all the time and effort that you can spend on it. If you're not careful, a forecast can turn out to be way off base. Did you ever hear the old computer hacker's expression, "Garbage in, garbage out"? The same is true of financial forecasts. Your prediction is only as good as the numbers that go into it. If the numbers are off the mark, look for one of the following reasons:

✔ Unrealistic or overly optimistic expectations

✔ Nonobjective assumptions

✔ Unchecked predictions

The following sections examine the financial statements that make up a financial forecast. After we explain how you can put these statements together, we point out which of the numbers are most important and which are the most sensitive to changes.

Piecing together your projected income statement

Projected refers to something that you describe or estimate in advance. When you construct your financial forecast, you should include *projected income statements* — documents that show where you plan to get your money and how you plan to spend it — for at least three years and for as long as five years into the future, depending on the nature of your business. You should subdivide the first two years into quarterly income projections. After two years, when your income projections are much less certain, annual projections are fine. (For info on income statements, flip to Chapter 11.)

Your company's projected income statements predict what sort of profit you expect to make in the future by asking you to project your total business revenue and then to subtract all your anticipated costs. The following should help you get ready:

- ✔ If you're already in business and have a financial history to work with, get all your past financial statements out right away. You can use them to help you figure out what's likely to happen next.

- ✔ If you run or are developing a new company and don't have a history to fall back on, you have to find other ways to get information on expected revenues and costs. Talk to people in similar businesses, sit down with your banker and your accountant, visit a trade association, and read industry magazines and newspapers.

The projected income statement has two parts — projected revenue and anticipated costs.

Projected revenue

Your company's projected revenue is based primarily on your sales forecast — exactly how much of your product or service you plan to sell. You have to think about two things: how much you expect to sell, naturally, and how much you want to charge. Unfortunately, you can't completely separate the two projections because any change in price usually affects the level of your sales.

Your sales forecast is likely to be the single most important business prediction that you ever make. If you get it wrong, the error can lead to mountains of unsold inventory or a sea of unhappy, dissatisfied customers — a financial disaster in the making. A company that sells souvenir T-shirts and that overestimates how many Stanley Cup T-shirts customers want to buy, for example, is left with an awful lot of worthless merchandise. By the same token, the corner toy store that underestimates how many kids want the latest action hero or Barbie outfit must answer to many frustrated parents and unhappy children — and suffer lost sales.

How do you make an accurate sales forecast? Start by looking at this formula:

Sales forecast = Market size × Growth rate × Market-share target

Look at the elements of the preceding equation:

- ✔ **Market size:** Estimates the current number of potential customers

- ✔ **Growth rate:** Estimates the speed of market growth

- ✔ **Market-share target:** Estimates the percentage of the market that you plan to capture

Because your sales forecast has such a tremendous impact on the rest of your financial forecast — not to mention on the company itself — you should try to support your estimates with as much hard data as you can get and with respect to your company vision and mission (see Chapters 3 and 4 for the scoop on vision and mission statements, respectively). Depending on your situation, you can also rely on the following guides:

✔ **Company experience:** If you have experience and a track record in the market, you can use your sales history to make a sales prediction. But remember that your sales are a combination of the size of the market and your share of the market. You may still need other sources of data (which we list in the following bullets) to help you estimate how the market and your share of it are likely to change in the future. Incorporating outside data also ensures that you take full advantage of all the growth opportunities available to you.

✔ **Industry data:** Industry data on market size and estimates of future growth come from all quarters, including trade associations, investment companies, and market-research firms (which we cover more extensively in Chapter 5). You can also get practical and timely information from industry suppliers and distributors.

✔ **Outside trends:** In certain markets, sales levels mirror trends in other markets, social trends, or economic trends (a phenomenon we describe in Chapter 13). Car sales, for example, tend to move with the general economy. So, when car dealers track what happens with the Gross Domestic Product (GDP), they get an estimate of where car sales are headed.

Even if a product is brand new, you can sometimes find a substitute market to track as a reference. When frozen yogurt first appeared on the scene, for example, its producers turned to the sales history of ice cream to help support their sales forecasts.

Don't forget to factor sales cycles into your forecast; in most of Canada, ice-cream sales freeze over from December to March, but hot chocolate heats up. Other markets may have other cycles. Retailers rake in most of their cash in the six weeks leading up to the Christmas holidays. Airlines do their biggest business during the summer months.

After you come up with your sales forecast, multiply it by the average price that you expect to charge for your product or service. The result is your projected revenue:

Projected revenue = Sales forecast × Average price

Where does the average price come from? You base your average price on what you think your customers are willing to pay and what your competitors charge (refer to Part II for more information on how to analyze your industry and customers). The price should also take your company's costs and your overall financial situation into account.

Now, put all the numbers together and see how they work. We use a company called Global Gizmos as an example. Sally Smart, widgets product manager, starts putting together a three-year revenue projection. Utilizing industry and market data along with Global Gizmos's sales history, Sally estimates that the entire market for widgets will grow about 10 percent a year and that Global Gizmos's market share will increase by roughly 2 percent a year, with projected price increases of approximately one to two dollars per widget (a very positive projection — you can't always assume that market share and prices will increase). She puts the numbers together in a table so that she can easily refer to the underlying estimates and the assumptions that support them (see Table 12-1).

Table 12-1	Widget-Revenue Projection for Global Gizmos		
Revenue Projection	*Year 1*	*Year 2*	*Year 3*
Projected market size (units)	210,000	231,000	254,100
Projected market share (%)	20	22	24
Sales forecast (units)	42,000	50,820	60,980
Average price	$26	$27	$29
Projected revenue	**$1,092,000**	**$1,372,140**	**$1,768,420**

Anticipated costs

After you complete your revenue projection, your foray into the future isn't finished. You still have to look at anticipated costs — the price tag of doing business over the next several years. To make life a little easier, you can break anticipated costs into the major categories that appear in a projected income statement: projected cost of goods sold, projected sales, general and administration expenses, projected interest expense, and projected taxes and depreciation (flip back to Chapter 11 for more details on all expenses). The following sections define these categories.

Projected cost of goods sold (COGS)

COGS, which combines all the direct costs associated with putting together your product or delivering your service, is likely to be your single largest expense. If you have a track record in the industry, you have a useful starting point for estimating your company's future COGS.

Although the following formula may look ugly, treat it as a simple way to calculate your projected COGS. Based on the assumption that the ratio of your costs to your revenue will stay the same, use this formula:

Projected COGS = (Current COGS ÷ Current revenue on sales) × Projected revenue

If you haven't been in business long, or if you're just starting a company, you don't have access to this kind of information. But you can still estimate your projected COGS by substituting industry averages or by using data from other companies that have similar products or services.

Although this ratio approach has the advantage of being simple, you should estimate your projected COGS by using more than one method. At the very least, you should sum up the estimates of your major product-related costs (materials, labour, utilities, facilities, and so on) to make sure that your projected COGS makes sense. This method is tougher, but it gives you a chance to make separate assumptions and projections for each of the underlying costs. You may be pleasantly surprised to discover that while your company grows and you stay in business longer, your projected revenue goes up faster than your costs do. The effect is called the *experience curve* (which we explain thoroughly in Chapter 14), and it means that your COGS-to-revenue ratio actually gets smaller in the coming years.

Sales, general, and administration

Sales, general, and administration (SG&A) represents your company's overhead: sales expenses, advertising, travel, accounting, telephones, and all the other costs associated with supporting your business. If your company is brand new, try to get a feel for what your support costs may be by asking people in similar businesses, cornering your accountant, or checking with a trade association for average support costs in your industry. Also, come up with ballpark numbers of your own, including estimates for all the major overhead expenses that you can think of.

If you have a mature business, you can estimate a range for your SG&A expenses by using two calculations. The first method projects a constant spending level, even if your company's sales start growing. In effect, you assume that your support activities will all get more efficient and accommodate your additional growth without getting bigger themselves. The other method projects a constant SG&A-to-revenue ratio. In this case, you assume that support costs will grow as fast as your revenue without any increase in efficiency. Because your projected SG&A costs are higher, this is the more conservative estimate. An accurate SG&A forecast probably lies somewhere in between. Given what you know about your company's operations, come up with your own estimate and include the assumptions that you make.

Interest expense

Your interest expense largely results from decisions that you make about your company's long-term financing. Those decisions, in turn, are influenced by your ability to pay your interest costs out of profits. Think about what sort of financing your business may need in the future (to acquire office space, computers, machinery, and so on) and what interest rates you may be able to lock in, and then estimate your interest expense as best you can. For more information on possible funding resources, check out Chapter 2.

Taxes and depreciation

Taxes certainly affect your bottom line, and you want to include your projections and assumptions in your anticipated costs. You can usually estimate the general impact taxes may have on the future by looking at their impact on your company now. If you're starting a new business, make sure to research tax rates for companies in your position. For the most recent guidelines, go to www.cra-arc.gc.ca on the Internet.

Depreciation, on the other hand, is an accountant's way of tracking the value that your purchases lose over time. As such, depreciation expense doesn't really come out of your pocket every year. You can estimate the numbers, but don't get too carried away. In the future, your depreciation expense includes a portion of those big-ticket items that you must buy to keep the business healthy and growing (computers, automobiles, forklifts, and so on).

When you plug the numbers into your projected income statement and calculate your net profit, be prepared for a shock. You may discover that the profit you expected to make in the first year or two turns into a projected loss. But don't panic: New business ventures often lose money until their products catch on and they begin to pay off some of the start-up costs. Whatever you do, don't try to turn a projected loss into a profit by diddling with the numbers. The point isn't to make money on paper; the point is to use the projected income statement as a tool that can tell you what sort of resources and reserves you need in order to survive until losses turn into predicted profits. And don't worry about your investors: They know better than anyone that new businesses take time to mature.

Estimating your balance sheet

The second part of your financial forecast is the *estimated balance sheet,* which, like a regular balance sheet (see Chapter 11), serves as a snapshot of what your company looks like at a particular moment — what it owns, what it owes, and what it's worth. Over the years, these snapshots (balance sheets) fill a photo album of sorts, recording how your company changes over time.

Your estimated balance sheets describe what you want your company to become in the future and how you plan to achieve your goal. The estimated balance sheets that you put together as parts of your financial forecast should start with the present and extend out three to five years in a series of year-end projections.

The projected income statements in your financial forecast project future revenue, costs, and profits; your estimated balance sheets lay out exactly how your company needs to grow so that it can meet those projections. First, you want to look at what sorts of assets you need to support the planned size and scale of your business. After you assess your necessary assets, you have to make some decisions about how you plan to pay for those assets. You have to consider how to finance your company — how much debt you plan to take on *(liabilities)* and how much of your investors' money *(equity)* you plan to use.

Assets

Your company's projected *assets* at the end of each year include everything from the money that you expect to have in the petty-cash drawer to the buildings and machines that you plan to own. Some are current assets, meaning that you can easily turn them into cash; others are fixed assets, which take much longer to get rid of (refer to Chapter 11 for detailed asset info). Don't be confused by the word *current;* we're still talking about the future:

- **Current assets:** The cash that you have on hand, as well as accounts receivable and inventories, add up to your current assets. How much should you plan for? That depends on the list of current liabilities (debts) you expect to have because you need to pay short-term debts out of your current assets. What you have left over is your working capital.

   Your estimates of future accounts receivable (money that future customers will owe you) depend on the payment terms that you offer and the sales that you expect to make on credit.

   Projected inventories (the amount of product in your warehouse) depend on how fast your company can put together products or services and get them to customers. The longer it takes to build products, the bigger the inventory level you may need, relative to your sales volumes.

- **Fixed assets:** Land, buildings, equipment, machinery, and other assets that you can't easily dispose of make up your company's fixed assets. Your estimated balance sheets should account for the big-ticket items that you expect to purchase or get rid of. Your capital purchases (such as additional buildings, more equipment, or newer machines) can play a major role in company growth, increasing both your revenue and the scale of your business operations.

Keep an eye on how each machine or piece of equipment helps your bottom line. If you plan to buy something big, make a quick calculation of its *payback period* (how long it takes to pay back the initial cost of the equipment out of the extra profit that you make). Is the payback period going to be months, years, or decades? If the payback period you foresee is longer than you want, consider an equipment lease as an alternative to an outright purchase.

Extruding better returns

A small, up-and-coming B.C. company (we'll call it Klever Kitchens) has made a big name for itself in the kitchen-accessories business. Klever Kitchens produces all sorts of newfangled gadgets and utensils for the gourmet chef — everything from pasta hooks to melon scoops. Because the company makes many of its products out of plastic, the owners face a decision about the purchase of a second plastic-extruding machine. They know that the investment is sound because the new $20,000 machine will allow the company to grow, and they expect it to generate an additional $4,000 a year in profit, resulting in an estimated payback period of about five years ($20,000 ÷ $4,000). The question is whether to pay for the extruder by borrowing the funds or by using some of the company's equity reserves.

The owners understand that accruing debt is a way to leverage the company. The bank already agreed to loan Klever Kitchens 75 percent of the $20,000 investment at a fixed 6-percent interest rate. But what do the numbers mean?

Return on equity (ROE) measures how much money Klever Kitchens makes on the money that it invests: ROE = (Added profit − Interest expense) ÷ Equity. By taking on debt, the owners expect to earn an additional $2,800 on their investment of $5,000 in the new extruder, for an ROE of 56 percent. That figure is almost three times the return that the company would receive by putting up the funds alone.

Acting like a financial crowbar, leverage allows Klever Kitchens to use other people's money to generate profits for the company. The risks are also a bit higher, of course, because the owners have to make added interest payments, otherwise they face losing the extruder and maybe the entire company. In this case, Klever Kitchens should borrow the funds because the rewards are well worth the risks.

Additional Plastic Extruder	No Leverage	Leverage
Liability	$0	$15,000
Equity	$20,000	$5,000
Added net profit	$4,000	$4,000
Added interest expense	$0	$1,200
Added profit minus interest expense	$4,000	$2,800
Return on equity (ROE)	20%	56%

While you plan for the future, you also want to keep track of your overall expected *return on assets* (ROA), which is your net profits divided by your total assets. This figure monitors how well you expect all your assets to perform in the future. If you compare your estimated ROA with industry averages, you get a measure of how competitive you can be.

Liabilities and owners' equity

Estimated balance sheets have to balance, of course, and you have to offset your projected assets at the end of each future year by all the liabilities (current and long-term) that you intend to take on, plus your projected equity in the company. Think about how leveraged you intend to be (how much of your total assets you expect to pay for out of money that you borrow). Your use of leverage in the future says a great deal about your company. It shows how confident you are about future profits; it also says, loud and clear, how willing you are to take risks for future gain. For more about how leverage works, check out the sidebar "Extruding better returns," in this chapter, or flip to Chapter 11.

Include the following liabilities and owners' equity categories on your company's balance sheet:

- ✔ **Current liabilities:** In this category, you estimate all the money that you expect to owe on a short-term basis in the future. Current liabilities include the amounts that you expect to owe other companies as part of your planned business operations, as well as payments that you expect to send to the tax people. You have to plan your future current assets so that they not only cover these estimated liabilities but also leave you some extra working capital (see the preceding section to find out how to predict future current assets).

- ✔ **Long-term liabilities:** The long-term debt that you plan to take on represents the piece of your company that you intend to finance. Don't be surprised, however, if potential creditors put a strict limit on how much they want to loan you, especially if you're new to the business. If buying a house without a down payment is hard, starting a company without one is almost impossible. The down payment is your equity contribution. In general, bankers and bondholders alike want to see enough equity put into your business to make them think that everyone is in the same boat, risk-wise. Equity reassures them that you and other equity investors have a real financial stake in the company, as well as tangible reasons to make it succeed.

  How much are lenders willing to loan you, and how large a down payment do you need to come up with to satisfy them? The answer depends on several things. If you're already doing business, the answer depends on your company's current debt, the maturity of your business, your business successes or failures, and your industry's prospects. If your company is new, financing depends on your track record in other businesses or on how well you do your homework and put together a convincing business plan. (Take a look at Chapter 2 for some additional financing tips.)

Before you take on a new loan, find out what kind of debt-to-equity ratios similar companies have (for help, turn to Chapter 11). Make sure that your company falls somewhere in the same range. As an additional test, run some numbers to make sure that you can afford the debt and the interest payments that come along with it.

✔ **Owners' equity.** The pieces of your company that you, your friends, your relatives, acquaintances, and often total strangers lay claim to get lumped together as *owners' equity*. Although the details of ownership can become ridiculously complex, the result of the process is fairly straightforward: All owners own part of your company, and everybody sinks or swims, depending on how well the company does. (Check out Chapter 2 for more information on investors and types of investment.)

In general, you can estimate your company's future benefit for the owners by projecting the return that you expect to make on the owners' investment (refer to Chapter 11 for the details). You can compare that return with the earnings of investors in other companies or even other industries.

During the initial stages of your company, equity capital likely comes from the owners themselves — as cash straight out of the wallet or from the sale of stock to other investors. The equity at this stage is crucial because, if you want to borrow money later, you have to show your bankers that you have enough invested in your business to make your company a sound financial risk. When the company gathers steam, of course, you can take some of your profits and (rather than buy the little sports car of your dreams) give them back to the company, creating additional equity.

Unfortunately, profits have another side — a down side residing in the red. Although you probably don't want to think about it, your company may lose money some years (especially during the early years). Losses don't generate equity; on the contrary, they eat equity up. So you have to plan to have enough equity available to cover any anticipated losses that you project in your projected income statement (refer to the section "Piecing together your projected income statement," earlier in this chapter).

Forecasting your cash flow

The flow of cash through a business is much like the flow of oil through an engine: It supports and sustains everything that you do and keeps the various parts of your company functioning smoothly. We all know what happens when a car's oil runs dry: The car belches blue smoke and dies. Running out of cash can be just as catastrophic for your company. If you survive the experience, it may take months or even years for your business to recover.

Cash-flow statements keep track of the cash that comes in and goes out of your company, as well as where the money ends up. These statements are crucial. Forecasting your cash flow helps you weather the financial conditions you may face. Projected cash-flow statements ensure that you never find the cash drawer empty at the end of the month when you have bills to pay.

Projected cash-flow statements should look three to five years into the future, and for the first two years, they should include quarterly or, better yet, monthly cash-flow estimates. Monthly estimates are particularly important if your company is subject to seasonal cycles or to big swings in sales or expenses, as they are for an ice cream business. (If you're not sure what a cash-flow statement looks like and how it differs from an income statement, flip to Chapter 11.)

You get a bonus from all this hard work: The effort that you put into creating projected cash-flow statements for the company gives you a head start when the time comes to create a budget for your business (see the section "Making a Budget," later in this chapter).

Exploring Alternative Financial Forecasts

Wouldn't it be nice if you could lay out a financial forecast — create your projected income statements, estimated balance sheets, and projected cash-flow statements — and be done with it? Unfortunately, the uncertain future that makes your financial forecast necessary in the first place is unpredictable enough to require constant attention. To keep up, you have to

- ✔ Monitor your financial situation and revise the parts of your forecast that change when circumstances — and your financial objectives — shift.

- ✔ Update the entire financial forecast regularly, keeping track of the accuracy of your past predictions and extending your projections another month, quarter, or year.

- ✔ Consider financial assumptions and scenarios that appear more optimistic and more pessimistic when compared to your best predictions, paying special attention to the estimates that you feel the least certain about. This comparison of scenarios — optimistic, pessimistic, and most likely — is called *sensitivity testing*. Creating the three scenarios shows you where the financial results differ. These differences reveal the most sensitive areas of your predictions.

Why take the time to look at different financial assumptions? For one thing, different assumptions show you just how far off your forecast can be if the future turns out differently than you expect. Also, the differences that you come up with can remind you that your forecasts are only that: forecasts. You have to prepare for alternative actions or directions — for example, marketing efforts or production plans to restrict spending — and these alternatives can help you respond and adjust quickly if the future is different than your original predictions.

Utilizing the DuPont formula

If you want to get a feel for what happens when you change any of the estimates that make up your company's financial forecast, you have to understand how the numbers relate to one another. The DuPont company came up with a useful formula that other companies have used since its inception.

The idea behind the *DuPont formula* is simple: to describe all the ingredients that play a role in determining your return on equity (ROE) — a number that captures the overall profitability of your company. ROE is your company's overall net profit divided by the owners' equity. But knowing that your ROE is 13 percent, for example, is like getting a B+ on a test. You think that you did relatively well, but why did you get that particular grade? Why didn't you get an A? You want to know what contributed to the grade so that you can do better next time.

By discovering what's behind your company's ROE, you have a way to measure the impact of your financial predictions on your profitability. The DuPont chart, shown in Figure 12-1, turns the formula into a pyramid, with the ROE at the top. Each level of the pyramid breaks the ratio into more basic financial ingredients.

Figure 12-1:
The DuPont chart turns the DuPont formula into a pyramid, with return on equity (ROE) at the top.

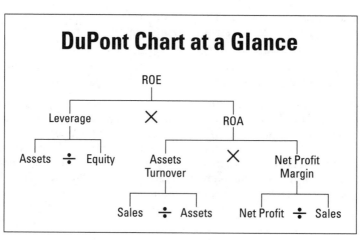

First level

ROE = Return on assets (ROA) × Leverage

You can increase your company's return on equity by increasing the overall return on your company assets or by increasing your leverage (the ratio of your total company assets to equity).

Second level

Leverage = Assets ÷ Equity

While your debt increases relative to equity, so does your company's leverage.

ROA = Asset turnover × Net profit margin

You can increase your return on company assets by turning those assets into more sales or by increasing the amount of money that you make on each sale.

Third level

Asset turnover = Sales ÷ Assets

Asset turnover is the amount of money that you take in on sales relative to your company's assets. The bigger your asset turnover, the more efficiently you turn assets into sales.

Net profit margin = Net profit ÷ Sales

Net profit margin is the profit that you make after subtracting expenses, divided by the amount of money you take in on sales. The larger your profit margin, the lower your overall costs relative to the prices that you charge.

Answering a what-if analysis

After you see the makings of the DuPont formula (outlined in the preceding section), you can start exploring different assumptions (for details see the earlier section "Constructing a Financial Forecast") and what happens when you change the financial forecast. With the DuPont formula, you can look at how those changes can affect your projected profitability, measured by your return on equity. The DuPont formula makes answering questions such as the following much easier:

- ✔ What if I cut prices by 3 percent?
- ✔ What if I increase sales volume by 10 percent?

✔ What if the cost of goods sold (COGS) goes up by 8 percent?

✔ What if I reduce company leverage by 25 percent?

If you get your computer and a spreadsheet program involved in the analysis (see your local computer guru for help, if necessary), you can ask ten what-if questions and get the answers before you have time to think of the next ten.

Making a Budget

The pieces of your financial forecast — the projected income statements, estimated balance sheets, and projected cash-flow statements — should create a moving picture of your financial situation tomorrow, next month, next year, and three or even five years out. You can see a much clearer financial picture in the near term, of course, because your viewpoint clouds up the farther out you try to look. Fortunately, you can use the best of your forecasts to make near-term decisions about where, when, and how much money to spend on your company in the future.

Making a budget for your company is one of the most important steps that you take when you prepare your business plan, and again while your company matures. Your budget, in effect, consists of a series of bets that you're willing to place, based on what you expect to happen in your industry and in the marketplace, in general. Your budget spells out the origin of your company's resources and where they end up going, and it helps ensure that you make the right financial decisions.

A budget is more than a collection of numbers. Your budget is also a business tool that helps you communicate, organize, monitor, and control everyday business. Your company's budget does the following things:

✔ Requires managers to communicate with one another so that they can agree on specific financial objectives, including revenue levels and spending targets

✔ Establishes roles and responsibilities for managers, based on how much money they become responsible for bringing in and how much they can spend

✔ Creates a standard way of measuring and monitoring management performance by keeping track of how well the departments meet revenue targets and spending limits

✔ Promotes the efficient and effective use of your financial resources by making sure that they point to a common set of business goals

Looking inside the budget

The rough outlines of your company's budget look a lot like your projected cash-flow statement. In fact, the cash-flow statement is the perfect place to start. Projected cash flow is a forecast of your company's projected money sources and where your funds may go in the future (check out the section "Forecasting your cash flow," earlier in this chapter, for a deeper look). Your budget fills in all the details, turning your financial forecast into a specific plan for taking money in and doling it out.

The *master budget* that you create should account for everything that your company plans to do over the next year or two. Although you spend your company's money in many ways, you can divide all the routes into short-term and long-term spending. In the short term, you use money to keep the business functioning every day, covering the costs and expenses of putting together and selling products and services. Over the longer term, you use money to invest in assets that make your company bigger, better, or more profitable.

If your company is small and you have only a few employees, a single master budget should be all that you need to keep your day-to-day finances on track, as well as to make decisions in the future. When your company gets a little bigger, however, you may want to examine your company's finances with more than one budget, each one covering a different aspect of your business. The following budget divisions make sense:

- ✔ **Operating:** All the costs that come with putting your product or service together, such as materials, supplies, labour, utilities, services, and facilities

- ✔ **Administrative:** The expenses of supporting your products and services, sales and advertising, administrative salaries, phone and fax lines, and travel

- ✔ **Financial:** The overhead expenses involved in managing your assets, including keeping your books, doing your taxes, controlling your product inventory, and keeping track of your accounts receivable (the money that customers owe you)

- ✔ **Capital:** Funds that you earmark for the purchase of big-ticket items, such as new equipment, computers, a company car, or additional office space

- ✔ **Development:** Money that you set aside for developing new products, opening branches in other cities, or marketing to brand-new groups of customers

When you need several budgets, such as those in the preceding list, you use a master budget to pull all the separate divisions together and make sure that they meet your company's larger goals and financial objectives.

Global Gizmos Company put together a budget for the next two years based on a financial forecast and its projected cash flow (see Figure 12-2). The company's master budget looks a great deal like one of its cash-flow statements (flip to Chapter 11 for a comparison). But the budget goes into more detail in dividing the broad financial objectives into actual revenue and expense targets for specific company activities. The company breaks down the cost of goods produced, for example, into the costs of raw materials and supplies, labour, utilities, and facilities.

Creating your budget

Somehow, people never find the right time to sit down and make a budget; they always have something much more important to do. This situation seems to hold true for household and company budgets alike. Why are budgets so hard to work on? Most people just don't like numbers. And putting together a budget means facing up to the realities of numbers on a page — something else that makes many people squirm. Often, people can't seem to find enough financial information around to make a useful budget. If you complete a financial forecast first, however, completing your company's budget is a breeze.

So, when should you begin? If you're just starting your business — or find yourself in a company without a budget in place — what better time than the present? If you're up and running, *when* you start the new budget cycle depends on your company's size. For big companies, the yearly budget process should begin six to nine months in advance. No wonder the job can feel a bit like never-ending drudgery! Most companies, however, should count on spending some serious time with their budgets three or four months before the next year arrives.

An established company can use its track record and financial history as starting points for next year's budget. But be careful: When you're a veteran, bad cases of budgetary lazities come easily when you can use last year's numbers as a shortcut to next year's numbers. Unfortunately, you can veer off financial course before you know it. A good compass for this situation is something called zero-based budgeting. When you insist on *zero-based budgeting*, you ask everybody — including yourself — to go back and start from ground zero to prepare the budget. Instead of depending on last year's budget numbers, you make full use of your financial forecast and build up a new set of numbers from scratch. The process, although more lengthy and effort-demanding, is worthwhile.

Master Budget

Global Gizmos Company

REVENUE AND EXPENSES		
	Next Year	**Year After**
Budgeted Revenue:		
Gross receipts on sales	$895,000	$970,000
Dividend and interest income	4,000	5,000
Total Revenue Available	**$ 899,000**	**$ 975,000**
Budgeted Expenses:		
Cost of goods produced	$ 600,000	$ 650,000
Raw materials and supplies	250,000	275,000
Labour costs	300,000	325,000
Utilities and facilities	50,000	50,000
Sales, general, and administration	$ 165,000	$ 170,000
Sales and distribution	90,000	95,000
Advertising and promotion	30,000	30,000
Product service	15,000	20,000
Accounting and office support	30,000	30,000
Interest expense	12,500	12,000
Taxes	22,000	24,000
Buildings, equipment, machinery	40,000	$100,000
Equipment and computers	35,000	25,000
Expanded warehouse	5,000	75,000
Development projects	10,000	15,000
New product development	8,000	5,000
New market development	2,000	10,000
Long-term debt reduction	2,500	2,000
Dividend distribution to owners	6,000	7,000
Total Expenses Out	**$ 858,000**	**$ 980,000**
NET CHANGE IN CASH POSITION	**$ 41,000**	**$ -5,000**

Figure 12-2:
The master budget resembles a projected cash-flow statement.

The budgeting process often gets a bad rap in the business world. Instead of viewing budgeting as a helpful business tool, business owners often rank budgeting among the greatest evils on earth, and managers often talk about budgets in unprintable ways. So what gives? When the budgeting process falls apart in a company, you can assume at least one of the following things happened:

- ✔ The executives handed down the budget to control the company's managers, taking away their ability to influence the business decisions that they were ultimately responsible for carrying out.

- ✔ The company based the budget on short-term thinking, ignoring long-term plans and strategic goals.

- ✔ The budgeted revenue and expense targets had nothing to do with the company's larger financial objectives or its real financial situation.

To make sure that your company's budget doesn't suffer these fatal flaws, take a close look at the following sections, in which we talk about two ways to put together a budget.

Top-down budgeting approach

The top-down approach to forming your budget is the simplest way to work through your company's financial plans. The process basically begins and ends with the people in charge. If you have a small company, you may want to invite some outside people — people whom you trust, such as your banker, accountant, or maybe a close business associate — to join you and offer their viewpoints, opinions, and expertise. The process goes like this:

1. **Put the finishing touches on your company's financial forecast, including the projected income statements, expected balance sheets, and projected cash-flow statements.**

   If certain pieces are missing or incomplete, try to get the information that you need or make a note that a necessary document is unavailable. (Check out the section "Constructing a Financial Forecast," earlier in this chapter, to form the pieces of the forecast.)

2. **Meet with your company's decision-makers (or your trusted group, if you're self-employed) to review the financial forecast.**

   Take time to discuss your general expectations about the future. Talk about the business assumptions that go into the forecast and the key predictions and estimates that come out of it. Ask everyone to think about alternatives.

3. **Meet again to explore possible financial alternatives.**

   After everyone has had a chance to reflect on the financial forecast, look at different sets of business assumptions and weigh their potential effects on the forecast. Continue to meet until the group either agrees or agrees to disagree about the future.

4. **Come up with revenue and expense targets for each of your company's major business activities or functional areas (whichever is more appropriate to your company).**

5. **Meet one last time after you draft the budget to review the numbers and to make sure that everyone is on board.**

    Put together a written summary to go along with the numbers so that everyone in the company knows what the budget is, where it comes from, and what it means.

Although top-down budgeting works well when you know all the people in your company on a first-name basis, the approach has its disadvantages when your company gets bigger. By including only the managers at the top, you run the risk of leaving out large chunks of the organization and losing track of your real business situation when it comes time to plug in the numbers. When your company expands, the need for a new technique becomes evident: enter the bottom-up approach, which you can read about in the following section.

Bottom-up budgeting approach

The bottom-up approach to creating your budget is an expanded version of the top-down process, but it takes into account the demands of a bigger company and more people who have valuable input. You still want to begin creating your budget by getting a group of senior managers together. That group should still spend time coming to a general understanding of, and agreement on, your company's financial forecast. But instead of forcing a budget from the top, the bottom-up approach allows you to build the budget up through the company.

Don't ask your group of senior managers to dictate the company's budget. At this point in the budget process, the bottom-up approach allows you to get managers and supervisors at all levels of the company involved. The process goes like this:

1. **Meet with senior managers and ask them to review the company's broad financial objectives for each of your major business areas.**

    Try to come up with guidelines that set the tone and direction for budget discussions and negotiations throughout the company. (See the section "Constructing a Financial Forecast," earlier in this chapter, to come up with objectives.)

2. **Ask the top managers to meet with their managers and supervisors at all levels in the organization.**

    Meetings can start with a recap of the budget guidelines, but the discussions should focus on setting revenue and expense targets. After all, these division managers actually have to achieve the numbers and stay within the spending limits.

3. **Summarize the results of the budget negotiations.**

   If necessary, get the senior group members together again to discuss revisions in the financial objectives, based on the insights, perceptions, and wisdom of the company's entire management team.

4. **Go through the process again, if you need to.**

   Make sure that every employee at every level of the organization is on board or at least understands the reasoning behind the budget and its numbers.

5. **Approve the budget at the top.**

   In this final pass, look at the overall budget not only in terms of current financial objectives, but also with respect to your larger business goals.

Part IV

Looking to the Future

The 5th Wave By Rich Tennant

"Well, I sort of have my own way of forecasting future business climates."

In this part . . .

Wouldn't life be easier if you had a crystal ball to see your future? We have some good news: Although you can't predict the future, you can *prepare* yourself for it. And planning for the future is a great way to cut down on wrong business moves that come with second-guessing.

In this part, we help you look to the future. We show you how you can manage the uncertainty that lies ahead by looking closely at where changes are likely to arise. We talk about how you can anticipate changes ahead of time, assessing what effect these changes could have on your business and how likely they are to really happen.

Instead of using a cystal ball or tea leaves, we help you shape your own future by thinking strategically. We introduce tried-and-true business strategies that have worked in the past and show you how to create your own company strategy for the future. Finally, we explore different ways your business can grow. We look at ways to extend your product line, expand into new markets, and branch out into new businesses.

Chapter 13

Managing Uncertainty

● ●

In This Chapter

▶ Tracking political, economic, socio-cultural, and technological trends

▶ Looking ahead with trend forecasting, scenario planning, and hedging

▶ Preparing your business for what may happen in the future

● ●

*C*hange defines life. When you get up in the morning, you expect to live through a day that differs in many ways from the day before. As far as we know, only Bill Murray in the classic movie *Groundhog Day* ever had to live the same day over and over again, and it almost drove him crazy.

All people expect change. At one time or another, no doubt, you've said, "I really need a change." But you don't often hear people say that they *want* a change or *like* change. Change makes the future uncertain, uncertainty makes planning difficult, and people like to plan. (After all, you *are* reading this book.)

Companies don't want or like change, either, and they come up with hundreds of excuses to try to keep business operations just the way they are. Here are some of the top excuses:

- ✔ It's never been tried before.
- ✔ We've tried it before.
- ✔ It's too radical.
- ✔ What we have is working fine.
- ✔ We don't have the time.
- ✔ We're not ready for it.
- ✔ Our company is different.
- ✔ We should, but . . .
- ✔ It's impossible.

Although companies try to avoid change, they can't escape it; nor should they try. Change is what makes a market work. Change allows companies to form and grow, products and services to get better, competitors to come from everywhere, and customers to go on shopping. Small or new companies often champion this change because they have little interest in maintaining the status quo. In a competitive marketplace, if you stop changing, you die. This is a harsh but true reality.

Good companies understand this fact but often have a hard time acting on it when they become successful — maybe because they have more at stake. The original Canadian stock exchanges listed the biggest and best Canadian companies of the era. Today, only a few of those original companies still appear on the TSX. Many operate in completely different businesses.

Across all industries, the list of companies whose stars have dimmed continues to grow:

- ✔ Dominion Textiles (major textile manufacturer)
- ✔ Canadian Pacific Airways (pioneered commercial aviation)
- ✔ Chieftain Products (originators of Scrabble)
- ✔ *Saturday Night* magazine (one of the first magazines published in Canada)
- ✔ Eaton's (revolutionized early retailing with its cash-only, one-price policy)

  See the sidebar "When retail giants roamed the land," in this chapter for details on retailers' decline.

Articles, documentaries, and entire books have been written on some of these companies, on their industries, and on their times. In each case, you can summarize the arguments by stating that each of these formerly successful companies failed because they didn't or couldn't change with the times. At some point, they each became frozen in the past, and that doomed them to extinction.

In this chapter, we prepare you for uncertain times. After all, your business plan should help you navigate through a constantly changing business environment. We start by defining the elements of change, including political, economic, socio-cultural, and technological trends. We look at ways in which you can anticipate change by forecasting trends and creating alternative scenarios. And we show you how to assess the possible effects of change and how to use innovation to take advantage of change.

Defining the Dimensions of Change

Events and forces beyond your control continuously change the business conditions around you. You can't fiddle with the laws of physics or human nature, but if you want your company to survive, you must keep track of changes when they take place. The experts call the practice *environmental scanning* — not the kind that Environment Canada does, but the kind that looks at anything that may affect your business situation.

Although thousands of factors can influence your business environment, you can simplify matters by looking at the major trends shown in Figure 13-1. (For the details, check out the following sections.) When radical changes threaten to reshape your industry and marketplace, you can bet that the underlying causes involve PEST trends — no, not the insect kind. PEST stands for broad political, economic, socio-cultural, and technological trends.

Canadian political trends

We won't grab any headlines by reminding you that the government has a profound effect on your company and your industry. From the rules and regulations that it issues to the tax policies and legal system that it supports, the government is a major player in your marketplace. Because of its sheer size and impact, the government sparks continuing national debate on how largely, how widely, and how deeply involved it should be in the day-to-day running of our economy.

Oh gee for O-Pee-Chee

If you've ever collected trading cards, you've come across the O-Pee-Chee (OPC) brand. The London, Ontario, candy company started selling sports cards of NHL hockey players with its bubble gum around 1933 and continued until the early years of World War II. O-Pee-Chee re-entered the arena in 1965 and had a few more decades of good plays with its own production of cards — including the all-time great Wayne Gretzky — and even tried licensing its competitor's cards. But where is OPC now? In a vintage collector category.

What happened? You guessed it: First, the political arena changed; then, the industry changed. Competitors saw a lucrative market and responded to the changing tastes of sports fanatics, young and old. With the popularity of hockey and baseball cards rising, manufacturers began producing trading cards for other sports, including basketball, football, and soccer. Now, fans buy and sell Upper Deck, Fleer, Leaf, and other, newer cards. The competitors offer premium cards with UV coatings, improved graphics, and catchy packaging — and the cards don't come with gum anymore. For too long, OPC stuck to what it had always done, then tried different cards off and on, but couldn't find the right formula. The brand was retired for a time, but one of the new competitors, Upper Deck, revived it recently. Will it succeed in the future? Only time — and the cards — will tell.

PEST Trends at a Glance

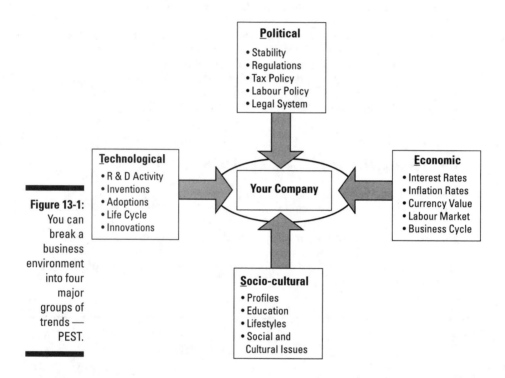

Figure 13-1:
You can
break a
business
environment
into four
major
groups of
trends —
PEST.

No matter which side of the more-or-less-government debate you stand on, you need to keep track of where the discussion is heading. Political actions at any level — municipal, provincial, or federal — can rapidly and dramatically alter your business environment, and you should include a summary of the relevant governmental trends in the "Business Environment" section of your business plan (see Chapter 1).

What kinds of issues should you watch for? Topics that arouse public opinion and finally lead to some sort of political reaction seem to have an eight-year cycle. During the first five years, nothing much happens. The issue may come up in an article here or an opinion poll there. But not until around the sixth year does the national press pick up on it in a serious way, and mounting public pressure finally results in some sort of government legislation. The earlier you spot a smouldering issue that may affect you, the more time you have to prepare a response. The following companies did just that:

- ✔ **Royal Bank of Canada:** After numerous complaints and investigative news reports about ATM inter-bank and "white label" transaction fees, as well as the Bank Act being overdue for review, the federal government began heated debates about regulating ATM fees. RBC, Royal Bank of Canada, expanded its already extensive network to more ATMs on college and university campuses, as well as within 1 kilometre of campuses, before laws were drafted.

- ✔ **Mattel:** After several negative reports, Mattel recognized the serious health issues and recalled toys containing lead paint before the government moved with new regulations.

What parts of government should you pay the most attention to? Think back to civics class (if you can remember anything more than shooting spitballs). At the federal level, government has three branches — Executive, Legislative, and Judicial — that work together to form laws. Each branch can affect your company.

Executive branch

The executive branch implements the laws. It consists of the following:

- ✔ **Head of State:** Canada is a constitutional monarchy, and as such, Queen Elizabeth II is the official Head of State. The governor general represents the queen in Canada.

- ✔ **Head of Government:** The political party with the most number of elected seats forms the government. The prime minister, who is the leader of the winning political party, sets the general tone and direction of the Canadian government. When Stephen Harper became prime minister, he reneged on Canada's commitment to the Kyoto accord, arguing that unless the developing world is brought on board with the developed world to fight global warming, the battle will be lost before it begins. Industries, such as oil and gas industries, that were primed to make adjustments have put changes on hold.

- ✔ **Cabinet:** The prime minister selects members of Parliament (MPs) to serve in the cabinet as ministers of departments.

- ✔ **Departments:** Each department head is a minister in the cabinet. Departments are created by the government (or Parliament of Canada) by statute or regulation. However, the prime minister has the power to appoint or dismiss a minister, as well as create or abolish departments, without the consent or involvement of the respective minister. Some notable departments include finance, health, fisheries, agriculture, industry, natural resources, environment, statistics, and foreign affairs. For a complete list, visit www.canada.gc.ca.

How may the federal government's agenda influence the future of your industry?

Legislative branch

The legislative branch makes the laws. This branch is made up of the executive branch, House of Commons, and Senate.

The House of Commons, which is made up of all the members of Parliament, writes the laws of the land. The Senate must approve these laws before the laws can receive Royal Assent from the Head of State. The House holds the nation's purse strings; only it has the authority to spend your federal tax dollars.

The House has authority to structure regulated industries, such as banking, transportation, and telecommunications. With the Bank Act backing him, a key member of the House and Cabinet, The Minister of Finance, single-handedly stopped the mergers of two sets of major banks. In both cases, the mergers were well underway before the banks sought input from the government.

The House created the Canadian Environmental Protection Act in 1999 (CEPA 1999) to ensure that Canada's air, water, and land remain clean and safe. As part of that effort, the House passed laws to increase the fuel efficiency of automobiles. Those laws, in turn, had a major effect on car size and design, as well as the materials manufacturers used to build every new car. Car manufacturers in the Greater Toronto Area thought these laws were unprecedented interference and a constraint on what automakers could do. Japanese car companies, however, viewed the new rules as a golden opportunity to break into the Canadian marketplace and provide car buyers with alternatives that could meet the new CEPA 1999 rules.

Today, deregulation is all the rage in the halls of Parliament. Are you going to discover new opportunities or see only threats?

Judicial branch

The courts apply the laws. The Supreme Court of Canada heads up the judicial branch; the Federal Court of Canada and superior courts of the provinces are also part of this branch. The judicial branch interprets all the laws that receive Royal Assent each year, so they have a profound effect on every industry in Canada.

The Supreme Court of Canada's ruling in 2005 that struck down Quebec's ban on private medical insurance rocked the nation. The ruling opened the door for a two-tiered system that the provincial and federal governments have worked diligently to disallow. If this two-tiered system goes forward, private health plans may see higher claims and end up passing down the cost to business clients. Will politicians and corporations lobby to have it reversed?

Although we focus here on the federal government, don't forget that provincial and municipal governments can also complicate your business life. Make sure that you keep current on their ever-changing rules and regulations. And on the other side of the coin, foreign governments can create just as many complications, often without the benefit of any advanced warning:

✔ The Mideast oil embargoes of the 1970s sent the entire Canadian economy into a tailspin, with unprecedented inflation rates and shortages that rippled through many industries. Today, however, Canada has one of the world's largest proven oil reserves, second only to Saudi Arabia.

✔ Major changes in the European community continue to create uncertainty for North American companies trying to predict the future look of their European customers and competitors. The 2002 introduction of a common currency, the euro, removed some major financial barriers related to corporate mergers and acquisitions, and the addition of 12 new members to the European Union between 2004 and 2007 changed the shape of European markets and customers. What's next?

✔ Asian governments that fail to enforce copyright protection create havoc in the music, movie, and software markets. And Asian countries that ignore child and prison labour laws cause problems and uncertainty for clothing and shoe retailers worldwide because those retailers must cope with international legal actions, customer boycotts, and bad public relations.

You may need a little help picking out the governmental activities and trends that can affect your business environment. Almost every industry has a trade association, along with an industry newsletter or two. These organizations, as well as Chambers of Commerce, devote much of their time and resources to keeping tabs on — and influencing — current events at all levels of government.

Economic trends

A bank account, a mortgage, a car loan, and credit cards seem to be straightforward financial arrangements that people take advantage of every day. When combined, these financial arrangements create the glue that holds our economy together. The economy, on a large scale, is complex and complicated, but the biggest mystery in economics is why no one seems to understand the basic forces at work.

Economics certainly sounds like science. People in the know always talk about it in terms of numbers — inflation rates, growth rates, interest rates, exchange rates, productivity levels, unemployment figures, price indices, blah, blah, blah. But when it comes to predicting the future levels of these indicators (and what they mean to consumers and companies), the science becomes rather subjective. No two economists are likely to agree on the direction, magnitude, or significance of the numbers.

However, economists do agree on some basic facts:

- ✔ Economic indicators constantly change.
- ✔ Indicators are sometimes predictable.
- ✔ Indicators somehow relate to the performance of the economy.
- ✔ The overall economy affects your business environment.

Obviously, economic uncertainty isn't very satisfying. But economic trends are important enough that you need to keep track of them, even if your information is incomplete. The most important economic trends for your industry should be incorporated into the "Business Environment" and "Financial Review" sections of your business plan (see Chapter 1). What numbers should you keep your eye on? It depends on your business.

If you sell new cars, for example, most of your buyers finance their purchases with leases or loans that have monthly payments tied to interest rates. So, low interest rates are extremely important to the overall health of the auto industry. Interest rates make or break the home-building market for the same reasons. If you're in the fast-food business, you need good, entry-level workers. Their ready availability hinges on wages and regional unemployment levels. As an exporter, you may want to examine exchange rates and the current level of the Canadian dollar against the U.S. dollar, euro, or yen.

The following paragraphs highlight four key economic indicators reflective of major trends in the economy that you should watch closely.

GDP

The *GDP* (Gross Domestic Product) is the total value of a country's annual production of goods and services. You should keep track of the change in GDP from year to year because that change reflects the current overall economy. Moderate, consistent growth in the GDP generally produces a healthy economy with expanding opportunities for many businesses. A drop in the GDP, on the other hand, often leads to lower demand for products and services, an increase in competition, and lower profits for everyone.

You can't always generalize based on the GDP, however. Businesses can go bankrupt when the economy is booming, and even in the worst of times, the entertainment industry rakes in cash. Don't rely solely on the GDP; look at how your industry and your company perform within the larger economy.

When retail giants roamed the land

The 1930s and 1940s were rough times around the world. But, all through the Great Depression and World War II, Canadians could still count on finding whatever they needed, from handbags to housewares, if they stopped and shopped at Simpsons or Eaton's in eastern Canada, at Woodward's or Spencer's in western Canada, or the Hudson's Bay Company in the northern territories. These giant retailers revolutionized one-stop shopping, and for decades, they fiercely battled for dominance of the mass-merchandising market in Canada.

When World War II ended, each company scanned the environment and came up with different predictions for Canada's economic future. The Hudson's Bay Company, Eaton's, and Simpsons saw a bright tomorrow in which pent-up demand, held in check by war and economic depression, would lead to unprecedented growth while Canadians rebuilt their lives. Woodward's and Spencer's saw the economic landscape very differently, betting that growth would be modest and business as usual.

Simpsons began a major expansion through a joint venture with Sears, Roebuck and Co. That strategy strengthened its catalogue division, rebranded existing stores to Simpsons–Sears, and built new stores under the Sears name in the booming suburbs. Eaton's expanded by acquisition and, in fact, purchased Spencer's in 1948. However, it eventually lost touch with its younger customers and became known as a retailer for the older Canadian. It closed its once-premier catalogue division in 1976, and in 2001, Sears purchased what was left of its stores. Woodward's retrenched, modestly expanded in western Canada, and suffered a gradual decline in operations.

The Hudson's Bay Company (HBC), Canada's oldest retailer, was the most aggressive with competitor acquisition, in both niche and geographic expansion. It purchased Simpsons–Sears (but had to divest of Sears stores to comply with competition laws), Woodward's, and Zellers. It also owns Home Outfitters and the Designers Depot.

HBC and Sears swept past their competitors and became the unchallenged retailers to an entire generation of Canadians. Today, trends have shifted yet again. HBC, now privatized by American Jerry Zucker, and Sears find themselves in a fight for their lives against the likes of Wal-Mart and Costco. And Simpsons, Eaton's, Spencer's, and Woodward's are true dinosaurs: extinct and almost forgotten.

Interest rates

Interest rates represent the cost of renting money — how much you have to pay a bank, for example, to use its cash for a certain period. Short-term rates apply when you borrow money for periods ranging from a month to two years. Long-term rates apply to loans that extend all the way out to 30-year home mortgages. As you can imagine, the cost of borrowing money affects every facet of the economy, from consumer spending to business expansion.

The Bank of Canada in Ottawa (the bank that holds the nation's bank account) sets the short-term interest rates. With the rise of the almighty credit card, short-term rates influence shopping habits: The lower the interest rates, the easier (and cheaper) it is for shoppers to buy on credit. So, if you want to start a retail business, you have to pay special attention to short-term interest rates.

Long-term interest rates rise and fall in the corporate and government bond markets. Long-term rates have a major impact on how easily consumers can afford houses, cars, and all other big and expensive purchases because consumers usually finance these items with long-term loans. Long-term rates, therefore, affect consumer demand for big-ticket items. Long-term rates also affect business decisions, such as building big new factories and buying expensive new equipment.

Inflation rates

Inflation, or a continuous rise in wages and prices, is a nasty habit that economies often suffer from. Consumers are the first to know when inflation rears its ugly head because prices go up, and money can't buy as much as it used to.

When inflation is high, companies find that resources and assets are more expensive for them, as well. They have to pay more for everything, from materials to employees' wages and benefits. Investors turn their attention to products that have intrinsic value, such as gold, real estate, and art — anything that protects them against less valuable money. Consumers may borrow more money, partly to pay the higher prices and partly because they can pay back today's cash with less valuable money. Lenders know the economic landscape, so interest rates go up. All these factors are a real drag on the economy over time, and inflation can lead to a recession if the government and the Bank of Canada don't attend to the problem.

Not all companies suffer equally from inflation, however. If you mine precious metal, pump oil, or sell real estate, for example, you can often do quite well during a period of inflation. If you operate any other business, however, you have to balance the broad economic trend against its effect on your industry.

Currency value

In today's global economy, the rise or fall of the Canadian dollar against the U.S. dollar, the euro, or the Japanese yen can have an enormous impact on your entire industry. Your suppliers, competitors, and customers may be anywhere in the world, no matter what industry you're in or how small your company is.

Currency values change daily. As a result, short-term fluctuations in the value of the Canadian dollar are unpredictable. The effects of longer-term currency trends, on the other hand, are easier to predict.

From mad to MADD

Too many tragic deaths have occurred from drunk drivers causing accidents. Loved-ones of the victims formed Canadian organizations such as PRIDE (Parents to Reduce Impaired Driving Everywhere), CAID (Canadians Against Impaired Driving), and PAID (People Against Impaired Driving), and worked tirelessly to stop impaired driving and support victims of this crime. In 1990, MADD (Mothers Against Drunk Driving) Canada was formed from the U.S. organization to create a national network with a powerful voice.

The new group attracted attention and members, striking a resonant chord across the nation. Members wrote articles, staged rallies, and mounted protests. Politicians took notice. Soon, Parliament held legislative hearings, and elected officials demanded action. Finally, the efforts of MADD Canada and its supporters paid off with new laws that changed everything from the minimum drinking age, the timing of "happy hours" in bars, and the advertising of alcoholic beverages to the arrest and sentencing of drunk drivers.

The laws changed the entire alcoholic-beverages industry, from advertisers and countless bars to nightclubs and restaurants across the country. And MADD Canada is still on the job.

When the value of the Canadian dollar is relatively low, for example, Canadian goods turn into bargains, so consumers around the world have a little extra incentive to buy Canadian. To compete, foreign competitors must lower their prices (and watch profits go down) or see their share of the market get smaller. Foreign companies also have a third option: come to Canada, build plants, and produce products to take advantage of the weak dollar. Toyota and Honda both built large production facilities in Canada to take advantage of the strong Japanese yen relative to the Canadian dollar.

The reverse is also true. A strong Canadian dollar leads to bargain prices on foreign products, a shift toward imports, and sometimes, the relocation of Canadian companies abroad to take advantage of cheaper foreign currencies. Many Canadian textile and garment companies relocated their production facilities to Asia to take advantage of weak local currencies.

Socio-cultural trends

Take two frogs and a skillet. Place the skillet on the stove and bring a small amount of water to a boil. Drop one of the frogs into the skillet. The frog jumps out of the skillet, onto the floor, and out the door.

EXAMPLE

Good ol' Canadian know-how

For 50 years, RONA operated a member-owned chain of old-fashioned hardware stores in central Canada. In the early 1980s, senior management recognized an emerging trend: the growing ranks of do-it-yourselfers (DIYers) and the increase in home renovations. The rookies lacked building knowledge and expected a great deal of helpful advice, and the contractors wanted better prices.

RONA, already well positioned with quality service, prepared for change. It formed a purchasing alliance with Ontario-based Home Hardware Stores and went on to acquire a number of building-supply chains across the nation. The new stores don't look anything like the old ones; most of the current, huge stores were built after 1994. Inside, you can find doors, windows, cabinets, counters, fixtures, siding,

lumber, tools . . . you name it. If you need help, they're the go-to people for how-to advice.

The company says that its upgraded 40,000-square-foot store is designed for men and women, contractors and do-it-yourselfers. It's targeting buyers who want the traditional hardware store in a bigger format. It even opened an online store in 2000, where customers can directly purchase a number of products.

RONA spotted an emerging cultural trend in the growing ranks of DIYers and home renovations, and it created a strategy and revised business plan to capture a big slice of the DIY and home-renovation pie. It employs 26,000 people in over 670 stores that generate close to $6 billion in sales annually.

Place the skillet back on the stove, this time filled with cold water and the second frog. As the water slowly heats, the frog sits there agreeably, never noticing the rising temperature. (Don't try this experiment at home unless you plan to have frog legs for dinner.) The moral? When you ignore the slow changes that take place around you, you boil.

Cultural changes don't happen overnight (after all, the greying of the baby boomers has taken many years). But the glacial speed of these trends reflects the glacial forces that lie behind them. The real danger lies in ignoring these trends simply because you can always worry about them later. Well, later always gets here sooner than you realize. Socio-cultural trends are often at the heart of new business opportunities, and you should address the ones that may be relevant to your industry in the "Business Environment" and "Company Strategy" sections of your business plan (see Chapter 1). Consider the cultural shifts we describe in the following list:

✔ **Demographic changes:** *Demographic* refers to the general profile of a specific population — anything from your company's customers to the citizens of a nation. Demographic data includes attributes that you may find on a national census form, such as age, gender, and family size.

Changes in the profile of a nation are certain to have profound effects on its economy and business. Canada, Western Europe, Japan, and the United States, for example, are all trying to come to terms with the slow aging of their populations. Their governments have to figure out how to take care of all these older people, and companies are trying to figure out how to sell them their products or services. (Flip to Chapter 6 for more info on customer demographics.)

✔ **Social changes:** A society is made up of the combined values, customs, and traditions that its people have in common. Social behaviour changes over time, of course, but people tend to give up their traditions slowly and grudgingly. Most Canadian schools still give their children the summer off, for example, even though most children no longer need to work on family farms.

But what happens to customs and traditions when the population changes — as people move from place to place, as families start to look different, and as new citizens bring along their own customs and traditions? Think of all the opportunities for ethnic restaurants (Chinese, East Indian, Korean, and Thai, for example) when new waves of immigrants move into different regions of the country. Any change in broad social behaviour, no matter how slowly it occurs, can have a dramatic effect on your company and on industries across the economy.

✔ **Lifestyle changes:** Changes in the way people live their lives affect how they work, what they buy, how they play, and where they live. About 25 years ago, for example, the health-and-fitness craze caught on in Canada. Today, the industry includes the makers of sports shoes, sportswear, exercise equipment, golf equipment, mountain bikes, kayaks, energy food bars, diet drinks, bottled water, and many other products.

Other major lifestyle changes that affect industries include

- Growing gender equality in every area
- Home-based businesses and telecommuting
- At-home shopping, education, and entertainment
- Multiple-career professionals
- Alternative family units
- People who continue to work past retirement age
- Workers who opt for early retirement

Technological trends

Technology breeds change, and change breeds technology. In the past 150 years, Canada has gone from buggy whips to the space shuttle robotics of

Canadarm 1 and 2, and from the telegraph to the Internet. A hundred years from now, people may look back at our era and marvel at how primitive our technologies were.

Every new technology doesn't change the world overnight. Most don't change the world at all, in fact. You could create a television show about the world's funniest inventions that pop up each week. For the most part, the technologies that succeed have been evolving for quite some time. No matter how fast a new technology takes over from the old, it usually follows a *diffusion curve,* which traces how a new technology catches on in an industry (see Figure 13-2).

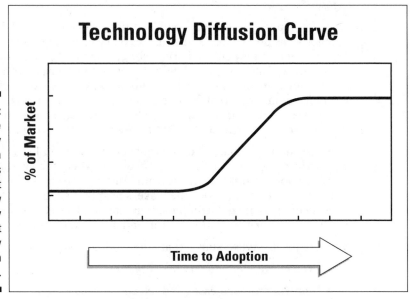

Figure 13-2:
The technology diffusion curve points out that when a new technology takes off, it usually catches on rapidly.

The diffusion curve demonstrates that it always takes a certain amount of time for any new technology to take off. When (or if) it does catch on, the technology usually sweeps through an industry quickly because companies don't want to fall behind. The technology reaches a plateau when most of the companies in an industry adopt the new technology.

Failing to quickly adopt a new technology that sweeps through your industry can be disastrous. The advent of compact disc (CD) technology, for example, put most manufacturers of vinyl records and cassette tapes out of business within a couple of years. In turn, memory sticks, MP3 players, and wireless access to the Internet are spinning CDs into a mature stage. And DVD technology turned VCRs into collector's items.

For the majority of new technologies that come along, reality lies somewhere between eureka and potential disaster. Think about the electronics industry: Transistors succeeded but didn't kill off their older cousins, vacuum tubes. The older technology managed to hang in there because, for certain applications, people still prefer tubes. After bandwagon jumpers held funeral services for radios (thought to be made obsolete by television), eyeglasses (considered to be outdated with the advent of contact lenses), and razor blades (not much use in the world of electric razors), these industries all turned around and actually grew bigger. Radio stations are some of the hottest properties around (people still hold value in listening to the car radio), designer eyewear is definitely in (fashion often trumps function in the eyes of the customer), and sales of safety razors never stopped expanding (most people like the closely shaved feel that razors provide).

What do these examples say about trends in technology? Although each industry is different, a few generalizations come to mind:

- ✔ Older technologies often have time to adjust to innovations.
- ✔ Older technologies can improve, even after they mature.
- ✔ New technologies usually begin by focusing on specialized markets.
- ✔ New technologies can create new customers, expanding the marketplace.
- ✔ Old and new technologies often live together for many years.

You may struggle to predict the coming of a new technology and what's going to happen when it arrives. To prepare yourself for possible changes in technology and the potential effects on your industry, review the major technologies that consumers currently use. For each technology, do the following things:

- ✔ Find out which research laboratories specialize in the technology and what technical journals and publications cover and report on it. Make sure that you check out academic, private, and government institutions.
- ✔ Attend major conventions and scientific meetings on the technology and subscribe to any relevant journals and publications.
- ✔ Monitor press releases on the technology and keep track of patents that innovators file in the field.
- ✔ Compare your company's capability to adapt to and apply technology to that of your key competitors.
- ✔ On a regular basis, re-examine the likelihood of a fundamental technological breakthrough and check the status of small, step-by-step process improvements in technology.

Although technologies within your industry may be unpredictable, you should track them over time and take them into account when you create your business plan. The technology advances in unfamiliar areas, however, have the potential to bite you while you sleep. When Xerox introduced its first copier in 1959, it basically stopped mimeograph machine makers cold. When Hewlett-Packard came out with its first hand-held calculator in 1970, slide-rule manufacturers took a fast slide into oblivion. So, you want to keep your eye on technology trends beyond your immediate industry. That way, you become better prepared for unexpected changes.

Anticipating Change

You probably have a hard time keeping track of what goes on around you; never mind trying to anticipate what's going to happen in the future. The point isn't to predict the future, however; leave that to the tea-leaf readers. Instead, your goal should be to understand what *may* happen so you can prepare yourself better than your competition can.

To do that, you need to estimate which of the many trends — political, economic, socio-cultural, and technological — will become the megatrend that produces tomorrow's innovation and makes tomorrow's entrepreneurs rich. What trend will have an influence on your industry, your strategies, and the competition?

Start by turning to the professionals and hearing what they have to say. Scan the publications that follow these trends. After time passes, you can judge which of them are most useful. Along with the *Financial Post* and *The Globe and Mail,* try the *Economist, Canadian Business, Profit, Report on Business,* and *FP Business Magazine,* among others.

You should also check out organizations that specialize in the future, including the MaRS Centre, Strategic Leadership Forum, Futures Canada, Global Business Network, and Applied Foresight Network.

Trend forecasting

You can use several tricks of the trade to peer into the future and decide whether a particular trend is likely to continue. Given the nature of the challenge, however, you may not want to rely on any one of these tricks too heavily. Each approach provides its own unique look forward.

Extrapolation

Sometimes, you can use mathematical sleight of hand to project a historical trend into the future. This process, called *extrapolation,* works particularly well for trends that don't change rapidly and that you can measure in numbers. The idea is fairly simple: You take your favourite trend (the inflation rate, for example) and assume that it will evolve in exactly the same way that it has in the past. Certain economic measurements, customer profiles, and even a few technology trends are likely candidates for extrapolation.

The easiest way to extrapolate a trend is to find someone who already did it for you, which means tracking down a magazine article or an academic paper. But don't despair if you have to do the job yourself. Computers make the job much easier, and the current crop of spreadsheet programs has buttons that you can click to generate an extrapolation, provided you have the historical data to get started, of course. Extrapolation is most useful in the "Financial Review" section of your business plan (see Chapter 1), where you make projections about your future financial situation.

Any sudden changes in a trend can mess up your extrapolation. Because the world and the global marketplace are more complex than they used to be, many trends are becoming less and less predictable, which makes forecasting more difficult — and the abrupt changes are exactly the ones you need to know about ahead of time. Judgment forecasting and Delphi studies may help you predict some of these changes.

Judgment forecasting

Judgment forecasting relies on the information, experience, and gut feelings of the people in and around your company to predict specific trends. Use a short questionnaire or a brainstorming session to get your managers, employees, suppliers, and even customers to give you their judgments about the future of particular trends. When these trends are important to your business, you should include them in the "Business Environment" and "Company Strategy" sections of your business plan (see Chapter 1).

Judgment forecasting isn't mathematical. It relies on the information and wisdom that your organization and business network already have to forecast specific trends in the future. You should use judgment forecasting periodically to stay one step ahead of the most recent events and changes in your business environment.

Delphi study

A Delphi study allows you to bring in the experts to talk about the future without necessarily having to pay an arm and a leg for their services. The idea behind the technique is simple. Say, for example, that you want to forecast trends in the use of solar energy to heat, cool, and provide electricity for entire housing developments. You know experts in the solar energy field can best address the question. Ideally, you could bring a group of them together for a face-to-face discussion of the issues. But that kind of forum is expensive and hard to organize. So, you use a Delphi study.

A *Delphi study* is a set of questionnaires that you put together to send to a group of experts when you have a particular question about the future. You summarize the answers and send the questionnaires out again to get another set of responses. A Delphi study is an inexpensive way to bring in the big guns without having to get them together in the same room.

Follow these steps to create an informative forum:

1. **Send a questionnaire to each of your hand-selected experts, asking for his or her judgment on an issue.**

   For this example, the issue is solar energy and the feasibility of solar-driven housing developments in the future.

2. **Summarize the experts' forecasts with your advisers, including what the majority of the experts say, the opinions of the minority, and any individual dissenting views, if they exist.**

3. **Send the summary back to each of the experts, along with a second copy of the questionnaire.**

   Ask the experts to review the first-round summary and then fill out and return the questionnaires again. Some experts may alter their original judgments and respond to new issues and concerns that you or other experts raise.

4. **Continue the process of responding and receiving feedback until you're satisfied that you and the experts have reached some common ground.**

5. **Incorporate the information on future trends into the "Business Environment" and "Company Strategy" sections of your business plan (see Chapter 1).**

Scenario planning

Sometimes, trends are too unpredictable or too numerous to track, so you can't project a single view of the future that seems to make any sense. *Scenario planning* allows you to imagine several complete versions of the future and consider how each version can affect your company's fortunes.

Military strategists use war scenarios all the time. So do experts in public health when they try to anticipate and prepare for the spread of a global epidemic. Scenarios can help your business imagine a variety of future prospects, too.

Start with a trend — the inflation rate, for example — and think about how you can create three or four alternative scenarios for the future, based on different levels of inflation. (For more information on inflation, refer to the section "Economic trends," earlier in this chapter.) Try to include a fairly complete description of what your business environment may look like in each case.

Don't hesitate to introduce another important trend into your scenario. Maybe your company's future is also tied to federal regulations that the government may announce sometime in the next five years; you can put together another set of scenarios that involve those regulations. But now you have two or three possibilities for regulation and two or three possible levels of inflation to juggle. Obviously, this situation can get out of hand rather quickly.

Experienced scenario jugglers are quick to point out the wisdom of working with no more than three or four scenarios at a time. Rather than add trend after trend into a growing set of scenarios, limit yourself to three complete scenarios based on different views of your industry in the future:

- ✔ An optimistic view
- ✔ A pessimistic view
- ✔ The most likely view

You may decide that low inflation, minimum regulation, and a technology breakthrough create an optimistic scenario, and high inflation, heavy regulation, and no technology breakthroughs create the pessimistic view. The most likely view falls somewhere in between. You should include the most likely view in the "Business Environment" section of your business plan (see Chapter 1).

You may want to create a business plan for the future by looking backward and doing what you've always done in the past. That method is easy and comfortable — and dangerous. Scenario planning isn't meant to predict the future; its real value lies in offering you new options and a wider range of possibilities to think about. Different business scenarios stimulate your imagination and bring to life compelling glimpses of your company's future.

Hedging your bets

What are the odds that something you forecast — a specific event, a particular activity, or a given scenario — will actually occur in the future? Fortunately, you don't have to dust off that crystal ball just yet. *Probability theory* is a respectable, age-old branch of mathematics. Probabilities are important because they present you with the likelihood that a prediction will come true.

You may understand more about probability theory than you think. If you flip a coin, for example, you have a gut feeling that half the time, you get heads. The odds of getting heads, therefore, are one in two. What other probabilities can you come up with? Here are some coin-flipping odds:

- ✔ Probability of flipping heads: one in two
- ✔ Probability of flipping two heads in a row: one in four
- ✔ After flipping three heads in a row, probability of flipping another heads: one in two

These probabilities are all based on *random statistics*. Every time you flip a coin, the singular outcome is random; it doesn't depend on anything else that happens before or around it. It doesn't matter if you flip three heads in a row; your next flip is still random, and flipping heads is still a 50-50 possibility. If you say "I bet I can flip two heads in a row," before you toss, you have one in four odds.

But many activities and events aren't random. The weather, for example, is certainly unpredictable and subject to change (no wonder we talk about it so much). But weather isn't random; many factors and forces influence it. What's the probability that the thermometer will hit the century mark tomorrow? The answer depends on your location and the season. The probability is higher in summer than in winter, and higher still during a heat wave.

Business trends of one kind or another are going to have a significant impact on your company in the future, so you should include references to them in many sections of your business plan: from the "Business Environment" and "Company Strategy" sections to the "Financial Review" section and even the "Action Plan" section (see Chapter 1). Many of the business trends that we look at in this chapter behave much like the weather: unpredictable and subject to change, but not random.

The probability of inflation, for example, reaching a certain level over the next six months depends on past inflation rates and on underlying factors such as economic demand, factory output levels, and wage pressures. With the pertinent info at hand, the experts tell us that they can forecast inflation, and their track records are about as good as weather reporters'. Still, everybody maintains an interest because forecasts are better than guesses.

Preparing for a Changing Future

Changes take place around you all the time. Some changes have a big effect on your company; you scarcely notice others. Some changes are obvious and predictable; others come out of nowhere. The critical questions you face are

- ✔ Which changes may actually take place?
- ✔ What do the changes mean for your industry?
- ✔ What impact do the changes have on your company?
- ✔ What opportunities and threats are created? (See Chapter 5 for more details on opportunities and threats.)

The impact that a trend or an event has on your business tells you how hopeful or worried you should be if your predictions do come true. A trend may be the best thing to happen to one industry and a complete disaster for another. An event may create a major opportunity for your company or have no noticeable effect at all.

A billion reasons to change

Toronto-based entrepreneur William (Bill) M. Tatham recognized that technology is a key driver of change today. He founded Janna Systems in his basement in 1990 and sold it ten years later for a cool $1.76 billion to his largest competitor, Sibel Systems.

In Janna Systems, Bill developed a world-class enterprise customer relationship management (CRM) solution for the financial services sector. He learned about financial services from the inside, and then applied what he knew to building innovative solutions for the unique needs of the sector. Banks needed to find, secure, and service customers, and nurture relationships. Janna Systems' product and service solutions enabled banks to better manage relationships

through traditional communication methods and via the Internet.

Keeping his hands on trends and his eye out for opportunities, Bill founded XJ Partners with his former management team to provide venture capital and advisory services to early-stage technology companies. He liked one of those companies, NexJ Systems Inc., so much that he's now its chairman and CEO. NexJ is a leading provider of user-friendly, enterprise-wide solutions, which enable NexJ's customers to manage change speedily. The software platform allows customers to rapidly design and build the exact solutions they need to meet their unique and specific requirements, with the least time to deployment.

Review the business trends and scenarios that you develop in the section "Anticipating Change," earlier in this chapter, and place the significant events or possible outcomes you foresee in one of the four probability/impact categories shown in Figure 13-3. Each category requires a different level of planning and investment on your part:

✔ High-probability, high-impact events demand careful preparation.

✔ High-probability, low-impact events call for routine planning.

✔ Low-probability, high-impact events require contingency planning.

✔ Low-probability, low-impact events suggest routine monitoring.

Figure 13-3:
The Probability and Impact Grid divides events into categories based on how likely they are to occur and what effect they may have.

Probability and Impact Grid

Probability

Impact			
	Contingency Planning	Careful Preparation	High
	Routine Monitoring	Routine Planning	Low
	Low	High	

If you need help figuring out which trends and scenarios belong in which categories, you can always open your wallet and call in the experts. But first, see what you can do on your own. Assemble a group of your colleagues and maybe one or two of your best customers for a brainstorming session on the future of your company. You may be surprised by the insights that come out of your get-together when you start the ball rolling. Here's what you do:

1. **Give the group members a fixed amount of time to review the trends and scenarios that you come up with and to throw in any new ones of their own.**

2. **Have someone make a list of the trends and scenarios that the group generates.**

3. **Put the complete list of trends and scenarios in front of the group.**

4. **Rank trends and scenarios, based on their potential to affect your company's future.**

5. **Rank these trends and scenarios again, this time based on the probability that they will actually occur.**

6. **Divide the trends and scenarios into the four probability/impact categories (refer to Figure 13-3).**

The Probability and Impact Grid tells you where to concentrate your investment in time and company resources. Placing the trends and scenarios that you generate into probability/impact categories gives you a place to begin. Don't go chasing after every trend. You should prepare for change, allocate time, budget resources, and plan for possible events based on a practical combination of probabilities and potential impact on your business.

Chapter 14

Thinking Strategically

● ●

In This Chapter

▶ Exploring business strategy

▶ Zeroing in on a focus strategy

▶ Using strategy to establish your market position

▶ Coming up with your own strategy

● ●

*I*n this chapter, we help you formulate a strategy for your company that ties in with your basic mission (see Chapter 4 to find out more about mission statements). We introduce several basic kinds of strategy that different businesses can apply across many industries. These off-the-shelf strategies include efforts to

✔ Be the low-cost provider.

✔ Differentiate your products.

✔ Focus on specific market and product areas.

We also talk about several other general strategic alternatives and answer a variety of important planning-related questions, such as

✔ What does it mean to become more vertically integrated as a company?

✔ What are the pros and cons of outsourcing a part of your business operations?

✔ How should a company act as the market leader or market follower?

We also give you some pointers about creating a strategic blueprint for your business. Include a summary of your strategic blueprint in the "Company Strategy" section of your business plan.

Applying Off-the-Shelf Strategies

Maybe you think your company's situation is absolutely unique and the issues you face are one-of-a-kind. In the fine details, every company is different. Of course, if you look through a microscope, every snowflake is also unique. But snowflakes have a great deal in common when you stand back and watch them pile up outside. Companies are like snowflakes. Although all the details give companies their individual profiles, companies and industries in general have remarkable similarities when you step back and concentrate on their basic shapes.

Master business strategist and Harvard University professor Michael Porter was one of the first to recognize and describe standard business profiles. Based on what he saw, he came up with three generic approaches to strategy and business planning. The generic strategies offer off-the-shelf answers to a basic question: What does it take to be successful in a business over the long haul? The answers work across all markets and industries.

Successful companies that follow one of the generic strategies recognize the tradeoffs involved in pursuing one strategy versus another and deliberately choose not to pursue a certain strategy in order to focus on the desired goal. For example, you may find it difficult to offer the highest quality product and the best service and still have the lowest price. Porter suggests that a company choose which generic strategy best fits its business goals and make business choices according to that strategy. Generic strategies boil down to the following standard approaches (highlighted in Figure 14-1):

- ✔ **Cut costs to the bone.** Become the low-cost leader in your industry. Do everything that you can to reduce your costs and deliver a product or service that measures up well against the competition.

- ✔ **Offer something unique.** Figure out how to provide customers with a unique and valuable product or service, and deliver your product or service at a price that customers are willing to pay.

- ✔ **Focus on one customer group.** Focus on the precise needs and requirements of a narrow market, using either low cost or a unique product to woo your target customers away from the general competition.

Cutting costs and offering something unique represent two generic strategies that work almost universally. After all, business, industry, and competition are driven by customers who base their purchase decisions on the *value equation* — an equation that weighs the benefits of any product or service against its price tag. (Refer to Chapter 8 for more information on the value equation.) Generic strategies simply concentrate your efforts on influencing one side of the value equation or the other.

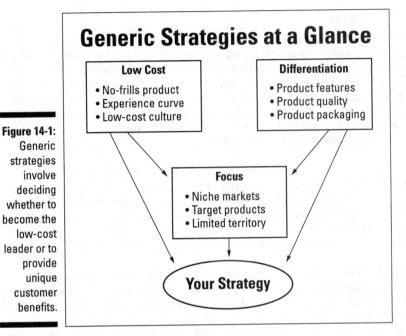

Figure 14-1:
Generic
strategies
involve
deciding
whether to
become the
low-cost
leader or to
provide
unique
customer
benefits.

Leading with low costs

Becoming the low-cost leader in your industry may sound pretty straightforward. In reality, it requires the commitment and coordination of every aspect of your company, from product development to marketing, from manufacturing to distribution, and from raw materials to wages and benefits. Every day, you find ways to track down and exterminate unnecessary costs. Find a new technology that simplifies manufacturing? Install it. See a region or country that has a more productive labour force? Move there. Know of suppliers that provide cheaper raw materials? Sign 'em up.

A cost-leadership strategy is often worth the effort because it gives you a powerful competitive position. When you market your company as the low-cost leader, you call the shots and challenge every one of your competitors to find other ways to compete. Although the strategy is universal, it works best in markets and industries in which price drives customer behaviour — the bulk- or commodity-products business, such as the large-scale purchase of grain, sugar, or oil, for example; or low-end, price-sensitive market segments such as Zellers retail shoppers or WestJet Airline customers who like the "get less for much less" offer of the airline.

The following sections describe the ways in which you can carry out a cost-leadership strategy.

No-frills product

The most obvious and straightforward way to keep costs down is to invoke the well-known KISS (Keep It Simple, Stupid!) principle. When you cut out all the extras and eliminate the options, you can put your product together on the cheap. A no-frills product can enjoy success if you can market it to customers that don't see any benefit in (or are even annoyed by) the bells and whistles in your competitors' products — half-hearted chefs whose microwaves sport a flashing 12:00, for example, or famous-writers-to-be who are baffled by their laptops or desktops.

In addition to removing all the extras, you can take advantage of a simple product redesign to gain an even greater cost advantage. Home developers replaced plywood with particle board, for example, to lower the costs of construction. Camera makers replaced metal components with plastic. And, of course, you can always follow the Neilson's solution: The company reduced costs at one point by making its chocolate bars a wee bit smaller.

As the old saying goes, "You get what you pay for." And companies that choose to compete on the basis of price typically sell products that don't sport the highest quality, the most features, or the best service in the marketplace. You must decide whether the strategic tradeoff is worth it. The term is "less for less." Some smart marketers, such as WestJet, still give great value and service while trimming the frills — along with the price — for a market position of "less for much less." Can you do the same?

Stripped-down products and services eventually appear in almost every industry. The most obvious examples today include

- ✔ **No-frills airlines:** Such as WestJet, CanJet, and Zoom Airlines

- ✔ **Warehouse stores:** Such as Real Canadian Warehouse Club and Costco, which offer a wide selection, low prices, and hardly any customer service

- ✔ **Bare-bones online brokerage houses:** Such as Questrade, TradeFreedom, and E*Trade Canada, which charge low commissions on stock and mutual fund trades with very little hand-holding or personal investment advice

Experience curve

Companies often attain or fall short of cost leadership based on the power of the *experience curve,* which traces the declining unit costs of putting together and selling a product or service over time (see Figure 14-2).

The curve measures the real cost per unit of various general business expenses: plant construction, machinery, labour, office space, administration, advertising, distribution, sales — everything but the raw materials that make up the product in the first place. The combined total of these costs tends to go down over time when you average them out over all the products that you make or services that you provide.

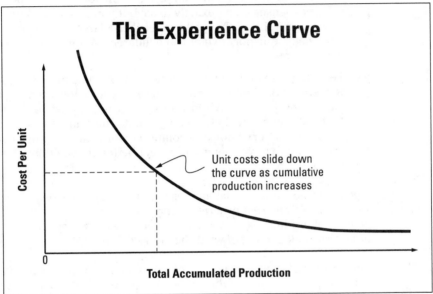

The underlying causes of the experience curve include the following:

> ✔ **Scale:** *Scale* refers to your fixed business costs, which are fixed in the sense that the amount of the product that you make and sell doesn't affect the costs. (Fixed costs usually include such things as your rent, the equipment that you buy, and some of your utility bills.) The more products you produce, however, the more immediate scale advantage you gain because the fixed costs associated with each unit go down automatically.
>
> Think about widgets for a moment. Suppose that you rent a building at $1,000 a month to house widget production. You add that rental expense into the cost of the widgets that you make so you don't lose money. Perhaps you turn out only ten widgets in the first month. No matter what they cost, you have to add $100 rent ($1,000 divided by 10 units) to the price of each widget. But if you can boost production to 100 units the next month, you add only $10 in rent ($1,000 divided by 100 units) to the price of each widget, reducing your rental costs per unit by a whopping 90 percent. Scale is good for business and your bottom line.

- ✔ **Scope:** *Scope* works a little like the scale effect, although it refers to the underlying cost benefit that you get by serving larger markets or by offering multiple products that share overhead expenses associated with business areas such as advertising, product service, and distribution. (Chapter 15 provides more information on your product portfolio.) These expenses aren't exactly fixed, but you do gain an automatic scope advantage if the ad that you run reaches a larger market or if your delivery trucks transport two or three different products to each of your sales outlets.

- ✔ **Learning:** As you learn, the overall cost of doing business goes down. Remember the first time you tried to tie your shoelaces? Big job. A lot of work. Now, you can do it in your sleep. What happened? The more you tied your shoes, the better you got at it. The same is true whether you work on a factory floor, at a computer workstation, or in a conference room. You (and your employees) get better at something the more you do it.

A general rule suggests that all these underlying causes result in what's known as an *80-percent experience curve:* Every time you double the total number of products you produce, unit costs go down by about 20 percent — or end up at 80 percent of what they were before.

The cost benefit that you get out of your company's experience varies and depends partly on your industry. Some industries don't benefit from experience effects at all. In industries in which the basic costs of raw materials are high, for example, you don't have much room to gain a big advantage through experience. Many service industries may not get much of an advantage from experience, either. It doesn't matter how good hairstylists become at what they do; it still takes them about an hour to wash and style each customer's hair, so company costs don't change (although customers keep coming back if they get compliments on how great they look).

Low-cost culture

You can sustain low-cost leadership only if every part of your company commits to keeping costs under control by reducing or eliminating expenses and unnecessary spending. This kind of commitment doesn't occur without the owners' leadership.

Perhaps more than any other strategy and business plan that you can pursue, the push to be the low-cost leader in your industry succeeds or fails based on how well you carry it out. Knowing where and when to bring in cost-saving technology may be one important aspect of your drive, for example. But at the heart of your plan, you absolutely need to figure out how to structure the company, reward your employees, and create the spirit of a lean, mean fighting machine.

In the end, your employees determine how efficient your company really is, and you have to set the right example. This may mean that as the owner of the company, you don't drive a company car or you try to avoid making personal long-distance calls from work. You can bet that your employees will see your example and follow your lead.

Low-cost leadership means exactly what it says. First, second, or third runner-up equals failure; you don't want to be first among equals. If you can't assume the low-cost leadership position, you run the risk of playing a part in your worst nightmare: a high-stakes, cutthroat industry in which price-war shoot-'em-outs threaten to destroy all the players. After all, if you don't have a clear leader, everyone's a challenger, and when low-cost challengers decide to battle for market-share advantage, they use price as their favourite weapon. If you happen to find yourself in such a Wild West industry, take action. Look for new and different ways to compete — alternative strategies that you can count on to reward you in the end.

Standing out in a crowd

Not every company can be the low-cost leader in an industry, and many companies don't even want to be. Instead, they prefer to compete in the marketplace by creating unique products and services, offering customers luxuries that they just have to have — products or services that they don't mind paying a little extra for. This strategy is known as *differentiation*.

Differentiation flourishes because companies can be different in many ways, which means that they can take different routes to success. Although the low-cost strategy that we discuss in the preceding section can easily produce a win-lose situation for many companies, differentiation often creates room for more players, with each company competing successfully in its own special way. The competition remains fierce, however, even with companies offering distinctly different products or services.

Businesses that can distinguish themselves from their competitors often enjoy enviable profits, and they frequently use those extra dollars to reinforce their unique positions in the marketplace. A premium winery — for example, Inniskillin Winery — earns its reputation based on the quality of its grapes and expertise of the winemaker, but it polishes that reputation through expensive packaging and promotional campaigns, as well as championing the Vintners Quality Assurance (VQA) standard to raise the bar for all Canadian wineries. These added investments make it more difficult for competitors to join in, but they also raise the cost of doing business. A maker of jug wine has trouble competing in premium markets. But at the same time, a premium winery can't afford to compete on price alone. No company can ignore cost, of course, even if it offers something unique. Wine-lovers may be willing to spend $20 for a special bottle of chardonnay, but they may balk at a $50 price tag.

After you set your product or service apart based on what it can do, how well it works, or the way that you package and distribute it, you need to develop these aspects into a successful differentiation strategy, creating a loyal set of customers along the way.

Because a differentiation strategy hinges completely on the relationship you create with your customers, stop and ask yourself several questions before you move ahead:

- ✔ Who are my customers?
- ✔ How do I best describe them?
- ✔ What are their basic wants and needs?
- ✔ How do they make choices?
- ✔ What motivates them to buy a product or service?

Check out Chapters 6 and 7 for more insights on customers. The following sections describe the ways that you can set yourself apart from the competition.

Product features

You can often find the basic outline of a successful differentiation strategy in what your product can or can't do for customers. After all, a product's features are frequently among the first factors that a potential buyer considers. How do your products stack up? Are you particularly strong in product design and development? (Chapters 9 and 10 may help you answer this question.) If so, you should consider how to leverage your strength in developing new features to make your company's products stand out.

Unfortunately, major product features represent big targets for your competitors to aim at, so differentiating your company based on major product attributes alone is sometimes hard to sustain over the long haul. Technology-driven companies — such as Research in Motion (RIM), Nortel, and Hummingbird — stay one step ahead of the competition by investing tremendous resources in research and development (R&D) and always offering the latest and greatest products.

You can sometimes discover ways to make your company stand apart by enhancing a product in more subtle ways. Offer your customers unique and clever options — bells and whistles that they appreciate all the more because they don't expect them. Examples include a camera that reminds you when your batteries are getting low, a car with a built-in global positioning system (GPS) and cellular technology, an insurance policy that makes it easy to keep track of what you own and then automatically updates your coverage, and software that actually removes itself from your hard drive when you want to get rid of it.

Product quality

When you offer a quality product or service that customers recognize, you take a big step toward standing out in the marketplace. In some sense, quality captures what differentiation is all about. Quality is what everybody seems to look for, and it often depends on the eyes of the beholder. Although customers can't always tell you exactly what quality is, they know it when they see it; and when they see quality, they like it — and may even pay a little extra for it.

Customers are likely to perceive the quality of your products a bit differently than they do the quality of your services. The differences between product and service quality are wide enough, in fact, that we treat the two separately in Table 14-1.

Table 14-1	Product and Service Quality Examples
Product Quality	*Example*
Performance	Do pots and pans get clean in the dishwasher?
Consistency	Is the restaurant's pasta special always tasty?
Durability	How long will the hiking boots last?
Reliability	Will the answering machine save all the messages?
Appearance	Does the watch have that special look and feel?
Brand name	Which stereo system is known for its quality?
Service Quality	*Example*
Capability	Does the dental surgeon know what she's doing?
Dependability	Will the newspaper be delivered in the morning?
Responsiveness	Can the tow truck arrive in time?
Integrity	How much should the lawyer be trusted?
Attentiveness	Does the bank teller smile and say hello?
Tangibles	Which airline has the cleanest onboard restrooms?

The different quality dimensions depend on your industry and on the customers that you serve. Even in a particular industry, different companies create successful differentiation strategies for distinct dimensions. The auto industry is a prime example of product differentiation. When you think of Porsche, for example, you think of performance; Volvo signifies safety; and Toyota and Honda are energy-efficient, reliable choices. These differences allow competitors to prosper in the same industry, each in its own way.

Competition is a bit different in service industries. For one thing, you have to face the importance of customers' impressions when you deal with services. By definition, a service is something that you can't physically hold; you can't touch it, feel it, or kick its tires. So customers face a bit of a quandary when it comes to making well-informed decisions. Figuring out what is and isn't a quality service is harder. How do you know whether your accountant is a genius or an Enron expat? Is the pilot of your flight an ace or just so-so? Is your dentist a saint or a sadist?

Based on this lack of insider information, customer perception dominates the service industry. When customers don't have all the data, they go with what they can see. No matter what other dimensions are important, the tangibles — equipment, facilities, and personnel — play a significant part in a customer's perception of service quality. As an airline executive recently quipped:

Filthy restrooms and dirty trays are bound to lead to engine failure.

Because customers can't evaluate the quality of an airline's engine-maintenance program, they look at the tangibles that they *can* judge, and they form their opinions accordingly.

It's all in the marketing

Following are some examples of effective differentiating strategies using patriotic advertising, unique selling location, and warranties and maintenance programs:

✔ Molson's popular "I am Canadian" campaign featuring Joe — the average Canadian — led to a surge of national patriotism, increased brand recognition, and numerous ad and comic parodies.

✔ Avon products look a great deal like cosmetics that you can buy almost anywhere, but the Avon Lady still gets the attention of women across the country who want to be pampered on their sofas with their favourite skin-care products.

✔ Kenmore appliances are sturdy and well built, but much of their popularity stems from top-to-bottom warranties, service, and maintenance programs that include routine house calls.

✔ Tim Hortons isn't just any donut and coffee shop — it's down-home Canadian, which is reinforced in its TV advertisements of customers on cross-country and international adventures, so intensely loyal customers go there for not just a coffee but a Timmy's.

A special kind of horsepower

Massey-Harris's humble origins began in 1847, in Newcastle, Ontario, making simple farm implements. Now, after 150 years of evolution and mergers, the Massey-Ferguson (MF) brand of AGCO builds bright red tractors and implements for every type of agricultural operation in all parts of the world, as well as lawn and garden equipment. MF makes some of the best agricultural equipment in the world, but its customers are impressed by much more than just equipment prowess. What really sets this company apart is its long-held philosophy to deliver more to its customers than equipment. As well as providing per-purchase advise, assistance with financing, online used-equipment purchasing, and repair training, it has a best possible back-up: global capability to deliver spare parts on short notice — within 24 hours.

No doubt a big and expensive promise. MF and AGCO invested decades creating a global service network with distribution depots that can fulfill its commitment, which of course means higher prices for MF equipment. But customers don't mind paying those extra bucks because they know how much is at stake if they have to shut down a huge agricultural process for want of a spark plug or fan belt. So MF sells peace of mind along with its machinery. Customers are so loyal and delighted that they regularly frequent the online Massey Mall (www.massey mall.com) to purchase logo products, gifts, collectibles, and memorabilia.

Product packaging

Customers often look beyond the basics to make the final decision on what to buy. In fact, your packaging may influence customers as much as the standard set of features that your product or service offers. You can't judge a book by its cover, as the saying goes — but many people *buy* books simply because of that cover.

You can develop an effective differentiation strategy based on product or service packaging — how and where you advertise, what warranties or maintenance agreements you provide, and where you decide to sell your product or service.

With creative advertising, attentive service, and sophisticated distribution, you can make almost any product or service unique in one way or another. If you don't believe us, check out the produce section in an upscale market. The market routinely identifies fruit and vegetable bins by country, province, or even farm of origin. Signs tell customers whether the farmers grew the produce with or without chemicals and specify the harvest date. Each combination represents a differentiated product that the market advertises, displays, and prices based on the unique benefits that the product offers.

Focusing on focus

The two generic strategies we talk about in the preceding sections concentrate on one side of the customer value equation or the other (check out Chapter 8 for more info on value equations). A cost-leadership strategy points out the price tag, and differentiation emphasizes the unique benefits that a product or service offers. The final generic strategy plays off the first two strategies: A *focus strategy* aims at either price or uniqueness, but it concentrates on a smaller piece of the action.

A focus strategy works because you concentrate on a specific customer group. As a result, you do a better job of meeting those customers' particular needs than your competitors who try to serve larger markets. The following sections discuss several ways to concentrate your efforts.

Niche markets

Small, well-defined market segments provide an opportunity not only to meet customers' needs, but also to exceed their expectations. If you direct your efforts to the high-end market segments, you may be well rewarded for your attentions when the money starts rolling in. Small, upscale hotels, for example, pamper their well-heeled customers with valets, free glasses of champagne, and even limousine service to restaurants and the airport. In some large cities, catering companies now focus on a growing niche — dieters hoping to shed unwanted pounds — by offering Atkins or South Beach diet menus, or personalized special-needs menus.

Customers are willing to pay a premium for this kind of service, and that premium can mean big profits. Niche markets don't have to be upscale, of course; factory outlet stores thrive by serving cost-conscious customers who have high-end tastes. Often, niche markets are too small to be of interest to larger firms. This makes them particularly appealing to small companies or to new businesses.

Targeted products

Companies that flourish through volume sales in large markets often ignore so-called specialty products and services — all those non-standard items and services that have limited appeal and market potential. Large market companies that do step into a specialty business are usually inefficient at it; size and overhead costs simply work against them. Specialty products and services spell potential opportunity for a business with a focused strategy.

Specialty hardware manufacturers, for example, have found a ready market for their new lines of old hardware. As it turns out, antique screws, hinges, doorknobs, and hundreds of other hard-to-find items are absolute necessities for turning rundown row houses back into elegant Victorian ladies.

Limited territory

Focusing on geography can result in cost advantages, better-served markets, or both. Where local tastes are strong or service and distribution costs are particularly high, for example, a regional business can flourish. Independent restaurants and grocery stores, television stations, and newspapers all attract a community of customers who want to buy regional products, patronize neighbourhood shops, and receive local news. Commuter airlines focus on regional service by offering frequent flights and the best schedules to out-of-the-way destinations, and they keep costs down by flying smaller planes, limiting facilities, and running bare-bones operations. For example, in 2001, Ultimate Ski Vacations Inc. found a niche by offering skiers non-stop weekend and mid-week flights out of a private executive terminal at Person International Airport to Mount Tremblant's International Airport at fair prices — which sure beat driving for seven hours. They've now expanded their niche by offering other departure points, western Canadian ski resort destinations, and ski packages. Oh, and don't forget the other season — golf. They have that covered, as well.

A focus strategy works especially well for the new kids on the block who want to establish a foothold in an industry in which the big guys have already staked out their claims. Instead of going after those fat, juicy markets (and getting beat up right away), you can avoid head-on competition if you focus on smaller markets, which may be less attractive to existing players. After you establish yourself in a niche market, you may want to challenge the market leaders on their own turf. Monte Carlo Inns, for example, started out as a small regional chain that offered specialized services for the business traveler. Now, the company is expanding nationally and internationally.

For small, established companies in a market, a focus strategy may be the only ticket to survival when the big guys decide to come to town. If your company has few assets and limited options, concentrating on a specific customer segment gives you a fighting chance to leverage the capabilities and resources that you have.

Customer loyalty is a potent weapon, even against much larger companies. Wal-Mart, for example, now finds it more difficult to move their superstores into small rural towns and even big cities because the residents rally around the local businesses and merchants that have satisfied them over the years, despite the fact that Wal-Mart probably has a wider selection of products at lower prices.

Unfortunately, a focus strategy is one of the most difficult generic strategies to maintain over time. Dangers lurk both inside and outside the company. If your market suddenly gets much bigger, you can count on intense competition down the road from much bigger players with much deeper pockets.

And if your market niche remains small, you face a powerful urge to spread your wings and expand into new and different markets, even though you can lose many of your original strengths and advantages.

Your best bet is to stay focused. Small companies have the best chance of sticking around over the long haul if they rally around a strategy and business plan that concentrate their resources and capabilities. Focus your energy on serving a specific market segment better than the competition. The history of business is filled with tales of smallish companies that took on more than they could handle — and those stories don't end well.

Changing Your Boundaries

Generic strategies form the basic building blocks that you can use to start assembling your company's business plan (see the section "Applying Off-the-Shelf Strategies," earlier in this chapter). But building blocks are just the beginning. Strategy should also address all the fine details that make your company and its goals unique. How do you take the next step? A successful strategy and plan depend on your business circumstances — what's happening in your industry and marketplace, and what your competitors are up to. These factors often determine what strategy can best serve your company. Don't forget your potential customers — and their needs, wants, and demands. Remember, demands are wants backed by buying power.

Doing it all — or just one thing

Every industry has its own special personality. The major forces at work are distinct, the activities are special, and the key players are unique. So take a moment to review your notes on the structure of your industry and the nature of your competition. (If you need some guidance, flip back to Chapters 5 and 8.) One of the characteristics that should jump right out at you is the range of activities that define your industry. *Vertical integration* is a measure of how many phases of the business you and your competitors are involved in.

Vertically integrated companies are involved in many parts of an industry, from supplying raw materials to selling products and services to customers. Other companies tend to focus on one or two major aspects of the business. Some breweries, for example, concentrate on one central activity: the brewing of beer. Vertically integrated breweries also get involved in growing the barley and hops; in making the beer bottles, labels, and cans; in trucking the beer around; and even in running the pubs that sell the beer to all those loyal customers.

The art and business of bread making

George Weston started out way back in 1882, using $200 to purchase a simple, single bread route from his boss. He successfully grew the business, eventually selling two operations to Canada Bread and going on to build a modest chain of bakeries in Ontario before his death in 1924. His son, Garfield, promised to continue expanding the business — but how much bread can you sell?

With roots in the bakery sector, Garfield achieved impressive growth through vertical integration. He bought companies in manufacturing — food and non-food, distribution and retail. So, when he finished buying all the companies he wanted, Weston's not only had a chain of grocery stores to sell its own bread, chocolate bars, and butter, it also supplied the sugar, milk, and cream that went into those products — plus, they provided the paper and cardboard that wrapped and boxed those products.

Integration was deep. Over the years, George Weston Limited's acquisitions included the pulp and paper companies E.B. Eddy Paper Co. and Somerville Industries; food processors Nabob Coffee, Westcane Sugar, chocolate company William Neilson Co. Ltd., and Donlands Dairy; and fisheries that hatch, grow, and process farmed salmon. Food distribution is operated under Loblaw Companies Limited with store banners of Loblaws, Atlantic Superstore, Provigo, the Real Canadian Warehouse, valu-mart, and Fortinos — to name a few.

Weston's has gone on to become one of the largest success stories of private-label marketing with the brands President's Choice, No Name, and Exact. It continues the strategy of vertical integration by increasing its offering of non-food products and services, such as financial services under the brand President's Choice Financial, and a points-based reward system to maintain and increase customers' loyalty.

Today, George Weston Limited is a publicly traded company headquartered in Toronto and is one of North America's largest processors and distributors of food products. The company has annual revenues in excess of $30 billion and international holdings in South America, Europe, Africa, and Australia. Now, that's a lot of dough!

Exactly where does your company stand in terms of vertical integration in your industry? This is an important question because it affects your decision about changing your boundaries and becoming more or less vertically integrated over time. Business gurus have coined a couple of terms to describe the strategic moves that you may decide to make:

✔ **Backward integration:** Extending your business activities in a direction that brings you closer to the raw materials, resources, and expertise that go into creating and producing your company's products

✔ **Forward integration:** Extending your business activities in a direction that brings you closer to the marketplace by involving the company in packaging, marketing, distribution, and customer sales

✔ **Divesting:** Reducing your company's activities to focus on specific aspects of your business by spinning off or selling other pieces of the company

Tables 14-2 and 14-3 describe some of the pros and cons of vertical integration.

Table 14-2	Pros of Vertical Integration
Pro	*Reason*
Efficiencies	If you're in charge, you may find it easier to coordinate activities at the various business stages along the way by combining related functions or by getting rid of overlapping areas to streamline your overall operations.
Resources	If you have a hand in the upstream (early-stage) activities of a business, you can guarantee that your company has access to the raw materials and resources that it needs to stay in business.
Customers	If your company is involved in downstream (late-stage) activities, you not only get to know a great deal about customers, but you also create lasting relationships and secure your own long-term access to the market.

Table 14-3	Cons of Vertical Integration
Con	*Reason*
Overhead	If you try to control all stages of your industry, you can run into extra expenses because of mismatched operations, idle resources, and added coordination costs.
Mediocrity	If your company is involved in a wide range of activities, being the best at any of them is much tougher, and the company risks becoming average in everything that it does.
Size and slowness	If your company is vertically integrated, your size often makes it difficult to quickly respond to change, and commitments to various parts of the industry leave you little room for flexibility.

Vertical integration has benefits and drawbacks, which explains why industries have seen swings in the popularity of vertically integrated companies over the years. The race to break up companies and concentrate on specific business activities follows a rush toward control of all aspects of an industry. And the cycle repeats.

One characteristic seems to hold true across the swings and cycles of vertically integrated companies within an industry: The most successful and profitable companies often do business at one of the two extremes of integration. Heavily integrated companies reap all the benefits of vertical integration; those that concentrate on a single activity eliminate all the costs and inefficiencies. Whatever you do, don't get stuck in the middle — with few of the benefits and too many of the costs.

Outsourcing and off-shoring

Today, standard business wisdom favours strategies that streamline companies, transforming them into leaner and meaner versions of themselves. After all, worldwide competition over the past two decades has made it more cost-effective to go out and buy the services and resources that you need rather than build them up inside the company. This practice is commonly known as *outsourcing* — or *off-shoring,* if you purchase those services and resources outside the country in the global marketplace. In each case, the clever idea is to take a piece of your business operations — your payroll system or your computer support, for example — and hire an operation on the outside to do it for you, saving you money.

Outsourcing can help you do what you do better. When you no longer have to worry about certain parts of your business, you can focus your energies on the operations that you do best and the activities that set you apart from the competition. In a recent survey of senior operating executives in more than 290 businesses in 19 countries, findings show that outsourcing is growing. Sixty-eight percent of respondents said that, as well as reducing costs and accessing additional talent and capabilities, outsourcing allows for more strategic flexibility and control over their business planning. Sixty-six percent also said outsourcing allows their companies to achieve better quality results, reinvent their business models, and drive innovation.

Which business functions do companies outsource most often? In that same survey, information technology came up as the most commonly outsourced activity at 57 percent, followed by the production or delivery of core products or services (53 percent), logistics and distribution (51 percent), human resources services (35 percent), sales and marketing (33 percent), innovation and R&D (32 percent), call centres (25 percent), and finance and accounting (24 percent). Outsourcing has grown more than 14 percent in the last decade, and the survey predicts continued growth.

If you decide to outsource a piece of your business, make sure to do your homework ahead of time. The companies you select as partners become a very real part of your business, so see how they fit in with the values and vision you have for your company (for a refresher on values and vision, flip back to Chapter 3). Their activities affect the way you work, the way your competitors react, and the way your customers see you in the future. So approach an outsourcing relationship like you would a marriage contract — as a serious commitment.

Leading and Following

No matter what industry you're in, you can divide your competition into two major groups: the market leaders and the market followers nipping at their heels. *Market leaders* are top-tier companies that dominate the marketplace, set the agenda for the industry, and make things happen; they occupy the driver's seat. The *market followers,* well, follow along. These companies work hard, think big, and keep the market leaders on their toes.

Depending on the market situation, companies in both groups behave very differently. Whether you already operate as part of an industry or you want to join one as a new business owner, you need to understand what motivates both the market leaders and the rest of the pack. The following sections explore some market strategies that focus on industry position.

Market-leader strategies

Market leadership varies, from the absolute dominance of one company to shared control of the industry by several leading players. If you enjoy a spot among the leaders, look at these possible strategic approaches:

- **Full speed ahead.** In this situation, your company is the clear market leader. Even so, you should always try to break farther away from the pack. You should strive to make the first move, whether you implement new technology and introduce innovative products, or promote new uses and set aggressively low prices. You should not only intend to stay on top, but also want to expand your lead.

- **Hold the line.** Your company certainly ranks high in the top tier of the market, but it doesn't have a commanding position of strength in the industry, so your goals centre on hanging on to what you currently have. Those goals may involve locking distributors into long-term contracts to make it more difficult for customers to switch to competing brands, or going after new market segments and product areas to block competitors from doing the same thing.

✔ **Steady as she goes.** In this case, your company is one of several power-ful companies in the market. As one among equals, your company takes on part of the responsibility of policing the industry to see that nothing upsets the boat. If an upstart challenger tries to cut prices, you quickly match those lower prices. You always scan the horizon for new competi-tors, and you work hard to discourage distributors, vendors, and retail-ers from adding new companies and brands to their lists.

Market-follower strategies

Market followers often take their cues and develop strategies based on the strength and behaviour of the market leaders. An aggressive challenger, for example, may not thrive in an industry that has a powerful, assertive com-pany on top. Fortunately, you can choose among several strategic alterna-tives if you find yourself in the market-follower position:

✔ **Make some waves.** Your company has every intention of growing bigger by increasing its presence in the industry, and you're willing to challenge the market leadership head-on to do it. Perhaps your strategy includes an aggressive price-cutting campaign to gain market share. Maybe you back up this campaign with a rapid expansion of distribution outlets and a forceful marketing effort. This strategy requires deep pockets, commit-ment, and the skill to force a market leader to blink, but in the end, your efforts could make you the leader of the pack.

✔ **Turn a few heads.** Your company enjoys success in its market niche, and you want it to stay that way. So although you don't want to chal-lenge the market leadership directly, you fiercely defend your turf. You have strengths and advantages in your market segment because of your product and customer loyalty. To maintain this position, you focus on customer benefits and the value that you bring to the market.

✔ **Just tag along.** You can easily point out companies that have settled into complacency. Frankly, they usually operate in rather boring industries in which not much ever happens. These companies are quite happy to remain toward the end of the pack, tagging along without a worry. Don't count on them to do anything new or different in the marketplace. (If you find your company in this position, you may be quite happy to tag along, too. If not, you should think about making a change while you're still awake.)

Experts tell us that only 10 percent of companies execute their strategy — they're the companies that excel in their field. So, after you finish crafting your master strategy, remember to include an implementation plan and mea-sure your progress monthly and quarterly. At the end of the year, you won't be one of those 90 percent who wonder what went wrong.

Working together: The power of standards

The world has become a very connected place over the last century. Today, planes, trains, automobiles, telephones, and the Internet connect nations and people. And we expect everything around us to connect as well: the television, the DVD player, the computer, the MP3 player, and the cellphone. What makes all these connections possible? Standards. Without standards — the technological details that everyone in an industry agrees upon — all the networks that define the modern world would simply disappear. Standards are such an important part of business in the 21st century that every industry imaginable has a standards committee that defines the rules for its particular technologies to follow.

If your company sets the standards in your industry, you gain a powerful advantage in the marketplace. In many markets, only one standard can exist. Microsoft DOS and Windows won out over the Macintosh operating system, and VHS videotapes triumphed over Sony Betamax. You don't have to worry that the CD or DVD you buy won't play in your particular CD player or DVD player because they all use the same standard format. The leaders don't always produce the best products available, but after a standard emerges, other companies find it almost impossible to unseat the market leader. Just check out what's happening with iPod clones or just look-a-likes — although less expensive, their market share is miniscule in comparison to Apple's.

Tailoring Your Own Strategy

You may feel overwhelmed by all the strategic possibilities and choices you have to make in devising a strategy for your company. Stop, take a deep breath, and remember: Strategy isn't a test that you take once and have to get a perfect score on the first time. Instead, it helps you decide how to do business over the long haul. Strategy is an ongoing process, so don't be alarmed if you can't immediately see how all the pieces fit together. And don't be surprised if you need to tinker with the "Company Strategy" section of your business plan along the way.

Coming up with the right strategy is something that you have the chance to work on over and over again — rethinking, revising, and reformulating. If you approach strategy in the right way, you don't ever finish the task.

As you begin to shape your strategy, let the following pointers guide you:

- ✔ Never develop a strategy without first doing your homework.
- ✔ Always have a clear set of goals and objectives in front of you.
- ✔ Reflect on your assumptions and make sure they reflect reality.
- ✔ Build in flexibility and always have an alternate strategy.

- ✔ Understand the needs, desires, and nature of your customers.
- ✔ Know your competitors and don't underestimate them.
- ✔ Leverage your strengths and minimize your weaknesses.
- ✔ Emphasize core competence (covered in Chapter 10) to sustain your competitive advantage.
- ✔ Make your strategy clear, concise, consistent, and attainable.
- ✔ Trumpet the strategy so you don't leave your organization guessing.

These guidelines aren't only helpful for creating a strategy, they're also useful for reviewing and revising one. Make sure you return to this list regularly as part of an ongoing commitment to your company strategy and business plan. How often should you review the "Company Strategy" section of your plan? It depends on how often changes occur in your industry and marketplace. Try to review the section at least once a year and whenever major changes occur.

Companies that take strategy and business planning seriously know that to hit a target, you follow the path of "ready, aim, fire" — not "ready, fire, aim." In other words, almost any strategy is better than no strategy at all. Companies that have clear strategies don't hit the bull's eye every time; no strategy can promise that. But these companies succeed in the end because they subscribe to a strategic process that forces them to ask the right questions and come up with good answers — answers that help them outshine the competition. And especially in a new venture, a clear and compelling strategy can help you attract funding and employees.

Chapter 15

Growing Up and Growing Bigger

. . . .

. . . .

*W*atching over a product or service while it makes its way through the cold, cruel marketplace is an awesome responsibility. It requires a major commitment of time and resources, as well as a great deal of careful planning. First, you have to understand what you must do to make the product a success. Which attributes and aspects should you stress? How do you make sure that people take notice (and like what they see)? How can you support and guide your product or service along the way, getting it into the right hands? You need to take advantage of opportunities when they appear. At the same time, you have to worry about lurking threats and competitive pressures.

Does this process sound a lot like rearing a child? Well, your product is your baby, and as any parent knows, you have to face one darn thing after another. Think about how many times you've heard a parent say, "You think they're difficult now? Just wait!"

Products and kids have a great deal in common — both of their worlds continually change, yet they eventually manage to grow up. A key difference for new businesses is that you must ruthlessly reinvent and reshape your product or service to respond to your markets and industry (something that you may want to avoid as a parent). For decades, the Dr. Spocks of the business world have poked, probed, pinched, and prodded products at all ages, and they've come up with a useful description of the common stages that almost all products go through. When you create a business plan, you have to plan for the changes in your product's life cycle.

In this chapter, we explain the product life cycle and what it means for your company. You find out about ways to keep your company growing. We also show you how to expand into new markets with existing products, as well as how to extend your product line to better serve current customers. We explore the opportunities and pitfalls of trying to diversify. You'll find out about strategic business units (SBUs) and several portfolio tools to help you plan and manage a growing family of products.

Facing Up to the Product Life Cycle

In business, the only constant is — you guessed it — change. The forces of change are everywhere, ranging from major trends in your business environment to the shifting tastes and demands of your customers to the unpredictable behaviour of your competitors. (For more info on change and how to prepare for it, check out Chapter 13.)

You may think that all these factors, stirred together, create a world filled with chaos and uncertainty. Sometimes, they do. But, normally, business changes follow orderly and even predictable patterns. Experts have plotted some of these basic patterns, and the cycles that they've come up with aptly describe what happens in the face of all the market turmoil and confusion.

One of these patterns — the *product life cycle* — illustrates what happens to a new kind of product or service after you launch it in the market. The cycle describes four major stages that a new product likely goes through:

- ✔ An introduction period
- ✔ A growth period
- ✔ Maturity
- ✔ A period of decline

The product life cycle is closely related to how eager people are to try out a new product or service. (For a refresher on customer personality types and the diffusion of innovation in the marketplace, flip back to Chapter 6.) Most product life cycles look something like Figure 15-1.

The curve traces your product sales volume over time. You can think about sales volume in terms of the revenue that you take in or the number of units that you sell. You may end up measuring the time scale in weeks, months, years, or even decades.

Every stage of your product's life cycle presents a unique set of market conditions and a series of planning challenges. The different stages require different management objectives, strategies, and skills. The following sections discuss what you should think about at each stage.

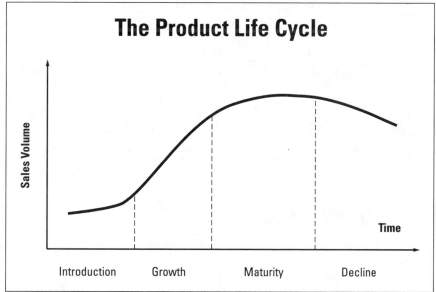

Figure 15-1:
The product
life cycle
represents
what's likely
to happen
to sales
volume for
a typical
product
over time.

Starting out

After you introduce a new kind of product or service in the market, that product or service begins to generate revenue. Because developing and launching something new is expensive, costs are relatively high at this stage and you normally don't find many competitors around. Growth depends on your company's ability to make the product, generate market awareness, and get customers to accept and adopt the new product.

At this stage in the product life cycle, your efforts focus on getting the product out the door or rolling out the new service — and ensuring that everything works according to plan. At the same time, you have to drum up plenty of interest while you struggle to create market awareness. Table 15-1 points out many characteristics of the introduction stage.

Table 15-1	Major Characteristics of the Introduction Stage
Component	*Characteristics*
Industry	One or two companies
Competition	Little or none
Key function	Research and development
Customers	Innovators and risk-takers
Finances	High prices and expenses
Profits	Nonexistent to negative
Objectives	Product adoption, building customer awareness
Strategy	Expanding the total market

Growing up

During the growth stage, the new product or service gains a reputation. If the product or service involves a new technology, the industry leaders agree upon *standards* — all the details that determine how the technology should work (see Chapter 14 for additional info). Demand rises rapidly, and sales increase. Competition increases as competing products jump into the fray to take advantage of an expanding market. Customers begin to develop brand loyalties, and companies tweak their product features to better serve customer needs — needs that you can now recognize (if you need a reminder, see Chapter 7).

In the growth stage, your priorities should turn toward meeting growing product demand, improving your product or service, and targeting specific groups of customers. Along the way, you have to fend off a growing crop of competitors. Table 15-2 highlights characteristics of the growth stage.

Table 15-2	Major Characteristics of the Growth Stage
Component	*Characteristics*
Industry	Many companies
Competition	Growing strength and numbers
Key function	Marketing

Component	Characteristics
Customers	Eager to try products
Finances	Variable prices and costs
Profits	Growing rapidly
Objectives	Sales growth and market share
Strategy	Establishing and defending position

Maturing in middle age

The growth of your product or service begins to slow in the maturity stage, when market demand levels off and new customers become harder to find. New competitors are also harder to find, so the competition stabilizes. Profits keep on growing, however, while your costs continue to fall. Changes in market share reflect changes in the value that customers place on the competing products, and an increase in market share for one product usually comes at the expense of its competitors.

At this stage, your attention should turn toward reducing costs and finally reaping the benefits of stable profits. Although you can easily feel comfortable at this stage, you need to keep a careful eye on the competition and begin to think about what happens in the final stage — decline. Table 15-3 identifies the characteristics of the maturity stage.

Table 15-3	Major Characteristics of the Maturity Stage
Component	Characteristics
Industry	Not as many companies
Competition	Stronger, but stable
Key function	Operations
Customers	The majority of buyers
Finances	Competitive prices and lower costs
Profits	At or near peak
Objectives	Cash flow and profit
Strategy	Maintaining competitive position

Riding out the senior stretch

At some point in a product's life cycle, sales usually start to fall off and revenue begins to decline. Competitors drop out of the market when profits all but disappear. Large-scale changes in the economy or in technology may trigger the decline stage, or the decline may simply reflect changing customer needs and behaviour. At this stage, you must redesign, reposition, or replace products still on the market.

When a product's life cycle begins its decline, your work shifts to redesigning your product or redefining its market. You can also come up with new uses or different kinds of customers. If all your attempts fail, you have to concentrate on ways to get out of the market so that you don't lose too much money. Table 15-4 shows various characteristics of the decline stage.

Table 15-4	Major Characteristics of the Decline Stage
Component	*Characteristics*
Industry	Few companies
Competition	Declining in number
Key function	Finance and planning
Customers	Loyal, conservative buyers
Finances	Falling prices and low costs
Profits	Much reduced
Objectives	Residual profits
Strategy	Getting out alive

Gauging where you are now

Take your product or service and see whether you can figure out its estimated position on the product life-cycle curve (refer to Figure 15-1). Even experts don't find this life-cycle placement an easy task. Do the best you can, but don't delude yourself about its position by being either too optimistic or too pessimistic. If you're stumped, ask yourself the following questions:

- ✔ How long has the product been on the market?
- ✔ How rapidly is the market growing?
- ✔ Is the growth rate increasing, decreasing, or flat?

✔ Is the product profitable?

✔ Are profits heading up or down?

✔ How fast are product features changing?

✔ How many competitors does the product have?

✔ Does the market now have more or fewer competing products, compared to a year ago?

Even if you feel confident about your product's position on the life-cycle curve, take the time to confirm your analysis. You're likely to get mixed signals from the marketplace, and the clues you find may even contradict one another. No two products ever behave the same way when it comes to the product life cycle. Unfortunately, acting prematurely on the evidence at hand can lead to hasty planning and a self-fulfilling prophecy.

Suppose that the widget manager at Global Gizmos Company detects a slow-down in widget sales. As a faithful believer in the absolute law of the product life cycle, she comes to the conclusion that the growth stage for widgets is finally coming to an end. What does she do? She begins to think about ways to reduce costs. Maybe she cuts the advertising budget and begins to phase out incentives for the sales force. What happens? Sales of widgets decline even further, just as she predicted. So she pats herself on the back for being the first to recognize the early stages of a worldwide widget decline.

But what if the sales slump is caused by a bit of bad weather, some delivery problems, or any number of other reasons? By substituting blind faith in a business textbook for her own good judgment and careful analysis, the widget manager actually aided a reversible outcome that she so confidently predicted in the first place.

What good is a business concept if you can't really count on it? Well, don't get us wrong. The product life cycle is a powerful planning tool if you use it to support — not replace — your own solid skills. When you deploy it as an early warning system, the product life cycle alerts you to potential changes, allowing you time to plan for a different business environment and to respond quickly when your product finally enters a new stage in its life. But you should always double-check what you think you see to make sure you don't mistake a temporary hiccup in sales for a full-scale life-cycle change.

Finding Ways to Expand

Face it — your product simply isn't going to be the same tomorrow as it is today. You may not plan to change it at all, but everything around your product is going to change. The world will take another step ahead. The economy, technology, your industry, and the competition will all change. As a result, your current and future customers may think about your company and your product a bit differently, even if you don't.

How can you find ways to grow and prosper as a company in the face of almost-certain product mortality? You probably have every intention of creating a new business plan when your product begins to age (beyond turning off the lights and locking all the doors). But which way do you turn? Doing nothing shouldn't be an option. But what alternatives do you have?

Fortunately, you don't have to invent the alternatives yourself; planning for long-term growth has been a philosophical favourite of management gurus for decades. One of the pioneers of business-growth techniques was a guy named Igor Ansoff. He came up with a simple matrix to represent the possible directions of growth (see Figure 15-2).

The road not taken

If we had to name the single product that had the greatest impact over the last century, we'd choose the automobile. But you may not have guessed that in the early days of the automobile. In the 1890s, bizarre four-wheel contraptions lurched around everywhere. They sputtered, sometimes careening forward, propelled by steam turbines, gasoline engines, electric motors, you name it — probably even by nuclear power, had it been around at the time. But the fledgling automotive industry faced a hurdle: getting folks to try these strange horseless carriages.

By 1905, after a bit of coaxing, the idea of automobiles as serious transportation began to catch on. Henry Ford introduced his Model T in 1908 and sold 10,000 of them for a hefty $825 each. In five years, annual sales rose to a half million cars, and by the mid-1920s, 15 million Model Ts had rolled off Ford's factory floor. Ford Motor Company drove the Model T up the product life-cycle growth curve and straight into its maturity. Ford produced almost half the cars in the world. Although the price of a T fell to $260 by 1925, the assembly-line efficiency and sheer volume of cars sold allowed profit margins to remain high. Business was good.

Business was *too* good, as it turned out. Henry Ford was successful at introducing, growing, and maintaining his product for many years. But he was so intent on reducing costs and expanding capacity that he failed to see the early signs of a decline. He didn't see that his beloved Model T was going out of fashion.

Ford should have looked ahead and adjusted his objectives and strategies for a new set of ground rules — guidelines governed by consumers who wanted more features and options. But he didn't. As a result, he was forced to shut down operations for most of 1927 while he retooled to compete against General Motors in a changing marketplace. During the course of that year, Ford lost $200 million and laid off at least 60,000 workers.

Figure 15-2:
The Growth
Directions
Matrix
describes
different
ways in
which your
company
can grow,
based on a
combination
of products
and
markets.

The Growth Directions Matrix captures nothing more than basic common sense: It says that if you want to make your business grow, you have to start somewhere. Start by taking advantage of where you are today and what you have to work with. How fast you grow in any direction depends on your capabilities and resources, as well as the rate of change in your industry. Consider the following ways in which you can move your company ahead:

✔ **Existing product, existing market:** Continue to grow by doing what you do now, but do it a little bit better. Customers will use more of your product or service more often and in more ways than before. Encourage people to use more toothpaste, for example, by encouraging them to brush their teeth (or, heck, even their dogs' teeth) more often. You can also increase your promotional efforts and marketing communication to encourage existing customers to use your product more often.

✔ **New market, existing product:** Grow in the short term by finding a fresh market for your existing product, either by expanding geographically or by reaching out to completely different kinds of customers. If you make baking soda, for example, get people who use baking soda in their favourite cakes and cookies to also put it in their refrigerators to keep them odour-free.

✔ **New product, existing market:** Grow by developing additional product features, options, or even a related product family that you hope will entice your existing customers. Think of the array of cranberry drinks you see available these days — everything from cranapple to crankiwi.

✔ **New market, new product:** Grow over the long term by going after new and unfamiliar markets with new and different products. Ford Motor Company, for example, used to make and sell prefabricated homes.

Without getting bogged down in a lot of details, try to come up with a dozen different ways to grow your company. Get yourself into the right frame of mind by reviewing your company's vision and mission statements. (Don't have 'em? Flip to Chapters 3 and 4 for everything that you need to know.) After you review the statements, complete the following steps:

1. **Identify three things that you can do right away to stimulate demand for your existing product in your current markets.**

   Offer rebates, start a sales promotion, hold a contest, or maybe come up with some new product uses.

2. **List three steps that you can take in the next six months to capture new markets for your existing product.**

   Create radio or television ads that target new customers; advertise in the local newspaper; use outdoor ads, such as billboards, outdoor benches, or bus shelters; start direct-mail and e-mail campaigns; or step up appearances at trade shows. Also, drive business to your Web site by including your Web address in all the forms of advertising that you use.

3. **Specify three developmental efforts that you can launch over the coming year to extend your current product line.**

   Enhance product features, add options or offer different sizes, or bundle products and services together. Talk to your customers and front-line staff to get a feel for evolving needs and demands.

4. **Describe three directions that you can take over the next three to five years that could move new products into new markets.**

   Engage in brainstorming sessions with colleagues or trusted advisers to come up with growth opportunities that play into current company strengths. Looking at the examples that other successful companies provide may inspire you — no one said you have to re-invent the wheel.

Many experts believe that any talk about brand-new products for completely new markets is really none of your business as a manager. These financial gurus think that managers are simply too biased to be objective when it comes to assessing totally new opportunities. They argue that you should return all your extra profits to investors and let them decide where to place their bets on the future. Unfortunately, investors have also made monumental mistakes in the past.

But the experts do bring up a good point. Although product innovation and expansion into new markets can be tremendously important to the growth and profitability of your business, growth in new directions is a very tricky — and risky — business. You should proceed in this particular direction only after you review your strengths and weaknesses as a company and assess all the opportunities and threats in front of you. For the complete low-down on SWOT (strengths, weaknesses, opportunities, and threats) analysis, check out Chapter 9.

Existing product and existing market

Many big-name companies have grown and achieved success by relentlessly pursuing a single business, a single market, or even an individual product decade after decade. When you see a Coca-Cola sign, for example, you imagine drinking a Coke. When you pass a Tim Hortons, you probably picture a coffee and donut. And when you hear the name Bell, Telus, or SaskTel, you think of picking up a telephone. But these companies haven't turned into billion-dollar corporations simply by launching their flagship products and letting the marketplace take care of the rest. Companies that largely depend on a single product spend enormous amounts of time and effort to continually rejuvenate and revitalize their core markets.

These companies invest heavily in the top-left box of the Growth Directions Matrix, shown in Figure 15-2. How do they make this single-box investment with success? They use these four main strategies:

✔ **Encourage greater product use.** You can increase demand by encouraging your customers to consume more of a product or service every time they use it. Maybe that means getting customers to feel good about buying more or giving them a better deal when they do. Customers may

- Buy larger bottles of cola because they can save money.

- Apply for more insurance coverage because you carefully show them that it's the prudent thing to do.

- Bundle their telephone, Internet, wireless, and cable access with one provider to gain better features and more savings.

- Opt for a packaged computer or stereo system that has extra components because they can easily assemble it all at the same time.

✔ **Generate more-frequent product use.** You can stimulate sales by getting customers to use your product or service more often. That may mean making the product more convenient, introducing it as part of a customer's regular routine, or offering incentives to frequent customers. Customers may

- Use toothpaste after every meal because of the hygienic value or for the greater sex appeal of whiter teeth and fresher breath.

- Regularly drink red wine at dinner because they've heard of its health benefits.

- Join a loyalty program and make extra purchases just to build more reward points.

✔ **Devise new uses.** You can expand your market by coming up with new ways for customers to use your product or service. That may include getting customers to use the product at different times, in different places, on novel occasions, or in unconventional ways. Customers may

- Snack on breakfast cereal during the day because you make it a low-calorie, healthy "comfort food."

- Put a radio in the shower and a DVD player in the car.

- Make digital videos of every imaginable event, from childbirth to pet funerals.

✔ **Woo customers away from competitors.** You can increase demand for your product or service the old-fashioned way: Take customers away from the competition. Although the result is sometimes a fierce and unwanted response from competitors, you can

- Create incentives for customers to switch from competing products, make the switch easy, and give them rewards for staying put with your product or service.

- Concentrate on becoming the most attractive low-cost provider around because of your unbeatable prices.

- Package a distinctive product so that it stands out in the marketplace.

- Focus on meeting or exceeding the needs of specific customer groups.

Companies that manage to grow in the same market with the same product do so by continually generating new demand and maintaining or even increasing their market share. Often, these companies succeed in slowing the product life cycle, extending its maturity stage almost indefinitely. In some cases, they even manage to reset the life cycle, pulling the product back into the growth stage by inventing new and creative products and uses, such as Research In Motion (RIM) does with its BlackBerry by expanding the product lines to the 8800 Series and Pearl. But steady and sustained market penetration based on a single product doesn't always work forever, and you sometimes have to look in new directions for growth.

How to build an empire going in the hole

The place: Hamilton, Ontario. The year: 1964. The result: a Canadian success story. When the first store opened, little did Tim Horton and franchisee Ron Joyce know that they'd be part of a major change in the way Canadians experience breakfast and coffee breaks. Their original goal was to offer top-quality, always-fresh products. The modest offerings consisted of only two products — coffee and donuts. However, they were already innovating with two original creations, the Apple Fritter and the Dutchie.

In the early '70s, food service experts predicted that people would eat two out of three meals a day away from the home because of people's increasingly busy schedules and full wallets. That prediction was good news for the 40 Tim Hortons stores. When customer demand grew and tastes changed, so did the number of stores and variety of products. By the end of the decade, Tim Hortons owned 100 stores and had introduced the phenomenally successful *Timbit* — a bite-sized donut hole.

That donut hole hollowed out a growth spurt for the fledgling chain. Over the next two decades, Tim Hortons expanded its franchise holdings across Canada, from coast to coast, and in a number of directions — market penetration, new markets, new products. In addition to their stand-alone stores, Tim Hortons opened locations in shopping malls, highway outlets, universities, and hospitals. Their standard locations offered 24-hour drive-through service, and the combo-unit locations housed both a Tim Hortons and a Wendy's. By the mid '90s, they opened the first U.S. store. However, the customer base and its tastes were maturing, and the competition positioned itself to satisfy those customers. Tim's countered the competitive move, and introduced more new products, including muffins, cakes, pies, croissants, and cookies, then soups, and chili. The successful donut chain also looked for new kinds of products and customers.

Timmy's, as the chain's fans affectionately call it, focused on satisfying loyal customers' on-the-go and dashboard dining demand. Bagels and sandwiches were introduced in the later '90s, along with specialty coffee drinks. Tim Hortons took advantage of market opportunities and leveraged its resources — locations, facilities, equipment, and very loyal customers — to expand its breakfast offerings, adding its Cinnamon Roll, Yogurt & Berries, and hot Breakfast Sandwich, and to launch lunch and dinner markets of sandwiches and wraps. The company is now traded on the New York and Toronto stock exchanges. It has more than 2,700 stores in Canada (almost twice as many as McDonald's), 345 in the United States, and 1 in Kandahar, Afghanistan. Not bad for a little Canadian company selling holes! By the way, the goal is still "always fresh."

New market or new product

At some point during the life of your company, a single product or service may not be enough to sustain an attractive level of growth in your business. Where do you turn? The Growth Directions Matrix (Figure 15-2) suggests that the most reliable and productive paths point to market expansion in the short term, as well as to extending your product line. These two directions for growth have the distinct advantage of building on capabilities and resources that you already have. Market expansion leverages your current product expertise, and product extension builds on your experience and knowledge of your current customers and the marketplace.

Successful big-name companies, such as Coca-Cola, Tim Hortons, Telus, and Chapters.Indigo.ca, are much bigger than just the flagship products and services that you associate with them. If you look closely at the ways in which they grow, they almost always do so through a combination of expanding into new markets and extending their product lines. Telus looks for new customers in both local and foreign markets, and it also offers a range of technology and service solutions, including contact centres and business process services. Coca-Cola enters new markets throughout the developing world by offering a family of cola beverages that includes Classic Coke, Diet Coke, and Caffeine-Free Coke. Tim Hortons is always open, offering breakfast sandwiches, Timbits, soup, sandwiches, and chili. And how about Chapters.Indigo.ca? It has gone from being Canada's largest online bookstore to being one of Canada's largest online sellers of everything from yoga mats to iPods.

New market

You can expand into a new market rather quickly by taking advantage of your current business model and copying many of your current business activities — producing, assembling, and distributing products, for example.

Going after new markets involves risk, however. New markets force you to conduct business on a larger scale. New markets mean wooing new customers and dealing with new competitors. When you enter a new market, you're the new kid on the block again, and you have to prove yourself at every step.

You can expand your market by moving into new geographical areas or going after new market segments:

- ✔ **Geography:** The most obvious way to grow beyond your core product and market is to expand geographically, picking up new customers based solely on where they live and work. This kind of expansion has many advantages. You not only do business in the same way as before, but you also have a head start in understanding many of your new customers, even with their regional differences. Because geographic expansion may require you to do business in unfamiliar areas or even in new countries, however, you have to pay special attention to how your company must change to accommodate the specific demands of your expanded market.

✔ **New market segments:** Sometimes, you can expand the market for your product or service by finding new kinds of customers. If you're creative, you can identify a group of customers that you neglected in the past. Look carefully at your product's features and packaging, how you price and deliver it, who buys it, and why they buy it. Also, reassess the customer benefits that you provide. Ask yourself how attractive a new market segment is in terms of its size and potential to grow. What strengths do you bring to the market? What competitors are already there? How do you plan to gain an advantage over the long haul? (Check out Chapter 6 for more on market segments.)

New product

If you want to extend the number of products or types of services that you offer, start planning well ahead of launching it into the marketplace. All too often, companies develop new product features, options, and major enhancements without giving much thought to the implications for the company's future direction and growth. Instead, a customer asks for this or that special feature, or a distributor requests a particular option or accessory, and before you know it, you have additional products to support.

The good news, of course, is that you already have customers. But you also have to be sure that your customers represent a larger market that benefits from your product extension. Also, the additional products need to make sense in terms of your business strategy and plan.

You can extend your product line or service by offering new features and options, or by creating related families of products:

✔ **New features and options:** The most common way to extend a product line involves adding bells and whistles to your product and giving customers the chance to choose which bells and whistles they want. The advantages are easy to tick off: You work from your existing strengths in product design and development, and you use your customers to help you decide which incremental changes to make. It sounds like the perfect game plan.

The danger comes from losing track of the bigger picture — where you want your company to end up. Individual customers, no matter how good and loyal they are, don't always reflect the direction of larger markets. So avoid creating a bunch of marginal products that you can't successfully sell or support. Instead, plan to develop a smaller number of products with features and options that you design to meet the needs of specific market segments.

✔ **Related product groups:** You may create a group of products based on a common element of some sort. You can develop a product family to use the same core technology, meet a series of related customer needs, or serve as accessories for your primary product.

You want the product group to look stronger in the market than the individual products do separately. That way, you reduce the risks inherent in product development, and the rewards are potentially greater. Take time to understand just how products in the group actually work together. Also, make sure that you address the separate challenges that each product poses in terms of customers, the competition, your company vision and mission (refer to Chapters 3 and 4, respectively), and your company's assets and capabilities.

Before you put your plans for growth into action, make sure that they draw on your company's strengths, reflect the capabilities and resources that you have available, and help maintain your competitive advantage. Think about the following questions:

✔ How well are you doing in the markets that you currently occupy?

✔ In what ways is the expanded market different from your current market?

✔ What parts of your business can you leverage in the expanded market?

✔ What functions and activities need to change to accommodate more products?

✔ How well does your extended product line meet specific customer needs?

✔ Is your extended product family stronger than each product by itself?

✔ How easily can you scale up your business to meet the expected growth?

✔ How will your competitive environment change?

Growth can be painful. It can take a company away from its roots and change that company's culture. You should think carefully about the tradeoffs; are they worth it personally and for all the stakeholders of the firm?

New product and new market

Has your company hit a midlife crisis? Do you find yourself searching for attractive new customers, sexy technologies, and aggressive competition? The need for rejuvenation comes to many companies at different times. A plan to move in new directions often involves diversifying the company, a move down into the bottom-right corner of the Growth Directions Matrix (refer to Figure 15-2). That corner, after all, is where the grass — and the profits — always look much greener.

You have to weigh the potential rewards against the challenges and risks that go along with diversification. Too many companies end up looking foolish when they try to figure out new tricks in unfamiliar businesses without much time to practice — and they have to face the financial consequences.

To improve your odds of success, start by doing your homework, which means researching all the new issues and new players. It's a daunting task and should be. The stakes couldn't be much higher.

Your chances of success improve substantially when you identify the ways that a potential new business direction relates to what your company already does. Even without the benefit of any existing product or market expertise, you can often discover aspects of a new business opportunity that play right into your company's core competence (flip to Chapter 10 for more on core competence). Here's what to look for:

- ✔ **Name recognition:** If you work hard to create a name for your company, you can sometimes make use of your brand identity in a new business situation. Name recognition is particularly powerful when the name has positive, clearly defined associations that you can carry over to the new product and market. Luxury-car companies such as BMW, for example, now give their names to expensive, upscale lines of touring and mountain bicycles.

- ✔ **Technical operations:** You can extend the resources and skills required to design, develop, or manufacture products in your industry — or perhaps the technical services that you offer — to support additional product areas. Research In Motion (RIM), a leader in wireless communications, is an expert in miniaturization, automation, and quality control. With those skills, it can acquire original technology or experimental products, and then go on to create product lines based on its expertise.

- ✔ **Marketing experience:** If your company has a great deal of marketing expertise available, you can put that expertise to good use to expand the awareness and strengthen the positioning of a new product. For example, small, independent developers come up with creative software products and then sell them to larger companies — companies that have the marketing muscle to successfully advertise, promote, and distribute the products — such as Google.

- ✔ **Capacity and scale:** Sometimes, you can take the excess capacity that your company has in production, sales, or distribution and apply that capacity directly to a new business area. You reap the benefits of a larger scale of operations and use your resources more efficiently. Many automobile dealerships around Canada, for example, reached out in the 1980s to show, sell, and service Toyotas and Hondas, permanently adding them to their North American car lines.

- ✔ **Financial considerations:** Persistent demands on your company's revenue, cash flow, or profits may inevitably point you in a new business direction. Although a financial opportunity by itself offers a fairly flimsy link to your existing products and markets, a new business may — just may — be justified on the basis of financial considerations alone. Large tobacco companies, for example, use their huge cash reserves to diversify into unrelated business areas that have brighter, smoke-free futures. Heck, they even buy interest in companies that make nicotine patches to help people kick the habit.

The temptation to set off in new directions and diversify into new businesses, creating brand-new products for brand-new markets, has bewitched and bothered business planners for decades. Unfortunately, the failure rate for new business ventures can be as high as 80 percent. And the most perplexing part of the puzzle is the fact that in the beginning, the ideas and research look so darn good on paper. Here are some examples:

- ✔ Campbell Soup Company thought that it had a winner when it decided to launch a family of juice drinks for kids. But its Juice Works brand struggled, in part because so many competitors had better brand-name recognition in the juice business.

- ✔ Federal Express set out to create the future of immediate document delivery by introducing a new computer network-based product. But loyal customers turned to FedEx to send hard copy, not e-mail, and the company got zapped by its Zap Mail service.

- ✔ CanWest MediaWorks decided that the media-savvy 18-to-34-year-olds needed a multi-brand media platform. But unable to compete in print, the company stopped the presses on the magazine *Dose* less than a year after starting it. They continued the e-zine at `www.dose.ca`.

A few companies, however, manage to succeed with new products and new markets time and time again. Roots is a very successful Canadian company that has designed and produced athletic wear for Olympic teams from Canada, the United States, Great Britain, and Barbados. But Roots started out 35 years ago producing only one product line — natural footwear. Today, it's a leading life-style brand known for its quality clothing, accessories, leather goods (both apparel and home design), timepieces, fragrance, and luggage. In addition, it develops custom products for hundreds of films, TV shows, concert tours, cultural events, and organizations. What's the company secret? It introduces new products that take advantage of the company's specific capabilities, resources, and expertise, plus it leverages its guiding values of quality, creativity, and integrity. In other words, the company moves out in new directions that have the best chance to benefit from its unique core competence (see Chapter 10).

Managing Your Product Portfolio

When you decide that you want to branch out with new products and into new markets, or to diversify into new businesses, you have to figure out how to juggle. What do we mean? You no longer have the luxury of doting on a single product or service. With more than one product and market to deal with, you need to figure out how to keep each of them aloft, providing each with the special attention and resources that it needs, depending on where it stands on the product life cycle (see Figure 15-1). You need the kind of organization and management provided by strategic business units.

Utilizing strategic business units

Juggling additional products and markets requires a bit of preparation, of course. The first thing that you want to find out is how many oranges and bowling pins — or products and services, in this case — you have to keep in the air at one time. Counting oranges and bowling pins isn't tough. For products and services, however, the following questions tend to pop up:

✔ How many products or services does your company have?

✔ When you add another feature or an option to your product, will the addition essentially create a new product that requires a separate business plan?

✔ When you have two separate sets of customers that use your service in different ways, do you really have two services, each with its own business plan?

✔ When you offer two different products, each of which you manufacture, market, and distribute in much the same way to the same set of customers, are you really dealing with one larger product area and a single business plan?

Often, these questions have no right answer, but taking time to think through the issues helps you better understand what you offer.

General Electric struggled with the questions in the preceding list in the late 1960s. The company had grown well beyond the original inventions of its founder, Thomas Edison; it wasn't just in the electric light bulb business any more. In fact, it was a diversified giant, with businesses ranging from appliances and aircraft engines to television sets and computers. The company had to figure out the best way to divide itself up so that each piece was a manageable size that the company could juggle with all the other pieces.

The managers at General Electric hit on the clever idea of organizing the company around what they called strategic business units. A *strategic business unit* (SBU) is a piece of your company that's big enough to have its own well-defined markets, attract its own set of competitors, and demand tangible resources and capabilities from you. Yet an SBU is small enough that you can craft a strategy for it, with goals and objectives designed to reflect its special business environment. By using the SBU concept, General Electric transformed nearly 200 independent product departments into fewer than 50 strategic business units, each with its own well-defined strategy and business plan.

Consider ways to reorganize your company around strategic business units. Each time you outline a separate business plan, you identify a potential SBU. How do you start? Because strategic business units often refer to particular product and market areas taken together, begin by following these steps:

1. **Break your company into as many separate product and market combinations as you can think of.**

2. **Fit these building blocks back together in various ways, trying all sorts of creative associations of products and markets on different levels and scales.**

    Think about how each combination may work in terms of creating a viable business unit.

3. **Keep only the combinations of products and markets that make sense in terms of strategy, business planning, customers, the competition, and your company's structure.**

4. **Determine how well these new SBUs mesh together and account for your overall business.**

    If you don't like what you see, try the process again. Don't change the way you define your products and markets — or the way you organize your business and allocate resources around them — until you're satisfied with the overall structure of the company.

Aiming for the stars

Managing a number of products or services is similar to managing a set of financial investments. Take your personal savings or retirement accounts, for example. Every financial counsellor tells you the same thing: You should spread your investments out to create a more stable and predictable set of holdings. Ideally, financial counsellors want to help you balance your financial portfolio based on how much money you need to earn right away and what sort of nest egg you expect to have in the future. Given your financial needs and goals, planners may suggest that you buy blue-chip stocks and bonds that generate dividends right away and also invest in more speculative companies that pay off well down the road.

Your company's products and services have a great deal in common with a portfolio of stocks and bonds — so much, in fact, that the juggling of your products and services is called *portfolio management.* To manage your product portfolio as professionally as financial experts track stocks and bonds, you need some guidance. *Portfolio analysis* helps you look at the different roles of the products or services in your company and determine how well they balance one another so that the company grows and remains profitable.

In addition, portfolio analysis offers a new way to think about strategy and business planning when you have more than one product or service to worry about.

To juggle your collection of products or services (or SBUs, if you divide them up, as we suggest in the preceding section), start by dividing them into two basic groups, depending on the direction of their cash flow: Put the ones that bring money into your company on one side and the ones that take money out on the other side.

Maybe you're surprised that you have two sides here. But because every product goes through a life cycle that likely includes an introduction stage, a growth stage, maturity, and then decline, different products naturally have different cash-flow requirements. (For more details, check out the section "Facing Up to the Product Life Cycle," earlier in this chapter.) You invest in products during their introduction and growth phases, and your mature products end up paying all the bills. Keep on juggling: You always need at least one mature product aloft to support the up and coming products.

You could make a first attempt at portfolio analysis now, using the two basic product groups: those that make money and those that take money. You just have to make sure that the first category is always bigger than the second. But the two categories don't help you figure out the future. Fortunately, the folks at the Boston Consulting Group (BCG) came up with an easy-to-use portfolio-analysis tool that provides some useful planning direction.

The Boston Consulting Group's Growth-Share Grid (see Figure 15-3) directs you to divide your products or services into four groups.

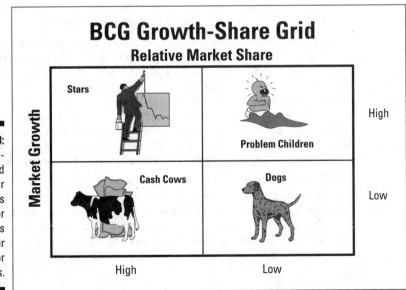

Figure 15-3: The Growth-Share Grid divides your company's products or services into four major groups.

You base your portfolio analysis on two major factors — market growth and relative market share:

- ✔ **Market growth:** Is the product or service part of a rapidly expanding market, or does it fall somewhere in a slow- or no-growth area? You use market growth to define your portfolio because it forces you to think about how attractive the product or service may be over the long haul. The exact point that separates high-growth and low-growth markets is rather arbitrary; start by using a 10-percent annual growth rate as the midpoint.

- ✔ **Relative market share:** Does your product command a market-share advantage over its nearest competitors, or does its market share place it down on the list relative to the competition? You use relative market share as a major characteristic to define your product portfolio because evidence suggests that a strong market-share position is closely tied to the profitability of a product. Separate your products into those that command the highest market share and those that don't.

Here's a review of the four types of products and services divided up by the Growth-Share Grid:

- ✔ **Problem children:** Products that have relatively low market share in high-growth markets. Problem children often represent newer businesses and are sometimes referred to as *question marks* because you aren't quite sure which path these products may take in the future. Because problem children are in expanding markets, they require plenty of cash just to tread water and maintain what market share they already have, but their relatively low sales generate little or no revenue in return. If you can substantially increase their market share over time — which means shelling out even more cash — problem children can blossom into stars. If not, you may have to give these products up.

- ✔ **Stars:** Products that have a dominant market-share position in high-growth markets. Every product wants to be a star. Stars usually have an expensive appetite — they need a lot of cash to fund continual expansion and to fend off competitors that want to get a piece of the turf. But their market-share advantage also gives these products an edge in generating revenue, high margins, and profits. So, stars usually support themselves, both producing and consuming large amounts of money. You shouldn't hesitate to step in and support a star product, however, if it requires additional resources to maintain its market-share lead.

- ✔ **Cash cows:** Products that have a major market-share position in low-growth markets. Because of their market-share advantage, cash cows generate a great deal of cash without requiring much in return. Their low-growth markets are mature, and the products are already well-established. The bottom line: You can milk cash cows to produce a cash surplus and then redirect that cash to fund promising products in other quadrants.

✔ **Dogs:** Products that deliver low market share in low-growth markets — and little else. Although many people are dog lovers, this particular breed is hard to love. Revenue and profits usually are small or nonexistent, and the products are often net users of cash. Although they require periodic investments, these marginal business ventures usually never amount to much, so you may want to turn your attention to more-promising product candidates.

Now, you can put all the pieces together to construct a Growth-Share Grid that represents your portfolio of products and services. Ideally, of course, you want to see mostly stars and cash cows, with enough problem children (the question marks) to ensure your company's future.

But the world isn't always ideal. Fortunately, you can also use the Growth-Share Grid as a tablet to sketch out what you plan to do with your products to balance them in the future. Just follow these steps:

1. **Sort through your company's products or services and get ready to put them in a blank Growth-Share Grid.**

   To see the grid format, refer to Figure 15-3.

2. **Place each product in its proper quadrant, given what you know about market growth and the product's relative market share.**

3. **Draw a circle around each product to represent how big it is in relation to your other products in the Grid.**

   Base the size of your product circles on revenue, profits, sales, or whatever measure is most convenient. The size of the circles measures the relative importance of each product to your company today.

4. **For each product in the grid, forecast its movement in terms of overall market growth and market-share position.**

   Use an appropriate time frame in regard to your industry and its rate of change.

5. **To capture this forecast, draw arrows indicating the direction of the movement and where you plan to have each product end up in the future.**

   Arrows that point outside the grid indicate that you plan to get rid of the products in question.

The BCG Growth-Share Grid, with its quirky cast of characters and its black-and-white view of the world, is hard to resist because it makes the complex and difficult job of juggling several business units or product portfolios seem almost effortless. After it first caught on nearly 30 years ago, however, the model became so widely overused and misapplied that the entire practice of understanding product portfolios went out of fashion. Today, of course, business owners understand that portfolio-analysis tools have their place, but businesses must use those tools sensibly. As the saying goes, if something looks too good to be true, it probably is.

Before you start moving your products around the Growth-Share Grid like pieces on a chessboard, remind yourself that the following strings are attached:

- ✓ Market growth is singled out as the only way to measure how attractive a market is and to determine if you want to be in business there. But growth isn't the only interesting variable. Markets may become attractive because of advances in technology, changes in regulation, and an increase in profits, to name a few.

- ✓ Relative market share describes how competitive you are and how profitable your company is likely to be. But market share is relevant only when you compete on the basis of size and sales volume. You can compete in other ways, including making your product unique in some way, focusing on a particular group of customers, or concentrating on service.

- ✓ The products you put on the Growth-Share Grid are linked only by the flow of cash in and out of the business. But you can think about how products and services may relate to one another and function together in other ways. You may decide to focus on the competition or market risk factors.

- ✓ The differences between a star and a cash cow (or a problem child and a dog) are arbitrary and subject to many definition and measurement problems. Without careful analysis and a dose of good judgment, you may cast your products in the wrong roles. You may end up abandoning a problem child too soon, for example, because you think that the product is a dog, or you may neglect and hurt a star product by labelling it a cash cow that you can simply milk for money.

Staying lean and mean

If you feel that the Growth-Share Grid we present in the preceding section doesn't represent your business situation (maybe you want something in Technicolor, maybe with a few more bells and whistles), you can find dozens of other models, methods, and tools that promise to guide you to the right answers with no muss and little fuss. Many of the other models claim to work particularly well for certain industries or in specific business conditions, and one of them may be just right for your company. Before you turn to the pros for guidance, however, you may want to take one more step in analyzing your portfolio on your own.

General Electric (GE), with the help of the consulting gurus at McKinsey and Company, came up with a portfolio-analysis framework that works with the strategic business units (SBUs) it defined within the company. (For a review of SBUs, check out the section "Utilizing strategic business units," earlier in this chapter.) The GE Framework is a little more complicated than the Growth-Share Grid, but you can apply it successfully over a wider range of business situations. You can see the GE Framework in Figure 15-4.

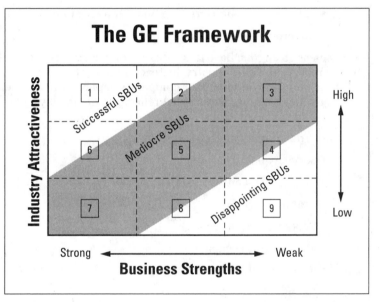

Figure 15-4:
The GE Framework arranges your company's SBUs in three diagonal bands and nine boxes, based on the strength of each SBU and its industry's attractive-ness.

The GE Framework may look a little confusing, but don't worry; we're here to help. The GE Framework creates two primary categories that shape your SBU portfolio analysis: industry attractiveness and your business strengths. Unlike the Growth-Share Grid, the GE Framework requires you to go on and define exactly what you mean by industry attractiveness and business strengths.

You may find coming up with what you see as attractive and what you con-sider a strength more ambiguous and less obvious than dealing with market-growth figures and relative market-share numbers. The following list should help you get started:

✔ **Industry attractiveness:** This category may include any number of com-ponents, depending on your industry. In most situations, however, you want to emphasize the factors that can lead to fatter returns on your SBU investments. Some of the factors that you should look at (in addi-tion to the overall market growth rate) are

- Industry size

- Industry ups and downs

- Intensity of competition

- Customer and supplier relationships

- Average revenue and profits

- Rate of innovation

- Entry and exit barriers (see Chapter 5 for more details)

- Government regulations

✔ **Business strengths:** Base this category on your specific business situation relative to your industry. Instead of relying on relative market share as the only indication of your company's capability to compete, you should include other factors that reflect your company's particular strengths and advantages, such as

- Product uniqueness

- Service quality

- Customer loyalty

- Brand recognition

- Costs and profitability

- Manufacturing capacity

- Research and development

- Patents

- Organizational skills

Rearrange your SBU portfolio so that every strategic business unit falls somewhere in one of the nine newly minted boxes (Figure 15-4 gives you a template). Depending on the location of each SBU, the GE Framework presents a set of planning guidelines. Here are the options that the numbered boxes suggest:

✔ **Protect your position.** Concentrate your resources and efforts on maintaining your strengths. Invest to grow at a fast but manageable pace.

✔ **Try harder.** Challenge the market leaders. Build up the strong aspects of your company and reinforce the vulnerable areas.

✔ **Be choosy.** Seek ways to overcome your business weaknesses. Keep an eye open for new opportunities if the risks are low.

✔ **Harvest.** Limit your investments and try to reduce costs to maximize your profits. Back away if you begin to lose ground.

✔ **Manage carefully.** Maintain your existing programs. Concentrate any new investments in promising areas with manageable risks.

✔ **Grow wisely.** Build on your competitive position. Invest in attractive areas in which you can gain or need to maintain an advantage.

✔ **Regroup.** Try to preserve your current cash flow. Defend your strengths and focus on areas that remain attractive.

✔ **Coast along.** Keep any further investment to the bare minimum. Protect the position that you have and try to sustain revenue.

✔ **Get out.** Cut your costs to the bare bones and avoid making any new investments. Bide your time until you can sell to the highest bidder.

Part V

Putting Your Business Plan into Action

"Einstein over there miscalculated our start-up costs and we ran out of money before we could afford to open a 24-hour store."

In this part . . .

Coming up with wonderful ideas, captivating strategies, and noble plans is great fun but the time comes
when you have to actually carry out your business plan.

In this part, we help you bring your plan to life. We look at
ways to organize your company and develop the procedures and systems that allow you to carry out your plan
as efficiently and effectively as possible. We talk about
ways to encourage leadership, develop business skills,
and create a company culture to help you achieve your
plan.

And don't forget to check out the Appendix. We show you
an entire sample business plan so that you have an even
better idea of how to lay out your plan.

Chapter 16

Shaping Your Organization

. . . .

In This Chapter

▶ Re-examining your business plan

▶ Creating an organization that works

▶ Putting the right procedures in place

. . . .

*W*hen you get close to completing your business plan, you need to make all the parts work together. If you need a little nudge to get under way, flip back to Chapter 1 for a refresher on the reasons you started your plan in the first place. And check out the Appendix for a good example of someone else's business plan.

Your next big step is arranging (or re-arranging) all your company's resources to put your plan into action. If you wanted to design a chair, a desk, or a sofa rather than your company, you'd probably think of the old adage

Form follows function.

This idea explains why chairs look the way they do — and why they look different from sofas. You spell out what your company intends to do — its *function* — in your business plan. Now, you must design a form for your company to support that function. The form your company takes can be as simple as you and your partners doing everything that needs to be done, or as complex as an organization with multiple functional areas and management levels.

For decades, business consultants have made their names and fortunes by coming up with different ways to design companies and organizations. What a surprise! We're quite sure that any number of these consultants would be happy to tailor a design just for you. But before you call one of them (and sign a big fat cheque), you may want to see what you can put together on your own. If you decide that you really do need professional help, your experience helps you ask the right questions.

In this chapter, we help you understand what you need to do to carry out your business plan. And we show you some ways to design your company with the six major facets shown in Figure 16-1. Three of these facets shape your company; the other three shape the people around you (check out Chapter 17 for additional people-shaping info).

Bringing Your Plan to Life

After you put your business plan down on paper, take the time to read it — and we mean *really* read it. Don't just check for typos and bad grammar; remind yourself of what it actually says. You may find it useful to have a trusted adviser read your plan, as well — someone not too close to the business — so you can receive some objective feedback. An amazing number of companies have business plans that nobody reads. Employees in those companies don't seem to know much about what the plan says about their business (other than the all-important numbers in the budget, of course).

Your business plan represents one of the six major facets of your company that help you reach your business goals (see Figure 16-1). Along with your organization and the procedures you put in place, it shapes your business. The other three facets — leadership, culture, and skills — prepare the people around you to make your business work (see Chapter 17 for details on how to rally your troops).

Figure 16-1:
To make your business a success, you should concentrate on these six major facets of your company, divided into two groups.

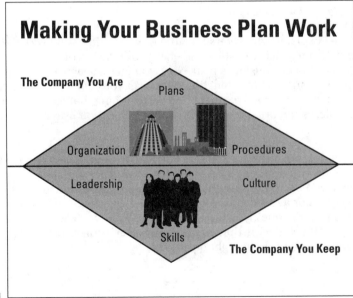

Making Your Business Plan Work

The Company You Are

Plans

Organization   Procedures

Leadership   Culture

Skills

The Company You Keep

Growing fast is hard to do

Consumers Distributing was a red-hot Canadian company from the '60s through to the late '80s. The concept was sound — a catalogue store offering a range of goods, from small appliances to toys to tools, at bare-bones discount prices. Customers selected products from a catalogue, filled out a slip with product codes, and waited for staff to fetch the items from the warehouse. How easy is that shopping experience? And how thrifty!

Now, this was before big box and discount stores showed up on every major corner. Consumers Distributing kept its costs down by using inexpensive warehousing, rather than expensive retail space, to stock product. This approach was novel. And customers caught on fast! From its humble beginnings of one store in Toronto in 1957, it grew to be an international catalogue retailer with 217 stores across Canada and the United States.

But Consumers had a pesky problem: It couldn't get rid of the perception of goods always being out of stock. In a store such as Zellers, available stock is on display in the store, and shoppers choose from what's available. At Consumers, shoppers chose from a catalogue. Because Consumers didn't have a current inventory system, clerks didn't know whether a product was in stock until they went to fill the order. After waiting in line, customers were sometimes told the product wasn't available. If they wanted an alternative, they had to go through the whole process again.

The company tried an aggressive approach to change the perception. It built several super stores that displayed the in-stock items and offered free home delivery or store-to-store transfers if items weren't in stock. With the purchase of a state-of-the-art inventory system, all stores were linked, so clerks could check stock real time and suggest alternatives. But all these changes were costly, and Consumers Distributing faced increasing competition.

Unfortunately, the chain couldn't make it work. Revenues dropped from $1.8 billion in '88 to $580 million in '95. Looking back, you can see what went wrong:

✔ The company's management wasn't quick enough to manage shoppers' perceptions.

✔ The company was financially overextended when the expansion strategy failed.

✔ The company was plagued by products frequently being out of stock.

Don't assume that you already know everything about your business plan. Because you're so close to all parts of it, you can easily miss the big picture. Step back and pay special attention to the broad sweep:

✔ Read your company's mission and vision statements as though you're seeing them for the first time. (Check out Chapters 3 and 4 for vision and mission statement info.)

✔ Consider the goals and objectives that you set for your company and ponder what they mean for the future. (See Chapter 4 for help on setting goals and objectives that make good business sense.)

- ✔ Review the strengths and weaknesses of your business and consider what they say about your company's opportunities and capabilities when it comes to making your plan succeed. (Chapter 10 helps you look at your company objectively.)

- ✔ Think about the different ways in which your company provides value to its customers and how these ways add up to your long-term advantage. (Chapters 6 and 7 show you how to examine your markets.)

If you expect people in your company to take the business plan seriously, you need to start with yourself. As you put your business plan into practice, stop and take a step back on a regular basis. Ask yourself these sorts of questions:

- ✔ Does the shape of your organization encourage the behaviour and skills that you need your employees to have?

- ✔ Do the procedures that you put in place make your company's organization stronger and more focused on your strategy?

- ✔ Do the business systems that you come up with make sense in terms of the kind of organization that you want to create?

- ✔ Does every last thing that you do support your working business plan and the company strategy behind it?

Putting Together an Effective Organization

If everybody in your company can fit comfortably into a Mini Cooper, you have a smooth organizational road ahead; you can arrange two or three people in only so many ways. But the mere fact that a structure is straightforward and flexible doesn't make it unimportant. Whether you have 2 or 2,000 employees, the way that you design your organization plays a major part in your business-planning success. No matter how big or small your company becomes, everybody involved still needs to know what his or her job is. All employees have to understand the special roles that they play in carrying out the business plan and in achieving company goals and objectives.

Where do you start? You can arrange your organization in several ways. The following sections discuss several of the most common structures.

Choosing a basic design

The simplest way to organize your small company is to put a trusted person at the top — an owner or senior manager — and have everybody else do whatever needs to get done. Describing how everyone fits in is easy because all employees are on an equal footing below the person in charge. Here's how the method stacks up:

- ✔ **Advantages:** You can usually find someone who's willing to do a job whenever it needs to be done. Because you don't devote many extra resources to managing the organization itself, the basic design is cost-effective.

- ✔ **Disadvantages:** The basic design really works only if your company has fewer than about 20 people. If your company is, or you want it to become, any larger, the person at the top can't keep track of everybody. At some point, you outgrow this style of organization if your company continues to grow. The basic design isn't always efficient, either. People end up doing jobs that they haven't done before, and experience often gets lost in the shuffle.

Focusing on a functional model

If you organize your company around business functions, you divide people into groups that center on what they do. You take all the engineers and put them together in one area and lump the marketing types together in another area. You put the operations people together in one area and all the financial folks in another. You need to make sure that some sort of general manager coordinates the various activities of the functional groups, of course. Here's how the method stacks up:

- ✔ **Advantages:** A functional organization works well if your business involves only one type of product or service. The organization is efficient because people excel at their particular tasks, and they perform each function in only one place. Also, every employee knows exactly what he or she is responsible for. The jobs in your company are well defined, and you have a clear-cut way to measure performance.

- ✔ **Disadvantages:** Unfortunately, a functional organization can all too easily turn into a bunch of separate silos standing side by side. The silos, each housing a different functional area, are almost always difficult to connect together; and without good communication, the functions begin to have separate goals. Operations, for example, wants to make the same product over and over again, whereas Marketing wants to sell different products to different customers. Each function may be efficient by itself, but the functions taken together aren't terribly flexible or effective in carrying out a larger business plan. Your general managers have to shoulder the responsibility of keeping communication open and constant.

Divvying up duties with a divisional form

If your company is big enough to be in more than one business, the best approach may be to organize by divisions. Each of your company's divisions can be responsible for a particular product, market, or geographic area (always adhering to company strategy and vision, of course). If your company is huge and diversified, your divisions may cover strategic business units, or *SBUs,* which are specific product-market combinations. (Refer to Chapter 15 for additional information on SBUs.) If you want, you can divide the major divisions in your company even further, often into separate business functions within each area. Here's how the method stacks up:

- ✔ **Advantages:** An organization made up of divisions that you base on products, markets, or SBUs encourages you to focus all your energy and resources on the real businesses that you're in. Managers inside the divisions can concentrate on their own sets of customers, competitors, and company issues. Senior managers can oversee how the divisions work together.

- ✔ **Disadvantages:** Because the separate divisions within your company often represent entire businesses, they sometimes compete with one another, perhaps going so far as to fight over the same customers. Also, separate divisions usually mean additional overhead costs because each division invariably has its own set of overlapping management layers and business functions (research, operations, marketing, service, sales, and finance). As a result, your company becomes less efficient and less capable of taking advantage of any scale economies that result from combining tasks.

Sharing talents with the matrix format

The matrix format organizes people along two dimensions, rather than just one. In a matrix organization, everybody works under two bosses and wears two hats. One hat may be functional; a person may be in the programming or auditing group, for example. The other hat may relate to special projects, such as one that needs a programmer and an auditor for six months. In the latter case, the programmer and the auditor report to both a functional manager and a project manager. Here's how the method stacks up:

- ✔ **Advantages:** The matrix format allows you to share talent, expertise, and experience among different parts of your company, applying resources when and where you need them. A matrix organization can be quite flexible in responding to business needs. At the same time, you maintain some of the efficiencies that you gain from arranging people by functions.

✔ **Disadvantages:** A matrix organization can be tricky to manage — and sometimes even disastrous. The format violates an important management rule: Don't give people two bosses at one time. Tension is bound to occur between the project manager and the functional manager, for example, and your employees get caught in the middle (check out the following section for managerial control issues). If you're not careful, the matrix format can lead to opposing priorities, clashing goals, and diverging ideas about how different dimensions should carry out your company's business plan.

Dealing with too many chefs in the kitchen

After you decide *how* to organize your company, you need to decide *how much* you want to divide it up. Ask yourself a simple question: If the guy who mails letters has a suggestion to make, how many people do you want the suggestion to pass through before it gets to the top of the organization? In other words, how many management levels do you want to have?

The number of tiers your management cake should boast depends a great deal on how big your company is and how you organize it. Managers can manage only so many people directly if they want to do a good job, and certain organizational structures simply require more managers than others. Always keep in mind one general rule: The more management levels you have in place

✔ The more control is concentrated at the top of your company

✔ The less flexible your organization is in the face of change

✔ The more costly your organization is to maintain

Finding what's right for you

How do you know what kind of organizational structure — and how much of it — is right for you? Unfortunately, the answer isn't always obvious. Depending on your company's size, how fast the company is changing, and the nature of your competition, certain ways of organizing seem to have an edge over others. The ones that combine several aspects of the common options we describe in the preceding sections seem to work best in practice.

Some companies try to stay efficient, flexible, and on target by keeping their organizations as simple as possible, using informal project teams when necessary, and reorganizing whenever changes in their industries and markets require it. A simple organizational structure tends to keep costs under control. Informal, temporary project teams create much of the flexibility of the matrix format without all the management confusion. A willingness to reorganize when your situation changes — your market expands, technology advances, or your company grows — can be a real strength.

Why do small companies stumble so often? Believe it or not, the biggest reason is that they have trouble handling their own success. A major stumbling block turns out to be an unwillingness of the people at the top to change the organization as a small company grows bigger.

Small companies tend to organize around a basic design, in which the owners or senior managers have their fingers on everything that the company does. Bigger companies can't work that way for long, and if the owners don't let go when the company needs to reorganize, the situation usually spells failure for an otherwise healthy enterprise.

Be sure to explore all your options when you go about creating or re-creating your organizational structure. Try to come up with a structure for your company that makes sense to you. The structure should also make sense to your major stakeholders, including the investors and lenders who have a financial interest in your business. (If you need a refresher on stakeholders, flip back to Chapter 2.) Only then can you put together an organization that allows your company a chance at long-term success and makes it easier for the company to fulfill its business plan.

Developing Effective Procedures

After you spend the time and effort to put together a business plan, you naturally assume that running your business automatically becomes easier. If you run a small company, you may not give any serious thought to what comes next. Now that you know what you have to do, you just go out and do it, right? Whether you make a sale, negotiate with a supplier, or keep track of expenses, you get the job done, even if you have to make up a way on the spot.

Unfortunately, informal procedures such as these (especially the ones that always change) don't work for long, even if your company consists of just you. Your customers and suppliers want to know what to expect when they deal with you, no matter how big or small your company is (so do the tax people, for that matter). People don't like to deal with tons of rules and regulations, unless they serve in the army. But all companies eventually have to come to terms with a set of guidelines that they want to use to remind everybody about their operating procedures.

When you start thinking about the procedures that you use to get things done in your company, you keep discovering new ones. To get started, ask yourself how your company

✔ Keeps track of customer sales orders

✔ Bills and credits customers

✔ Handles customer complaints

✔ Recruits and trains new employees

✔ Determines wages, salaries, and benefits

✔ Reimburses employee expenses

✔ Develops capital and operating budgets

✔ Manages product inventory

✔ Creates new products and services

✔ Monitors the industry and the competition

And don't forget business-planning procedures. For years, managers and management gurus alike pretty much ignored the systems and procedures that made companies run. Face it — systems and procedures are b-o-r-i-n-g. As a result, you can trace back many of the standard operating procedures still in use today to a time when business meant manufacturing, distributing, and selling products. Period. But times change — and companies change with them. So you need to make sure that your systems and procedures are current and functional.

During the late 1980s, businesses began to wake up to the fact that some of these boring old systems were holding them back. Enter *re-engineering* — the smart idea that you should take a close look at all your company's procedures to see if they really make sense, given what your company actually does. When companies jumped on the re-engineering bandwagon, they discovered that they used standard procedures just because companies had always done the procedures that way. Today, following suit is simply not good enough, especially with your competition breathing down your neck.

Determining which systems you need

Try to take the basic idea of re-engineering to heart when you develop your business procedures. Carry out business activities in your company because they make sense, not because you want to follow a tradition or trend. Take a moment to think about a few of the essential systems that you're most likely to need as you go forward:

- ✔ **Accounting system:** The right accounting methods, principles, and even software can mean the difference between knowing what you have and losing track of where your money comes from and where it goes. Income statements, cash-flow statements, and balance sheets are indispensable to your business. (Turn to Chapter 11 for all the financial information that you can handle.) You need to have a reliable accounting system in place if you want to be able to put your financial records together in a way that you can trust. *Accounting For Canadians For Dummies,* by John A. Tracy and Cécile Laurin (John Wiley & Sons Canada, Ltd.), can help you understand accounting essentials.

- ✔ **Budgeting system:** Your company should have procedures that allow you to create a complete financial picture today and to project your future needs (refer to Chapter 12 for more on financial planning and budgeting). Make sure that your budgeting process covers your short-term needs and encourages long-term investments.

- ✔ **Personnel system:** People are a big part of your company, even if you're the only employee right now. No matter how many people make up your company, you should have a system in place that rewards employees for their hard work and also encourages them to think about their continued contributions over the long haul.

- ✔ **Information systems:** Unfortunately, you don't have a quick-and-dirty way to keep up with what's going on in your industry and markets. You need to have a process to capture facts and figures when and where they become available, and you need an information system to make sense out of that data after you have it in hand. Consider your customers: You should keep track of everything that you know about what customers want, what you've done for them in the past, and what they expect from you in the future (check out Chapter 7 to get better acquainted with your customers). While you're at it, set up a similar system to keep track of your competitors (see Chapter 8).

- ✔ **Planning system:** We spend this entire book talking about business plans. But all the great planning ideas that you come up with may as well remain in your head if you don't set up a system to develop them inside your company. After you have a business plan, you also have to put a planning process in place to keep the plan alive. (See the section "Bringing Your Plan to Life," earlier in this chapter, for helpful hints.)

Measuring effectiveness

You can measure the effectiveness of your systems, strategy, and goals by using management tools. One of the most popular is *Balanced Scorecard,* which is a performance measurement framework developed by Drs. Robert Kaplan and David Norton. It looks at specific financial and non-financial data about your company's systems, activities, and results. These data are called *benchmarks* or *key performance indicators.* Here are a few examples:

- ✔ **Financial indicators:** Revenue, profit, cash flow

- ✔ **Customer value indicators:** Customer satisfaction, customer loyalty

- ✔ **Internal business process benchmarks:** Productivity, rate of improvement

- ✔ **Employee performance benchmarks:** Knowledge, skills, employee satisfaction

In addition to acting as a valuable measurement tool, Balanced Scorecard helps an organization to

- ✔ Identify the important actions it should take, such as marketing efforts, improving processes, and employee training

- ✔ Establish how employees can identify success, both in their own performance and for the company overall

- ✔ Keep staff focused on the company's critical success factors

Their framework has proven to be very valuable. Top corporations around the world have implemented Balanced Scorecard as a tool and guide for measuring, managing, and improving performance. A number of software development companies and business consulting firms have developed programs and processes to help organizations adapt the framework to a customized balanced scorecard for their specific needs.

For the do-it-yourselfer, business consultant and author Peter R. Niven crafted an easy-to-read, practical road map and guide for creating an effective balanced scorecard in his book *Balanced Scorecard Step-by-Step: Maximizing Performance and Maintaining Results,* 2nd Edition (Wiley).

Chapter 17

Leading the Way

· ·

In This Chapter

▶ Promoting leadership in yourself and others

▶ Acquiring the necessary business skills

▶ Establishing your company culture

▶ Nurturing your company vision

· ·

The key to success in business is seizing opportunities. Right now, your business plan represents an opportunity. One of the biggest mistakes that companies make is not taking full advantage of the business plans that they work so hard on. We've seen companies use their plans to raise loads of money and put together a dynamite management team — only to toss the plan into a top drawer somewhere and forget about it. Six months or a year later, the owners wonder why their business is sputtering. We've watched entrepreneurs with great ideas and a sound business strategy never get their companies off the ground because they fail to follow through with their plans.

If you ask successful business owners how they made it, they usually list two things: They had a solid business plan in place, and they stuck to that plan. Putting your business plan together isn't enough; you have to lead the way and put your plan to work.

What business areas do you see or envision as the most important pieces of your company? Maybe you think of your business mainly in terms of the products that you offer or the services that you provide. Maybe the image that first comes to mind is of a building or a warehouse with your name and logo on top. Perhaps you think of the organization, your way of doing business, and the reputation that you want to cultivate. Your company is a combination of these services, images, and ideas. But most importantly, the people around you define your business — who they are, how they act, and what they're capable of doing.

If you want your business to be successful, you must create a culture that promotes your business plan and ensures it gets carried out. Even the best plans fall short if no one implements them, and successful implementation of a business plan requires strong leadership. You have to lead and encourage others to assume leadership roles. And you have to make sure the people around you develop the skills they need to do their jobs better.

Encouraging Leadership Roles

If you want your people to follow you into the future that your business plan lays out, you have to lead them. But what does it really mean to be a leader, and how can you encourage others to take on leadership roles?

Leadership abilities and management skills are two very different things. Leadership certainly is part of what it takes to be an exceptional manager, but leaders have a more general capacity to influence others and persuade them to behave in certain ways.

Effective leaders lead in many different ways, depending on the circumstances at hand. When you find yourself in different business situations, you have to be prepared to alter the way that you lead. Consider the following leadership styles:

- ✔ **The boss:** Sometimes, you simply have to tell people what to do, either because they don't know how to proceed or because you have definite ideas about what should happen next. Even when you lead as the boss, however, remember that you get the most out of people by giving them good reasons to carry out what you ask of them.

- ✔ **The adviser:** If you want your people to take on responsibility over time, you have to let them go off and try to accomplish the tasks that you give them on their own. In your advisory role, timing is everything because you need to develop a sixth sense for when to step in with support and give just the right amount of advice. Make sure your people know how to ask for help when they know that they need it. Sometimes, you lead best when you allow people to make mistakes — they can grow from the experience.

- ✔ **The colleague:** When you bring people into your company and develop strong working relationships over time, your leadership may become almost invisible. On the surface, you behave more like a colleague — one among equals. In this case, you lead in subtle ways and often by example. If you demand the best of yourself, others excel in your shadow. If you meet deadlines, your employees strive to meet them, too. This brand of leadership is based on mutual respect, and it can turn into one of the most powerful forces and potent assets that you have to make your company a success.

When you reflect on your leadership talents and those of the people in your company who work closest to you, you may wonder whether talented leaders are born or whether they can be made. It's hard to say which statement is true. Some people are natural leaders. You can easily impart basic management skills to someone, for example, but instilling leadership abilities in them requires much more effort and patience.

The Canadian Army claims that it can create leaders out of raw recruits. Although you may argue about its success rate, the Army has come up with leadership techniques, procedures, and programs based on one simple piece of wisdom:

> *Don't ask those you lead to do anything you wouldn't be willing to do yourself.*

The Army provides good advice for aspiring leaders in any situation and in every walk of life.

Developing Business Skills

Your employees are responsible for turning your business plan into reality. You can't simply pick any bunch of random people who are willing and able to work (not if you want your plan to work, that is). The people you bring on board must have the right skills to do what you ask them to do.

The right skills today are different than they were just 10 or 15 years ago. You still want your people to be tops in their own areas, of course, whether they work in engineering, operations, marketing, or sales. But they also need to have more general abilities that allow them to succeed in the company that you want to build for the future. In short, the people around you should excel in one or more of the following activities:

- ✓ **Managing information:** Employees should be able to deal with an avalanche of information on almost every imaginable aspect of your company. You need people who can not only organize the bits and pieces of data, but can also make sense out of the data and then go on to make business decisions that take advantage of the information.

- ✓ **Thinking independently:** Employees should be able to tackle business issues when those issues crop up. You can't afford to have too many people around you who do only what managers tell them to do. If you want to get the most out of your company, your people have to take initiative, think on their own, and come up with answers to the business problems that they face every day.

✔ **Working in teams:** Employees should be able to get work done as part of a group. The need for speed in a complex business world makes it hard to get anything big accomplished without pooling resources, talent, and expertise. Whether you need to solve a technical problem, assemble a product, or deal with a strategic issue, you count on a team of people to get the job done.

✔ **Dealing with change:** Employees should be able to complete tasks in different ways, take on new responsibilities, and adapt to unfamiliar situations. Industries don't stand still anymore, and if you want your company to keep up, you need people around you who can keep pace with a constantly changing business world.

✔ **Acquiring new skills:** Employees should be able to keep on expanding their ability to perform their job. If you want your company to move forward, your employees have to move ahead, as well. Provide avenues for employees to continue their professional education and encourage them to master new skills.

A leader on leadership

Successful entrepreneur and corporate leader Ted Rogers started with one tiny FM radio station in downtown Toronto in 1960 and manoeuvred it into the communications conglomerate Rogers Communication Inc. (RCI). Rogers controls an empire of $14 billion in assets and has 22,500 employees in Canada.

His impressive portfolio includes Canada's second-largest telecommunications company (by revenue), largest wireless phone carrier, biggest cable television monopoly, and largest radio network; it also includes a national chain of video stores, most of Canada's consumer magazines, and the country's only national television shopping channel. Rogers also owns the Toronto Blue Jays baseball team and the stadium in which it plays — the Rogers Centre, formerly the Toronto SkyDome.

When author Caroline Van Hasselt, for her book *High Wire Act: Ted Rogers and the Empire that Debt Built* (Wiley), asked Ted Rogers what advice he would give budding entrepreneurs, he was quick to offer up these tips:

✔ Have adequate financing.

✔ If you have a vision, never give up control.

✔ Surround yourself with good people — hopefully, better than you.

✔ Follow your instincts.

According to Rogers, these are the most important characteristics of an entrepreneur (and leader):

✔ Hard working

✔ Motivated

✔ Resourceful

✔ Persistent (never give up)

Like him or hate him, Rogers is definitely a big personality with big ideas, a big voice, and big success. Although he manages with a tough-love technique, he's been known to be humble, charming, witty, and caring. Rogers made sure that he had solid advisors behind him and strong corporate lieutenants beside him with strong teams backing them.

When your company grows and changes, you have to decide how your employees should acquire the necessary leadership skills to achieve company success. Do you invest in inside training to develop all the business skills that employees need, or do you go out and buy the necessary expertise, bringing in new people who already have the backgrounds that you want? Going outside is certainly faster, but developing and promoting people from within your company can create a more engaged, dedicated workforce and a much stronger organization in the long run.

Creating the Right Culture

Don't worry: Promoting culture doesn't mean forcing everybody to go to the opera or the symphony on a regular basis — although we do support the arts. Your company culture comes from the common attitudes, beliefs, and behaviour of the people involved in your organization. In that sense, company culture resembles a nation's culture. But remember: People aren't born working for your company, and they don't grow up in it, either. When you attempt to create a company culture, you bring together people of different backgrounds and try to give them a common outlook.

Your company culture may focus on offering the best technology, the finest products, the highest level of customer service, or the lowest costs; or it may focus on being the most innovative, fastest growing, or any combination of these areas.

You want these attitudes to translate into the way in which your employees act. If your employees base their behaviours on a set of shared beliefs, you can always count on the people around you to do the right thing in any business situation. Company rules and regulations look good on paper, but a company culture provides a sturdier set of guidelines for encouraging employees to behave in an appropriate way.

Unfortunately, you can't order people to have a particular point of view, so you have to take advantage of less direct methods to change attitudes and influence behaviour. Leadership plays a powerful role in this task. The strongest company cultures often thrive in companies that have effective leaders — Ted Rogers and Rogers Communication Inc., for example.

Here are some ways you can use leadership skills to create a strong company culture:

✔ **Mission, values, and vision:** Use your position in the company to talk about the company's mission, the values that you think are important, and the vision that you have for the business (check out Chapter 3 for a vision statement discussion and Chapter 4 to put together your mission statement). Reinforce the ideas that really matter. Make sure that everybody is always aware of why you think each person is a part of your company and what you want each person to ultimately accomplish.

✔ **Actions and activities:** Set an example for everyone around you to follow when it comes to the attitudes that you want to see and the behaviour that you want to promote. If you want your company culture to value customers, for example, go out and visit customers. If you want people to focus on profits, ask questions about profitability every chance you get. If innovation is critical to your company's success, search out the innovators, and then acknowledge and reward them.

✔ **Rituals and rewards:** Set up rewards inside your organization to support the company culture and the behaviour that you want to promote, and then endorse and identify yourself with that behaviour. Offer customer-satisfaction awards, for example, and attend the ceremonies. Set profit targets and hand out bonuses when employees meet them. Make a big deal out of innovations that work and see to it that employees aren't punished when they try something new and it doesn't pan out.

Your company culture can be one of the keys to making your business plan work. If the culture you create doesn't support your mission and goals, it can turn into a stumbling block. You can't change your company culture overnight, so you have to pay close attention to the attitudes and outlook of the people around you. You have to put in time and effort to encourage the shared behaviour that you expect to see across the company.

Following Through with Your Vision

In the end, your business plan represents the ultimate vision of what you want your company to become, right down to the last market initiative and financial projection. A company vision creates a sense of shared commitment and direction (see Chapter 3 for more info on creating a vision statement), and you can use your business plan to communicate your vision to everyone who has a stake in your company. To keep your business plan a living, breathing document that conveys and refreshes your company vision, make use of the following suggestions on a regular basis:

✔ Reproduce your mission and vision statements in company newsletters, employee handbooks, and even on business cards. (Chapters 3 and 4 provide all the details on vision and mission statements, respectively.)

✔ Refer to your business plan whenever appropriate — during marketing strategy meetings or new product development forums, for example.

✔ Use the plan as a yardstick to evaluate all programs and initiatives.

✔ Use financial targets to evaluate actual performance on a regular basis, such as every month or quarter. Adjust your plan or actions accordingly.

✔ Use your business goals and objectives as the primary guide when you conduct employee performance evaluations. (Check out Chapter 4 for help in setting your business goals and objectives.)

✔ Actively enlist feedback from everyone in the company when you prepare to assess and revise your business plan.

Part VI
The Part of Tens

"The financial section of our business plan didn't take in to account the product loss associated with office politics."

In this part . . .

Keeping on top of your game means staying in shape, keeping current, and making the right moves. A business plan needs the same kind of rigor to keep a company in condition.

In The Part of Tens, we start by reviewing ten signs that your business plan may need freshening. We list the ten most important questions to ask yourself about your business plan while you work on it. Finally, we point out the ten things that you never ever want to be caught doing (while business planning, of course).

Chapter 18

Ten Signs That Your Business Plan Needs Refreshing

*Y*ou should always revisit your business plan at least once a year. But if you operate in a rapidly changing industry, you may face times when you absolutely have to do an unscheduled review of your strategy and plan. This chapter gives you ten warning signs that your business plan needs attention.

Your Business Goals Change Abruptly

Even the best business plan requires adjustments when conditions change. But if your company drastically changes course, you need to meet with your management team and look at your business plan from the bottom up. Take the time you need to do a complete review and update your business plan to reflect a rational course change that addresses the problems you identify. See Chapter 4 for more details on setting business goals and objectives.

You Don't Meet Your Plan Milestones

Your business plan sets out a strategy and action plan for meeting your goals and objectives. Deadlines are one of the engines that propel your business forward. What do you do if the company begins to miss deadlines and important projects start to fall behind schedule? Sit down with your staff and figure out why the schedule you set for your company isn't working. Identify the source of the problem, including aspects of your current business plan that may not be realistic. With the help of your team, brainstorm solutions that can get you back on track. If you can't catch up, revise your planning schedule so that employees don't become frustrated.

New Technology Makes a Splash

Technological innovation can alter your business landscape entirely — changing what your customers want, how your business operates, and who your competitors are. A shift in technology can make existing products obsolete and create a market for new products or services almost overnight. So, when a new technology appears on your business horizon, you need to reassess your business plan. Fast. Sit down with your management team and consider how this new technology should change the way you do business or the customers you aim to serve. Lay out plans for how you can use the new technology to your advantage. Check out Chapter 13 for tips on how to manage changes in your business environment, including changes in technology.

Important Customers Walk Away

Customers always keep an eye out for a better product or service, or a better deal. Losing a few customers is part of doing business. But if you start to notice that a lot of your customers are going elsewhere, something's wrong. Your competitors may be stronger than you think, your efforts may be falling short, or the market itself could be changing. Whatever the reasons, the defection of important customers is an alarm signal you can't afford to ignore. One way to get more information: Ask departing customers why they want a change. And talk to your sales force for further insights. After you research and gather tips and information, adjust your business plan accordingly. Flip back to Chapters 6 and 7 for tips on understanding your customers.

The Competition Heats Up

You need to know the competition if you want to compete successfully. So, if an important new competitor sets up business in your market, you should revisit your competitor analysis and adjust your business plan accordingly. Keep in mind that competition isn't necessarily a bad thing. It usually forces you to focus on what you do best and develop ways to do it as efficiently as possible. But to respond effectively to a new competitive threat, you need the right plan in place. Check out Chapter 8 for the full scoop on tracking your competition.

Product Demand Falls Sharply

If you see an unexpected drop in your current sales figures, move quickly to diagnose the problem. You may have a mismatch between the features you offer and the benefits customers want, a problem with quality control, or a breakdown in customer service. Or perhaps the competition has moved ahead of you. Don't panic. Take time to identify the reasons behind the change in sales and revise the appropriate parts of your business plan — product design, operations, and marketing strategy, for example. Flip back to Chapter 9 for a review of your business capabilities and an analysis of your company's strengths and weaknesses.

Revenues Go Down or Costs Go Up

You won't find a clearer sign that your company is in trouble than when revenues go down or costs go up. But all too many business owners ignore the warning signs until it's too late. Why? Because for most businesses, things don't usually go wrong overnight. Costs rise gradually; revenues slowly drift downward. By the time the warning bells go off, the business doesn't have time for a simple fix. You should revisit your business plan — namely, the financial plan you have in place — at the first signs of a profit squeeze. See Chapter 11 for more information on financial statements.

Company Morale Slumps

The morale of the people who work for you is critical to your success. If morale slumps, you may see productivity and quality decline, as well. At the first sign of grumbling among your staff, talk to the key people around you and find out exactly what's wrong. Perhaps your planned goals and objectives are unreasonable, which creates frustration rather than motivation in the company. Or maybe your employees see a mismatch between your stated mission and your plan of action, creating confusion and indirection. Perhaps you don't have procedures in place to recognize and reward a job well done. Review and revise your plan to calm the company waters. Check out Chapters 16 and 17 for new ways to communicate your business plan and motivate your employees.

Key Financial Projections Don't Pan Out

Face it: Predicting the financial future of your company is part science and part guesswork. Plenty of situations can come out of the blue to disrupt even the most conservative financial projections. If your projections begin to look a little wobbly, don't wait until they topple. Sit down with your key staff members to review all the assumptions that went into your original projections and make a detailed list of the things that may change your forecasts. Work up a revised set of financial projections based on the new reality. If necessary, revise your action plan, as well. For more info on how to create financial projections, see Chapter 12.

Too Much Growth, Too Fast

You don't hear anyone complaining if business is booming. But many business owners don't realize that companies can grow too fast — and that can spell trouble if they haven't prepared. Product quality or customer service can suffer, for instance, or manufacturing may not be able to keep up with demand. Some companies even find that their basic organizational structure no longer fits their new size. If you experience similar growing pains, look back at your business plan to identify the parts that need to change in order to accommodate the good news — and your increasing size. See Chapter 15 for the inside scoop on how to best manage your company growth.

Chapter 19

Ten Questions to Ask about Your Plan

The planning process is done. Your plan is ready. Or is it? Before you unveil the final draft of your business plan, ask yourself and your trusted advisers ten simple but important questions.

Are Your Goals and Mission in Sync?

The goals you set for yourself are the results that you absolutely, positively intend to achieve. To a large extent, your goals determine how you set priorities and how you run your company. (They also play a big role in your success.) Make your goals consistent with one another so that you don't run in different directions at the same time. In addition, tie your goals to your company's mission so that you always head in the right direction. For more info on your mission and goal setting, flip back to Chapter 4.

Can You Point to Major Opportunities?

Opportunity knocks only once, the saying goes. So you need to hear the knock when it comes. Your business plan should highlight the major opportunities that you see heading your way (in technology, markets, or distribution, for example) and outline the actions that your company intends to take now to be in a position to take advantage of those opportunities down the road. Have a trusted associate or acquaintance read your forecast to see whether the same opportunity seems to jump out. Chapter 5 talks about ways to spot business opportunities.

Have You Prepared for Threats?

You may be tempted to put on rose-coloured glasses and see a bright and sunny future ahead. Now's the time to take those glasses off and get real. Your plan stands a better chance of success if you paint an objective picture — including the bad news along with the good. That way, you're prepared for the eminent dangers that come with starting a business. Make sure your business plan acknowledges the biggest threats that loom on the horizon (a market slowdown, new regulations, or increasing competition, for example) and offers concrete ways to prepare for them. Chapter 5 points out how you can identify and prepare for threats. If you recognize threats before your competition does, you can often turn a threat into a real business opportunity.

Do You Know Your Customers?

Customers are the lifeblood of any business. The more you know about your customers — who they are, how they act, and what they want — the more you know about your company. Customers tell you how to succeed in the market-place. Your customers are so important to your company that you can't afford to leave them out of your business plan. You should answer three questions:

- Who's buying?
- What do they buy?
- Why do they buy?

Your plan should explain how your company intends to serve customers better than any of your competitors. Check out Chapter 7 to get better acquainted with your customers.

Can You Track Your Competitors?

Your competitors are around to make life interesting. They always try to woo your customers away, promising products or services that have better value (more benefits, lower prices), and you can't ignore them. You have to be able to identify your competitors — how they do business and where they plan to go in the future. Competition represents a big piece of your business environment. Your business plan should cover what you know about your competitors and — more important — how you intend to keep track of them on an ongoing basis. Chapter 8 talks about the methods you can use to keep an eye on the competition.

Do You Know Your Strengths and Weaknesses?

Business plans typically concentrate on a company's strengths. Yes, they're worth boasting about, but you also need to consider your weaknesses. You may find it hard to be objective in making an honest assessment of what your company does well and what it can do better. But your company's strengths and weaknesses determine your odds of success when you look ahead. Strengths and weaknesses refer to your company's capabilities and resources — how well they match up with the capabilities and resources that you need to have in place to be successful.

In your plan, list your company's capabilities and resources — from management skills or research expertise to operations and distribution strength or a loyal customer base. But be sure to describe how each of these capabilities or resources is either a strength or a potential weakness, given your business situation and the industry in which you compete. Turn to outside people if you need objective feedback. Chapter 9 helps you discover your company's strengths and weaknesses.

Does Your Strategy Make Sense?

Sure, you should know where you want to go, but you also need to know how to get there. Strategy is what makes your business plan happen. Make sure your business strategy pulls together your company's strengths and weaknesses, the opportunities and threats that your company faces, and your business goals.

Base your business plan, from beginning to end, on an overall strategy that makes sense. Your company should have a strategy that you ground in reality and that makes reasonable assessments and assumptions about what's happening and what's about to happen — a strategy that logically and rationally looks at what you can accomplish and how long it may take. Flip to Chapter 14 for more information on strategy.

Can You Stand Behind the Numbers?

Too many high-flying companies have come crashing down in recent years, victims of unrealistic and sometimes even phony numbers on the balance sheet. Make sure the numbers you outline are rock solid. Think of all your financial statements as your company's report card — one that answers some big questions. Do your customers love you? Are your competitors afraid of you? Are you making the right business choices? An income statement presents the bottom line, the balance sheet shows what your company is worth, and the cash-flow statement keeps track of the money.

Your current financial statements tell everybody how well you're doing. But many people are more interested in your financial forecasts, which say what you expect the numbers to be in the future. Just because your forecasts include official-looking numbers, however, doesn't mean that the predictions will necessarily come true. If you want to paint an honest picture of your company, your business plan should include a realistic financial portrait, based on assumptions that you believe in and numbers that you trust. Chapter 11 paints a financial picture for you.

Are You Really Ready for Change?

Everything around you — from technology to competition and your market — is going to be a little different tomorrow, no matter what business you're in. To keep up, you have to think two or three steps ahead. You must look carefully and continually at what may happen in the world and how it may affect your company. Although your business plan paints an honest picture of how you see your company, the plan should also acknowledge the fact that you don't have a crystal ball. So present some options. Include one or two alternative business scenarios, asking — and answering — the question, "What if . . . ?" See Chapter 13 to look at some more scenario planning.

Is Your Plan Concise and Up-to-Date?

Ultimately, a business plan is a tool for communication. Make sure yours gets the important messages across. Your plan should certainly capture all the essentials about your company and its situation; but remember, none of the information can be of use to anyone if your business plan is too long, impossible to read, or outdated. So take time to read over your plan. Is it easy to understand? Is it easy to navigate? Did you know where to find all the details? Have an advisor read your plan and ask the same questions. Objective feedback can provide you with invaluable perspective.

Chapter 20

Ten Business-Planning Never-Evers

In This Chapter

▶ Making a plan and sticking to it

▶ Respecting both your customers and your competition

▶ Being bold in your business

▶ Sharing your plan and making it count

*T*his chapter lists ten of those easy-to-make, "I can't believe I did that" planning miscues. We list them so that you have a better chance of not making these mistakes yourself. But if you happen to make them anyway, at least you know that you're not alone.

Failing to Plan in the First Place

We're probably preaching to the choir here because you're already reading this book. But neglecting to plan is a business sin so grave that it always merits a short sermon. Planning isn't easy. After all, you don't come across any right or wrong answers, and nothing's guaranteed. But the planning process leaves your company better prepared to face an uncertain future.

Although a business plan may not solve all your problems, it helps. Planning makes you a better manager and makes your company, no matter how large or small, more competitive and more likely to succeed over the long haul. And in case you want a cross-reference to a chapter with more information on the business plan, we suggest you read, well, this entire book.

Shrugging Off Values and Vision

Perhaps you find it invigorating to jump right into the thick of things. You're itching to line up your products and services, seize the opportunities in front of you, and face down your competitors, one by one. This situation is the business version of a roller-coaster ride, and we can't deny its appeal: ups, downs, and hairpin corners. But roller coasters end up right back where they start — and so will your company if you don't stand back and spend some time on the values and vision that set you off in the right direction.

You set up your company's values and vision statements to remind you where you want to go and what you want to become. Together, these statements are your business compass, so don't start your journey without them. Check out Chapter 3 to put together your statements.

Second-Guessing the Customer

Everybody knows the cliché "The customer is always right." Well, it isn't considered a cliché for nothing. Whether you're trying to satisfy an individual customer face-to-face or attempting to figure out what an entire segment of the market needs and wants, ignore what customers tell you at your own peril.

This idea seems so obvious that we hardly find it worth repeating. But you may be surprised by how many companies approach the marketplace with a "We know just what you're looking for" attitude. Just remember that if you don't listen to your customers, your competitors will. Chapter 7 gets you closer to your customers.

Underestimating Your Competition

Sometimes, you can get so involved in working on your own product or service that you forget the other people out there who are working to develop and market the same product or service. As the competitive heat intensifies in your industry, your competition gets smarter and grows in number.

Keeping tabs on your competitors is just as important as listening to your customers. After all, if you want to stay ahead of the pack, you have to know what the rest of the pack is up to. The more you know about your competitors, the better equipped you are to beat them at their own game. Flip to Chapter 8 for more competitive advice.

Ignoring Your Strengths

Why does the grass always seem a little bit greener in the other company's yard? It usually isn't all that green when you get up close and look carefully, of course. But you face a real temptation in the business world to think that other companies have all the right answers, the better way of doing things, and the correct approach.

Oh, you can always learn from your competition — no doubt about it. But what works for one competitor isn't necessarily the best way for you. So don't forget to catalogue your company's unique strengths and use them to your advantage in the marketplace. Turn to Chapter 9 to spot your strengths.

Mistaking a Budget for a Plan

Putting together your company's budget is one of the most critical steps in the business-planning process. In a budget, after all, you make all the really big decisions about how much money to spend and where to spend it. Your budget plays a large role in determining what your company plans to do in the months and years ahead.

But don't ever mistake your budget for your business plan. The bulk of your plan is all the work that you do up front, before you begin to put your budget together. All the analysis of your industry, customers, competitors, and your-self helps ensure that your financial decisions are the right ones — the ones that move your company closer to your larger business goals. Chapter 12 provides tips on putting together a budget.

Shying Away from Reasonable Risk

Some people jump out of airplanes; others refuse to lace up a pair of skates. Some of us don't mind betting the farm; others have trouble buying a lottery ticket. But no matter how you feel about risk, no business venture is risk-free, especially in today's competitive markets.

Doing business means taking risks, and creating a business plan can help manage those risks. Don't shy away from making a bold business move — after you do your homework, assess the risk, and deem it a reasonable step to take. A good entrepreneur is a reasonable risk-taker. Chapter 5 clues you in on how to maximize opportunities and recognize threats.

Allowing One Person to Dominate a Plan

Nobody has all the right answers (at least, no one we've met). So no matter how big or small your company is, don't create a business plan alone. Even if you're the only one running the show, get other people you trust involved in the planning process — at the very least, find trusted advisers to review what you've done and provide an outside perspective. (Flip to Chapter 1 for a discussion of whom you should involve in your business-planning process.) If you run a bigger company, involve as many people with different points of view as you can in your planning process. The more viewpoints you get, the stronger your business plan becomes. Just be careful not to let the process become too democratic: Chaos doesn't promote progress.

Being Afraid to Change

All people end up making changes in their lives. Sometimes, you don't have much choice in the matter. Most people, however, prefer to go on doing the same things that they've always done, especially if they do them well. Companies aren't much different. Changing the way that you do business or the kind of business that you do isn't easy, and change is particularly hard if you already enjoy success. But a good business plan alerts you to changes that your company should make before the industry, your markets, or your competition forces you to make them — changes that allow you to be more responsive to customers, more competitive, more efficient, and more successful, all while following the company vision. Chapter 13 starts you down the road of managing uncertainty.

Forgetting to Motivate and Reward

A business plan isn't useful if it never gets out of your head or off the page. Your business blueprint needs to translate into the efforts and activities of all the people in your company — and it needs to make sense. Chapter 16 points out ways to bring your plan to life and communicate it to others.

You have to link your strategy to your vision, link your vision to the company mission, and link your mission to the goals and objectives that you set. Take these pieces of the plan and link them to the ways in which you motivate and reward the people around you. Chapters 3 and 4 discuss vision, mission, and goals and objectives; Chapter 17 points out ways you can become a more effective leader.

Appendix

A Sample Business Plan

Sometimes, you have to see something up close and personal before you really understand what it's all about. Viewing a real live business plan should get you much closer to putting your own plan on paper.

Your written business plan says something about all the important parts of your company. After all, you want to convince people — and yourself — that your company knows what it's doing. If you want to persuade people of anything, however, they have to actually sit down and read what's in front of them. So you want to be clear, concise, and to the point, and it doesn't hurt to spend some time with your prose, either.

Here we show you a sample business plan. (We changed some names and some of the numbers to protect the innocent.) By reviewing the plan in some detail, you can understand how to construct a business plan of your own.

Network Components, Inc. (NCI) Business Plan – CONFIDENTIAL!

Executive Summary

Company Overview

With the proliferation of client/server architecture and the use of on-line transaction processing (OLTP), on-line analytical processing (OLAP), as well as intranet/Internet servers in corporate enterprise computing, increased server capacity has become necessary to handle the expanded processing load — that is, processing power, memory, data storage, and so on. In turn, this has led to the computer cluster as a means to meet this need.

A computer cluster is a group of compute nodes (single, SMP, and so on) that are connected by a network and act together as a single system. The cluster architecture provides increased fault-tolerance and the ability to grow processing power by simply adding new compute nodes to the cluster (they are highly "scalable"). For such scalable cluster systems to be constructed, a new network, called System Area Network (SAN), must be implemented. Necessary features of these SAN systems include high bandwidth, low latency, low overhead, and scalability. Our firm, **Network Components, Inc. (NCI),** has developed a proprietary high-performance network architecture that possesses these features, based on completely open technologies. We believe that cluster computing will become the next dominant architecture for the expanding server market over the next three to five years — as do many other informed industry analysts.

▶ Technology and Products

NCI is developing a SAN architecture called *Tera*Net©, which consists of an SCI-PCI network interface (*Tera*Link©), an SCI-based switch (*Tera*Switch©), and an SCI interface to mass storage devices such as RAID, Magneto-Optical farms, Tape Libraries, and so on. NCI hardware and driver software will be compatible with all major software Mbytes/throughput on the SCI network with 2.1GB/node-to-node bandwidth and latencies of 2–5 μs.

This architecture uses two proprietary technologies developed by NCI founder Dr. Fritz von Honecker. These technologies include a novel approach to resource management and intelligent network interface architecture. A critical feature of *Tera*Net© is the use of an intelligent I/O system that handles all intra-node traffic, alleviating costly compute node processor intervention — and that, in turn, provides complete scalability for adding nodes to the cluster. Full production prototypes are expected by November 2008, with initial *Tera*Link© tests completed by December 2009.

▶ *The Market Opportunity*

Initial customers for NCI will be server manufacturers who provide volume and mid-range server systems for corporate enterprise computing. Each of the principal network operating system developers has announced the updated release of clusterable operating systems, including Microsoft Windows Vista, Linux BProc, and Sun Solaris Cluster. Initially, the now-defunct Zona Research projected an $8.9 billion market for corporate intranet server systems and $1.95 billion in Internet server sales by 1998. However, intranet server revenues grew at >200 percent CAGR, while IDC reports that NT-based server unit sales increased at 85 percent CAGR from 2002 to 2005. Worldwide revenues in 2006 for the x86-based server market reached $25.8 billion with shipments of 6.9 million servers and will continue to expand by 7 percent annually to reach 10 million units by 2011.

When valued-added resellers (VARs) become involved in cluster-server development, NCI expects to use both a push and a pull marketing strategy. The key to the push strategy will be the development of strategic relationships with the larger VAR firms. The pull strategy will be implemented through advertising to IT/IS managers/developers to raise their awareness levels of the underlying cluster network. The corporate end-user market will be supplied through the use of both direct sales and distributors.

▶ *Competition*

There are two key vendors currently providing or planning to provide SAN architecture hardware and software within the coming year. These competitive technologies include Dolphin's Express SCI-PCI interconnect and Myricom's Myrinet. In each case, NCI's *TeraNet*© technology will outperform competitors. More importantly, Dolphin Express and Myrinet are proprietary technologies, whereas NCI will provide completely open network architecture. We believe that NCI will have a distinct competitive advantage over these rivals.

▶ *Funds Requested*

The company is currently at the seed stage of financing, with an initial $150,000 investment completed from a group of private individuals. This current investment provides capital for the development and production of alpha production prototype hardware. NCI is seeking additional Stage One financing of $1.5 million by Q4 2008. Use of these funds includes completion of both 2- and 64-bit versions of our product and the development and fabrication of an SCI Link Controller ASIC. Within 9 to 12 months of closing on Stage One financing, NCI anticipates the need for an additional $3 million in Stage Two financing; we project a positive cash flow from Q3–Q4 2010.

▶ *Exit Strategy*

NCI projects that it will either be acquired or that it will implement an IPO. This choice will be determined by the board of directors based on market developments and the firm's competitive situation. It is not possible to predict at this time when either of these options might occur.

1. NCI Business Plan

▶ The Company

With Microsoft, Linux, and Sun each developing a clusterable operating system, producers of volume and mid-range servers are beginning to provide cluster-based server systems. Cluster servers are single or Symmetric Multi-Processor (SMP) systems that, when connected, act as a single system. There are two classes of these systems: (1) fail-over and (2) fully scalable.

Simple fail-over systems provide a mechanism for the migration of active processes from one node to another. This provides increased uptime for the server by being tolerant against single-node system crashes, as well as system hardware and software upgrades. These fail-over systems can be connected by standard high-speed networking technologies, for example, Fast Ethernet, Fibre Channel, ATM, and so on. Beyond a few compute nodes, these types of systems yield little or no performance enhancement.

Scalable systems not only provide fault tolerance, but also enhanced performance as nodes are added to the cluster. Applications can be distributed over multiple compute nodes, providing superior performance when compared with single nodes. In order for applications to communicate/coordinate activities in this distributed environment, high-speed, low-latency, scalable networks must be implemented. Traditional networking technologies cannot provide these features. Therefore, a new class of network must be used. NCI has developed a novel network architecture based upon open standards, which will enable scalability in these clustered systems.

The mission of Network Components, Inc., is to become the leading provider of high-performance network systems for use in computer clustering, enabling the construction of powerful, scalable, fault-tolerant server systems from low-cost, commodity hardware. NCI's network architecture called *Tera*Net© consists of a node-to-node interconnect (*Tera*Link©), a switch (*Tera*Switch©), and connectivity to mass storage devices, such as RAID, tape, magneto-optical systems, and so on. *Tera*Net© has several major advantages over competitive technologies, including performance, scalability, versatility, and openness. There are currently no available SAN systems that will outperform *Tera*Net©. The use of a proprietary (patent-filed) intelligent I/O system allows *Tera*Net© to handle all inter-node I/O traffic, alleviating I/O overhead on the process nodes. Because the additional traffic from added compute nodes does not provide additional overhead on other compute nodes in the cluster, *Tera*Net© systems are completely scalable.

▶ Current Company Status

NCI is a start-up company with superior technical expertise. An early prototype of the SAN *Tera*Link© interface board, connecting a PCI bus to an SCI network, has been evaluated in a system test at Lawrence Berkeley National Laboratory. The prototype implements a patent-pending proprietary resource management technology (this was invented by the founder of NCI), which has been found to be fully functional and verified.

▶ *NCI Objectives*

NCI's full SAN architecture will be delivered to the market within 12–18 months. In order to reduce the overall capital necessary for this extended period, NCI plans to initially market the product to producers of proprietary cluster-server systems. By providing these customers with a solution to their requirements for a high-speed interconnect, NCI will be able to profit from high-margin products in the early stages of the company's development. In order to attain positive cash flow as early as possible, as well as complete development of the product, NCI plans to implement the business in three phases, described below.

~ *Phase I* ~

NCI is currently in the early stage of Phase I development and expects to complete this phase no later than December 2008. Product development for this phase is expected to provide proof of principal for the interconnect product. Potential strategic partners will also be identified during mid-Phase I. By allowing customers to provide software support for integration of NCI products into their proprietary systems, NCI will significantly reduce overhead and manpower costs. Organizationally, NCI anticipates the recruitment of a chief executive officer (CEO) during this first six months. Prior to Phase II, the CEO will provide strategic consulting, industry networking, and so on.

~ *Phase II* ~

Phase II development will be implemented in quarter-based stages. Several iterations of board development are expected during the first two quarters of Phase II.

▶ *Quarter 1*

By QI, a small customer/strategic partner base is expected to have been identified. NCI anticipates further testing and development of the *Tera*Link© product, which will be made available to strategic partners. By mid/late Q1, 50 *Tera*Link© boards will be produced. *Tera*Link© sales will be made to customers interested in a solution in which they provide much of the software development. Development of the NCI SCI ASIC will begin by early Q1 2009. NCI plans to hire six additional employees during Q1 2009, including two software developers and one each of a firmware developer, hardware engineer, business development manager, and administrative assistant.

▶ *Quarter 2*

During Q2, NCI expects to sell the first working *Tera*Link© interface boards. Working system prototypes of customers' cluster servers, using the NCI interconnect product, should be available during this period. An additional 100 *Tera*Link© interface cards will be produced. Hiring during this period will include a second software/firmware developer and a product quality control/assembly/customer-support technician.

▶ ***Quarter 3***

Development and refinement of the complete SAN product line will also be pursued. NCI anticipates additional sales of 100 *Tera*Link© boards to a small customer base, while late in Q3, NCI plans production of an additional 200 *Tera*Link© cards. Strategic alliances and relationships with OEM customers should also be developed in this time period. An additional support technician will be hired during Q3 2009.

▶ ***Quarter 4***

NCI anticipates completion of development and fabrication of the NCI SCI ASIC in early Q4 2009. Development of the *Tera*Switch© product line will begin by early Q4. Additional *Tera*Link© board sales are expected to rise to 200 during this final quarter of Phase II. Late in Q4, NCI plans to have a fully operational and functional *Tera*Net© solution available for customers. Ramping of *Tera*Link© production will begin in Late Q4. Complete full *Tera*Net© systems integration should occur at this time. Additional hiring during this phase, including engineers and marketing personnel, will bring total NCI employee headcount to 19.

~ *Phase III* ~

Within 18 months of initial seed funding, NCI plans to have a full release of *Tera*Net©. The hardware and software components of the architecture will be fully developed, allowing integration of the NCI open SAN technology in NT-based cluster server systems. Product expansion and *Tera*Net© enhancements will be ongoing during this period. First year full production sales are expected to be 8,500 *Tera*Link© units and 600 *Tera*Switch© units. It is expected by the end of Phase III (Q4 2010) that NCI will employ 28–32 people.

2. *Markets and Competition*

▶ ***The Enterprise Server Market***

International Technology Group reports that the typical Fortune 500 firm had 8 gigabytes (GB) of corporate data in 1979. In 1990, the number had grown to 28,000GB; to 400,000GB by 1999; and to 161 billion GB (exabytes) by 2006. Between 2006 and 2010, data added annually will increase to 988 exabytes. In order to access and utilize this information, new classes of powerful business applications have been developed. These new applications require huge amounts of processing power, storage capacity, and communication bandwidth. Database-driven servers able to run on-line analytical processing (OLAP) applications, as well as serve interactive Internet and intranet sites, are quickly becoming the staple in corporate enterprise computing.

One architectural implementation of these systems uses symmetric multi-processors (SMP). These computers have a global view of system resources, including memory, disk space, tape storage, and so on. Therefore, as the number of processors in a given system is increased, eventually the performance rises only slightly due to competition for access to the resource; thus, these systems do not scale well with the number of users or as increasing processing power becomes necessary. Also, this architecture leads to single points of failure, minimizing fault tolerance in the system.

One type of multi-processor server system gaining attention in the enterprise market is the clustering of single and multi-processor computers. By clustering computers in a share-nothing environment (meaning each computer has its own memory, disk space, and so on), systems can scale by simply adding compute nodes to the cluster. A mechanism can be implemented in which, if a compute node or process fails, the process being executed can be migrated to another processor in the cluster, allowing for a completely fault-tolerant system. Separate servers can also be assembled into a single computing facility, making these systems more easily managed while affording IT groups the flexibility to grow beyond single machines. By providing fail-over services, clustered systems can be utilized as extremely high-availability corporate Internet/intranet servers, allowing for nearly continuous service or "webtone." Additionally, as the number of accesses or "hits" increases, Internet/intranet server performance can be enhanced by simply adding nodes to the cluster, providing nearly unlimited scalability.

▶ *The Cluster Interconnect Market*

For simple fail-over solutions, any number of network protocols and architectures can be used, but to build truly performance-scaleable cluster server systems, a new class of network technology must be employed. These would be high-speed, low-latency, low-overhead networks that can facilitate message passing from CPU to CPU to coordinate processor activities, as well as CPU-to-I/O and I/O-to-I/O communications. The network framework used in clustering has been called the "system area network" (SAN). Currently, all commercially available multi-processor cluster systems are based on proprietary SAN technology. Clustering multiple processors to build servers for corporate enterprise applications is a market with a tremendous growth potential if an open SAN technology is made available. NCI intends to provide an industry-standard open SAN technology to meet this need.

According to a survey of 400 large companies conducted by Oracle Corporation, the average computer downtime event results in a $140,000 loss in the retail industry and $400,000 in the securities industry. Yet clusters can provide 99.99 percent uptime, yielding average downtime costs of only $84,000 per year. By reducing system management needs and providing fault-tolerance against costly downtime while increasing system performance, cluster servers — and ultimately the NCI SAN technology used to construct these architectures — can pay for themselves within 6 to 12 months.

▶ *Alternative Network Technologies (Fail-Over)*

It might appear that cluster interconnect technologies would be compatible with high-end networking protocols, Fast or Gigabit Ethernet, Fibre Channel, or Asynchronous Transfer Mode (ATM). Although useful as possible client-server components, traditional networking is insufficient for clustering interconnects. For example, one very important aspect of a cluster interconnect is its message passing latency and overhead. The NCI network allows extremely low latency message passing (typically less than five microseconds) with zero processor overhead. This compares with several hundred microseconds to millisecond latency and processing overhead per message for LAN (local area network) and WAN (wide area network) architectures.

In Table 1, we compare standard networking technologies with NCI's TeraNet©. Note that although several of these networks claim to have similar throughput, the complex protocols involved in using them for data transport significantly reduces the throughput.

Table 1: Comparison of Standard Networking Technologies with NCI's TeraNet©

	Fast Ethernet	*Gigabit Ethernet*	*ATM-155*	*Fibre Channel*	*NCI TeraNet©*
Throughput	12 MB/s	100 MB/s	155 MB/s	2.13 Gbps	2.1 Gbps
Latency	ms	ms	100 µs	100 µs	2–5 µs
Processor Overhead	Large	Large	Large	Large	N/A
NIC Cost	$25	not required	615	$940	$800
Switch Cost	$80	$150 (8)	$15,000 (4)	$3,925 (8)	$3,000 (8)

(The numbers in parentheses are the number of ports)

For each of the standard technologies listed in Table 1, the processing overhead is very large, with similarly large latencies. For environments where distributed applications must communicate between the various processors, this latency will severely impede performance and scalability.

~ *Market Size and Development* ~

Market reports and projections for an open SAN market segment are difficult to obtain due to the market infancy. However, by providing a general overview of the current and projected number of NT server sales, Intel-based application servers, and the projected revenues for intranet/Internet servers, we can provide a plausible scenario for NCI revenue projections.

Microsoft has recently announced a schedule for deploying Windows Server 2008 (formerly Windows Server 2003), which will eventually provide clients with a single system image of the clustered server and enhance cluster management. The release is scheduled for February 2008. Windows Server 2008 shares much of the same architecture and functionality of Windows Vista, with a variation called Server Core. Server Core is a scaled-back installation, which does not include many features that are not core server features such as .NET Framework or Internet Explorer. Beta 1 has been in the market since 2005, and Beta 2 with WinHEC was released in spring 2006, followed by Beta 3 in spring 2006. Sun's Solaris Cluster Technology was released in late 2000. Capabilities to cluster 8 and 16 nodes were anticipated by 1998 and 1999, respectively; however, the technology today supports from 2 to 100 nodes.

As Windows Server 2008, Linux BProc, Sun's Solaris Cluster, and so on become increasingly accepted, corporate IT managers will begin migrating enterprise server systems from proprietary SMP architectures to open clusters of single processor and SMP systems. This new technology will enable smaller to mid-sized businesses to begin utilizing some of the more processor-intensive applications and fail-safe features, which have historically been cost prohibitive. Therefore, along with crossover from the SMP market, a significant portion of the low-end x86-based server market has adopted cluster systems and clustering technology. Prices for the major categories of servers are displayed in Table 2.

Table 2: Category Pricing of Servers

Category	Unit Price
Volume servers	< $25,000
Midrange Enterprise servers	$25,000–$499,999
High-end Enterprise servers	$500,000 or more

It is expected that the majority of these servers will be application servers, where fault tolerance and scalability are essential. Table 3 displays the forecast shipments of x86-based servers worldwide. Industry analysts predict that when scalable clustering becomes fully available, 20–30% of the x86-based server market will use clustering capabilities.

Table 3: Forecast Shipments of x86-Based Servers (Worldwide)

Year	Units Shipped
2006	6,900,000[1]
2007	7,383,000
2008	7,900,000
2009	8,450,000
2010	9,000,000
2011	9,680,000

([1]Actual shipments; source: DataCenter.com [Feb. 27, 2007])

Since the greatest volume of clusterable computers will be utilized by corporations for application and Internet/intranet servers, we forecast revenues for the server market for Internet/intranet and higher-end servers worldwide in Table 4. Notice that while the annual growth rate is 7 percent in shipment of units, revenue AGR is lower at 5% due to competitive pricing and production cost reductions.

Table 4: Forecasted Revenues Worldwide Server Market (in Billions)

Year	x86	Other	Total
2008	$28.4	$29.7	$58.1
2009	$29.9	$31.1	$61.0
2010	$31.4	$32.7	$64.1
2011	$32.9	$34.3	$67.3

(Forecast based on worldwide revenues in 2006 of $52.7 billion; source: DataCenter.com, [Feb. 23, 2007])

▶ *Revenue Projections*

In 2009, NCI plans to market and sell to the segment of the cluster-server market that needs high-speed interconnects for proprietary server systems, thus integrating *Tera*Link© into their overall system design. NCI estimates board sales to these customers of 350 units (150 in FY09), with the majority of these in Q4. Assuming the NT server market continues to grow at 7 percent AGR, we estimate 29.9 million x86-based servers sold in 2009. During 2009, we expect only 5 percent of the total x86 server market will use clustered systems. Because the majority of clusters in 2009 will be simple fail-over systems, NCI projects that only 10 percent of the cluster market will use high-speed interconnects. We also expect that in 2009, the average number of nodes in a cluster will be two. Therefore, the projected 350 interface cards sold in 2009 represents an 0.8 percent market share for NCI.

It is expected that the open x86-based cluster server market will become mature with the Phase II release of Microsoft's Windows Vista software, due in early 2008. Initial discussion with several large multi-processor server suppliers indicates, conservatively, an initial market of *Tera*Link© interface boards to be 12,000 units. NCI estimates that on average for every 16 *Tera*Link© boards sold, a *Tera*Switch© will be implemented. In 2010, the projected number of x86 servers sold is 9 million. Conservatively, we estimate that 15 percent of these will be clustered systems with two nodes. We also expect that the number of cluster systems with high-speed interconnects will increase to 25%. Assuming that NCI can double its market share to 5 percent in 2010, NCI projects the sale of 8,500 *Tera*Link© (32- and 64-bit) units and 600 *Tera*Switch© units. With an average price of $1,612 for *Tera*Link© and $800 for *Tera*Switch©, NCI expects to generate revenues of $14.0MM in FY10 (see Table 5, below).

Table 5: Expected Revenues of NCI for FY 2010

Est. Number of x86 Servers Sold =	9,000,000
X % That Are Clusters	15%
= Number of Clusters	1,356,674
X % That Are High-Speed	25%
= Number of Clusters	339,168
X Average Number of Nodes	2
X % Est. NCI Market Share	2.5%
= *Tera*Link© Revenue	8,360 @ $1,612 ea = $13,476,320
+ *Tera*Switch© Revenue	555 @ $800 ea = 444,000
= Projected Total NCI Revenue	$14,238,000

► Competition

There are currently two competitors providing non-SCI-based system area network (SAN) interconnect technologies: Myricom, Inc.'s *Myrinet* technology and Dolphin Interconnect Solutions' Express.

Myricom, a privately held corporation located in California (currently with 50 employees), introduced its high-speed, low-latency SAN technology called Myrinet in 1994; it claimed 60 MB/s point-to-point for large message sizes (10KB) and at least 40 µs latencies. It later released its second product, Myri-10G. It is operating in numerous clusters in over 50 countries and in 20 percent of the Top 500 supercomputer list of 2005. Myrinet PCI cards cost $750, while 8-port switches are $3,500–$3,990, yielding $850 per port to implement a Myrinet system. NCI expects Myricom will continue to dominate the demanding scientific and engineering market, but will likely only be a niche player in the open Intel-based server market.

Dolphin Interconnect Solutions is a privately held company that emerged out of an ASIC design house in Oslo, Norway. Currently, Dolphin is the principal provider of CMOS SCI chips. It has announced that it has perfected the Dolphin Express interconnect technology with the innovative Dolphin Express Supersockets software. It boasts that it can enable users of MySQL Cluster to achieve superior database performance. Although Dolphin will be a prominent competitor in the SAN interconnect marketplace, NCI's patented flow control and resource management architecture will provide an edge over this competitor in price and performance. Additionally, NCI expects the initial clustering methodologies to be widely varying. Because NCI provides a CPU at the network interface, while Dolphin does not, it will take Dolphin much longer to adapt to the changing environment, giving NCI a significant edge in system implementation.

~ *Response of Competitors* *to NCI Entry into Market* ~

Dolphin could potentially be very competitive and possibly underbid NCI products. It has established sales channels and has several critical strategic alliances, which provide a reasonable lead time. One principal concern is Dolphin's SCI link controller chips, necessary for any SCI-based network products. Dolphin could essentially starve the entire market of these chips in hopes of capturing greater market share. This is the principal reason NCI believes the development of an alternative SCI link controller ASIC will be necessary, not only for NCI but also for the SCI-based market, in general.

Myricom is expected to remain a niche player in this market. It will primarily continue to supply research institutions and governmental customers with its product. Currently, however, Myrinet does not have enough market share to impact NCI's strategy.

3. Marketing and Sales

▶ Customers

Initially, NCI products will be sold to providers of enterprise-class server systems who wish to add a clustering option to their portfolio of products. Providers of these systems and market size are shown in Table 6.

Table 6: Market Share of Server Shipments Worldwide (2006)

Company	% Market Share	Revenue (Billions)
IBM	37.9	$19.
HP	26.8	$14.1
Dell	9.7	$0.5
Sun Microsystems	9.7	$0.5
Fujitsu/Fujitsu-Siemens	4.1	$0.2
Others	11.8	$0.6

▶ NCI Market Strategy

Initial customers will be providers of volume to mid-end x86-based server systems looking to provide a cluster solution, without developing in-house SAN technology. Many of these principal customers have the resources to develop a SAN technology. However, the availability of an open SAN architecture that is ready to integrate into their server systems, is affordable, and meets their performance requirements is clearly a better solution. NCI expects that the cluster and subsequent SAN market will evolve in three distinct phases.

▶ Phase I

Phase I is expected to dominate the sale of clusters until Q3–Q4 2010. Although VARs will begin cluster development and integration in Q1 2010, volume sales to these customers is not expected until 2011. Sales to top-level server companies require this to be an executive sales strategy, as each sale will entail multi-hundred-thousand- to multi-million-dollar transactions, and the decision to use a given SAN system will be made by senior executives and senior engineers at the given server company. Direct contact and in-house demonstration with test systems integrated into the company's full cluster-server systems will provide the bulk of market communication during the first 12–18 months. Trade show participation will be limited to one to two shows per year, initially, because primary sales will be through direct executive channels.

▶ *Phase II*

During 2010, NCI expects an increase in the number of VAR's building cluster-server systems for clients. This will coincide with the release of Microsoft's Cluster Server software, which provides improved system-management tools and initial development of a single system image for the cluster. During the increase in the number of VAR cluster-server providers, NCI expects to engage additional sales personnel. For the VAR market, NCI plans to use both push and pull marketing strategies; push strategies will again be implemented as direct sales channels from both executives and sales associates. Demonstrations will also be provided both in conjunction with server manufacturers and NCI sponsored cluster-server conferences. NCI plans to tightly integrate customer support with customer education programs during the early phases of this market development.

On the pull side, NCI plans promotion in the principal business journals, which cover enterprise/corporate computing topics. These magazines include *Computer Reseller News (CRN), VAR Business, EE Times, Computer World, PC Week, Network World, INFOWorld, Ent,* and *Information Week,* among others. Because corporate end-users typically have more intimate relationships with VAR suppliers than manufacturers, NCI will attempt to raise the awareness of the IT/IS specialists at the enterprise level in an effort to have them contact/question their VAR product providers concerning NCI products.

During this market development, NCI expects to participate in three to six trade shows per year. These shows will include Hot Interconnects, Storage Networking World, INFOWorld, LISA, and Massive Technology Show. During this phase, a customer support manager and team will be developed in order to handle the assumed increased customer volume.

▶ *Phase III*

Finally, during 2011–2012 — when Microsoft Windows Vista is expected to become truly scalable — NCI expects to develop direct corporate accounts as end-users. Not only will these corporate customers be developing and integrating new cluster systems, but they will also be using NCI hardware/software to upgrade their current scalable systems. Advertising will be expanded to include all relevant enterprise/Intel/Internet/intranet trade magazines.

4. The Products

NCI intends to supply open System Area Network (SAN) interface and switch products in the form of an initial product called *Tera*Net©. *Tera*Net© consists of several independent components, including *Tera*Link©, the PCI-SCI interface card, and *Tera*Switch©, an SCI switch product.

*Tera*Link© provides the interface between the local bus of a given host system and the SAN interconnect fabric. NCI expects to initially offer this product in a PCI form factor, allowing it to be used in PC/Intel-based computer systems. Both 32- and 64-bit versions of this interface card will be produced. Because development from PCI to the PMC (embedded [VME] computer systems) form factor is trivial, NCI expects to eventually offer this product, as well. Despite the large market segment of PCI-based computers, there are also other systems not using PCI as the local bus standard (for example, SGI). NCI intends to eventually produce follow-up products that interface to those buses, as well.

The second product is a scalable network switch, *Tera*Switch©. This switch allows the construction of any architectural compute fabric in the clustered system. Even with a 500 MB/s network link, as additional nodes are clustered, intra-cluster communication will begin to suffer. The *Tera*Switch© product allows the construction of clusters much larger than eight nodes.

A third product, expected to be completed 9–12 months after Stage One funding, is the generic SAN SCI ASIC (Application Specific Integrated Circuit). This SCI interface chip will be used in both the NCI *Tera*Link© interface card and the NCI *Tera*Switch© product. This ASIC provides the chip-level interface between the *Tera*Link© board and the SCI network. NCI will make this ASIC commercially available as a stand-alone chip product and logic core, in order to further promote an open SCI-based SAN architecture.

▶ *Applications*

*Tera*Net© will be used in clustered server environments where continuous, fail-safe operations and applications and performance are critical issues. The SCI network implements a shared memory approach to all I/O. This means any processor or agent in the system can directly access any other resource in the system by simply reading from or writing to it. This concept grants minimum latency access to any system resource. This low-latency, high-bandwidth network will provide the environment for applications to be fully parallelized to enhance performance, similar to Massively Parallel Processor (MPP) type systems. Supercomputer-level performance will be attainable by clustering individual and multi-processor nodes. Large enterprise-level intranet/Internet server installations will be the primary application environment; this technology can also be utilized as a high-speed, point-to-point interconnect in any application where high throughput is necessary.

▶ *Product Advantages*

The most important feature of the NCI SAN bridge architecture is the combination of the data transfer controller with a micro-controller CPU. The firmware for this processor can be updated in the field by downloading new update/configuration software. The availability of the CPU to system vendors allows offloading time-critical parts of higher level network or clustering protocols from the host CPU onto the appropriate network bridge. Complex self-test and monitoring functionality can be implemented with minimal cost. Customized server configurations are also more easily implemented because the I/O controller is a programmable CPU.

The most important feature of the SCI network is its scalability, meaning that the aggregate bandwidth of a switched SCI network scales linearly with its size. Therefore, as more nodes are added to the network, the aggregate bandwidth becomes higher.

▶ *Present Product Status*

A prototype SCI–PCI interface was completed in January 2007 and has been tested for one year. Dr. von Honecker, the founder of NCI, was the principal investigator of the R&D project leading to the implemented design. The basic flow control concept has been implemented and its functionality completely verified. The second hurdle, the micro-controller or the full data transfer controller, was not implemented in this prototype.

The full design of the *Tera*Link© product is currently under way. The design of the data transfer controller is 80 percent finished and completely simulated at this point. There are very few design risks remaining with respect to its overall functionality. The implementation of Commercial-Off-The-Shelf (COTS) chips in the architecture has been discussed in detail with various chip designers. The architecture described was well within the design limits of these devices. Fully functional and tested alpha prototype boards will be ready in Q4 2008.

Product development is also ongoing. With $150,000 in capital in place, it is expected that alpha prototype production boards will be available in December 2008. Further development will continue as the boards are installed in the clustered systems of NCI's initial customers. Given adequate funding, beta products are expected to be available by May 2009.

▶ *Manufacturing*

NCI expects that all SAN components will be manufactured off-site, as a volume of 200,000 *Tera*Link© interface cards does not warrant the creation of an independent production facility. NCI expects to have a two-to-three person production team that oversees the production process at the fabrication house. Outsourcing these products allows costly resources to be more effectively utilized, along with significant savings in time-to-market. Later, some of the COTS chips on the *Tera*Link© board will be merged into a proprietary ASIC in order to reduce production costs. Unit production costs for the *Tera*Link© interface boards and *Tera*Switch© are projected as shown in the following table:

	FY 2009	FY 2010	FY 2011	FY 2012	FY 2013
TeraLink©	$1,200	$960	$700	$580	$400
TeraSwitch©	$500	$500	$320	$280	$250

5. Risk Analysis

In evaluating an investment in NCI, a prospective investor must particularly consider the risks involved. NCI believes the primary risk in the overall venture is the current lack of experience in the management team. A senior management team that has successfully taken a product from inception to market will be needed for success of the venture. As mentioned earlier, NCI is currently searching for a CEO with a proven track record in the computer/networking industry. Another risk factor involves NCI's markets and competition. A principal concern has been the widespread establishment of Tandem's ServerNet in the industry prior to full release of NCI's product line. Although Tandem had a significant head start in this market, NCI expects that only early pioneers purchased this product. Also, with the acquisition of Tandem by Compaq and then Compaq acquisition by Hewlett-Packard (HP), NCI expects competitors of HP to become reluctant to using ServerNet as their primary SAN architecture. Software for clustering more than two Intel-based processors will not be available from Microsoft, Novell, or IBM until Q3 2009. NCI believes few end-users will have developed preferences of clustering interconnect technology by NCI's product release date. Additionally, the NCI SAN product provides a significant performance increase over Tandem, Digital, and Dolphin SAN systems.

6. Financial Data

Financial projections have been developed for FY 2009–2013 (FY for NCI is October 1–September 30). The financial projections for Pro-Forma Revenues, the Pro-Forma Income Statement, the Pro-Forma Balance Sheet, and the Pro-Forma Cash-Flow Statement are shown in Tables 7–10.

▶ Investment

The company is currently seeking an additional $1.5MM in Stage One capital investment for the purpose of reaching the beta stage of product development for the TeraLink© interface board (both 32- and 64-bit versions), as well as for developing the NCI SAN ASIC. Following seed and State One investments, NCI expects to obtain an additional $3MM in order to complete prototype development for the TeraSwitch© product, complete development of the TeraNet© system, attain full integration for the components in the TeraNet© system, and bring the technology to market.

Any purchase of securities of NCI will not be registered under the Securities Act of Ontario or other applicable securities laws and regulations. Accordingly, such securities of NCI may not be resold unless they are subsequently registered under the Securities Act or other applicable laws, or an exemption from registration is obtained. NCI has no current plans to register any of its capital stock under the Securities Act or any other applicable laws. In addition, in the event that NCI should register its capital stock, there is no assurance that a purchaser of such securities would be able to include any securities owned in such initial registration or any subsequent registration. In the absence of such registration, there is no existing public or other market for the NCI securities, and it is not anticipated that any such market will develop. Moreover, the transferability of the stock is subject to certain restrictions. Consequently, investors may be unable to liquidate their investment when they desire, or anytime in the near future.

Table 7: NCI Pro-Forma Revenues by Product (FY 2009–2013)

Units	FY 2009	FY 2010	FY 2011	FY 2012	FY 2013
PCI-32 NT	150	6,475	9,500	7,500	0
PCI-64 NT	0	1,885	22,000	67,500	175,000
s.k.u. 3	0	0	0	0	0
SCI Switch	0	556	2,520	6,000	14,000
Total Units	**150**	**8,916**	**34,020**	**81,000**	**189,000**
Prices:					
PCI-32 NT	$2,000	$1,500	$1,250	$1,000	$750
PCI-64 NT	0	2,000	1,250	1,000	750
s.k.u. 3	0	0	0	0	0
SCI Switch	0	800	700	600	500
Revenue:					
PCI-32 NT	$300,000	$9,712,500	$11,875,000	$7,500,000	$0
PCI-64 NT	0	3,770,000	27,500,000	67,500,000	131,250,000
s.k.u. 3	0	0	0	0	0
SCI Switch	0	444,800	1,764,000	3,600,000	7,000,000
Total Revenue	**$300,000**	**$13,927,300**	**$41,139,000**	**$78,600,000**	**$138,250,000**

Table 8: Pro-Forma Income Statement (FY 2009–2013)					
	FY 2009	*FY 2010*	*FY 2011*	*FY 2012*	*FY 2013*
Revenue:					
NT Product Sales	$300,000	$13,927,300	$41,139,000	$78,600,000	$138,250,000
Total Revenue	$300,000	$13,927,300	$41,139,000	$78,600,000	$138,250,000
CGS	162,110	8,356,380	23,860,620	43,230,000	74,655,000
Gross Margin	137,890	5,570,920	17,278,380	35,370,000	63,595,000
(% of Revenue)	46%	40%	42%	45%	46%
Operating Expenses:					
R&D	1,148,841	1,671,276	5,348,070	8,646,000	13,825,000
(% of Revenue)	383%	12%	13%	11%	10%
Sales & Marketing	280,489	974,911	2,056,950	7,074,000	12,442,500
(% of Revenue)	93%	7%	5%	9%	9%
Gen'l. Admin.	197,117	835,638	1,645,560	2,358,000	2,765,000
(% of Revenue)	66%	6%	4%	3%	2%
Total Operating Exp (% of Revenue)	1,626,447 542%	3,481,825 25%	9,050,580 22%	18,078,000 23%	29,032,500 21%
EBIT	($1,488,557)	$2,089,095	$8,227,800	$17,292,000	$34,562,500
(% of Revenue)	496%	15%	20%	22%	26%
Tax Expense	0	417,819	2,303,784	4,716,000	9,677,500
Net Income:	($1,488,557)	$1,671,276	$5,924,016	$12,576,000	$24,885,000
(% of Revenue)	496%	12%	14%	16%	18%

Table 9: Pro-Forma Balance Sheet (FY 2009–2013)

	FY 2009	FY 2010	FY 2011	FY 2012	FY 2013
Assets:					
Current Assets					
Cash	($1,488,121)	($4,998,668)	($1,558,853)	$5,228,216	$23,804,616
Net A/R	148,500	5,878,125	7,328,475	12,969,000	22,811,250
Inventory	66,000	1,996,367	3,577,500	6,331,003	7,193,688
Total Current Assets	(1,273,621)	2,875,804	9,347,122	24,528,219	53,809,554
Gross Fix Assets	77,500	185,500	327,000	506,500	651,500
Less Accum Dep	12,492	57,517	153,717	282,783	431,250
Net Fixed Assets	65,009	127,983	173,283	223,717	220,250
Total Assets	**($1,208,612)**	**$3,003,787**	**$9,502,405**	**$24,751,936**	**$54,029,804**
Liabilities					
Short-Term Liab.					
Acct Payable	87,768	2,153,072	2,508,939	4,485,902	7,550,743
Salaries	48,750	106,750	185,358	260,872	348,524
Taxes	0	417,819	575,946	1,179,000	2,419,375
Total S-T	136,518	2,677,641	3,270,243	5,925,774	10,318,642
Long-Term Liab.	0	0	0	0	0
Total Liab.	**$136,518**	**$2,677,641**	**$3,270,243**	**$5,925,774**	**$10,318,642**
Equity:					
Preferred Stock	138,000	138,000	138,000	138,000	138,000
Common Stock	5,427	5,427	5,427	5,427	5,427
Ret. Earnings	(1,488,557)	182,719	6,106,735	18,682,735	43,567,735
Total Equity	**($1,345,130)**	**$326,146**	**$6,250,162**	**$18,826,162**	**$43,711,162**
Liabilities + Equity	**($1,208,612)**	**$3,003,787**	**$9,520,405**	**$24,751,936**	**$54,029,804**

Table 10: Pro-Forma Cash-Flow Statement (FY 2009–2013)

	FY 2009	FY 2010	FY 2011	FY 2012	FY 2013
Beginning Cash	$0	($1,488,121)	($4,998,688)	($1,558,8534)	$5,228,216
Sources of Cash:					
Net Income	(1,488,557)	1,671,276	5,924,016	12,576,000	24,885,000
Add Depr/ Amort	12,491	45,026	96,200	129,066	148,467
Issu. of Pref Stock	138,000	0	0	0	0
Issu. of Com Stock		5,427	0	0	0 0
Plus Changes In:					
Acct. Payable	87,768	2,065,304	355,867	1,976,963	3,604,841
Salaries Payable	48,750	58,000	78,608	75,514	87,652
Taxes Payable	0	417,819	158,127	603,054	1,240,375
Total Src of Cash	**($1,196,121)**	**$4,257,425**	**$6,612,818**	**$15,360,597**	**$29,426,335**
Uses of Cash					
Less Changes					
Net Acc/Rec	148,500	5,729,625	1,450,350	5,640,525	9,842,250
Inventory	66,000	1,930,367	1,581,133	2,753,503	862,685
Gross Fixed Assets	77,500	108,000	141,500	179,500	145,000
Total Uses	**$292,000**	**$7,767,992**	**$3,172,983**	**$8,573,528**	**$10,849,935**
Changes/Cash	($1,488,121)	($3,510,567)	$3,439,835	$6,787,069	$18,576,400
Ending Cash	($1,488,121)	($4,998,688)	($1,558.853)	$5,228,216	$23,804,616

Index

• *C* •

Notes

Notes

Notes

BUSINESS & PERSONAL FINANCE

978-0-470-83878-5

978-0-470-83818-1

Also available:

- Buying and Selling a Home For Canadians For Dummies 978-0-470-83740-5
- Investing For Canadians For Dummies 978-0-470-83361-2
- Managing For Dummies 978-0-7645-1771-6
- Money Management All-in-One Desk Reference For Canadians For Dummies 978-0-470-15428-1
- Negotiating For Dummies 978-0-470-04522-0

- Personal Finance For Canadians For Dummies 978-0-470-83768-9
- Small Business Marketing For Dummies 978-0-7645-7839-7
- Starting an eBay Business For Canadians For Dummies 978-0-470-83946-1
- Stock Investing For Canadians For Dummies 978-0-470-83925-6

HOME & BUSINESS COMPUTER BASICS

978-0-471-75421-3

978-0-470-11806-1

Also available:

- Blogging For Dummies 978-0-471-77084-8
- Excel 2007 For Dummies 978-0-470-03737-9
- Macs For Dummies 978-0-470-27817-8
- Office 2007 All-in-One Desk Reference For Dummies 978-0-471-78279-7

- PCs For Dummies 978-0-7645-8958-4
- Web Analytics For Dummies 978-0-470-09824-0

FOOD, HOME, GARDEN, HOBBIES, MUSIC & PETS

978-0-7645-9904-0

978-0-470-15491-5

Also available:

- 30-Minute Meals For Dummies 978-0-7645-2589-6
- Brain Games For Dummies 978-0-470-37378-1
- Dog Training For Dummies 978-0-7645-8418-3
- Home Improvement All-in-One Desk Reference For Dummies 978-0-7645-5680-7

- Knitting For Dummies 978-0-470-28747-7
- Origami Kit For Dummies 978-0-470-75857-1
- Violin For Dummies 978-0-470-83838-9

INTERNET & DIGITAL MEDIA

978-0-470-25074-7   978-0-470-39062-7

Also available:

- eBay For Canadians For Dummies 978-0-470-15348-2
- MySpace For Dummies 978-0-470-09529-4
- Pay Per Click Search Engine Marketing For Dummies 978-0-471-75494-7

- Search Engine Marketing For Dummies 978-0-471-97998-2
- The Internet For Dummies 978-0-470-12174-0
- YouTube For Dummies 978-0-470-14925-6

HEALTH & SELF-HELP

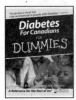

9780-470-83370-4   978-0-470-15307-9

Also available:

- Breast Cancer For Dummies 978-0-7645-2482-0
- Depression For Dummies 978-0-7645-3900-8
- Healthy Aging For Dummies 978-0-470-14975-1
- Improving Your Memory For Dummies 978-0-7645-5435-3
- Living Gluten-Free For Dummies 978-0-471-77383-2

- Neuro-linguistic Programming For Dummies 978-0-7645-7028-5
- Pregnancy For Canadians For Dummies 978-0-470-83945-4
- Understanding Autism For Dummies 978-0-7645-2547-6

EDUCATION, HISTORY & REFERENCE

978-0-470-83656-9   978-0-7645-2498-1

Also available:

- Algebra For Dummies 978-0-7645-5325-7
- Art History For Dummies 978-0-470-09910-0
- Chemistry For Dummies 978-0-7645-5430-8
- French For Dummies 978-0-7645-5193-2

- Math Word Problems For Dummies 978-0-470-14660-6
- Spanish For Dummies 978-0-7645-5194-9
- Statistics For Dummies 978-0-7645-5423-0
- World War II For Dummies 978-0-7645-5352-3